The Preston Model an Wealth Building

CW01511804

Through a deep examination of what has become known as the 'Preston Model', this book explores an innovative approach to local economic development that utilises economic democratisation to realise both social and economic objectives.

The first part of the book examines the main strands of the Preston Model framework and what makes it different to other urban regeneration schemes: the combination of local anchor institution procurement to generate and retain local wealth, and the development of co-operatives to fill gaps in local supply chains. The chapters in this section consider the Preston Model as viewed through different lenses: politics and society, community, economics, democracy, trade unionism, language and communication, education, and transferability. The second part explores the influences and applications of the Preston Model, in theory and practice, in selected locations and various circumstances worldwide. This includes discussion of key ideas such as economic democracy, social enterprise, and the creation of capacity for co-operative self-government, alongside essays on prominent international examples of similar approaches, which can inform and in turn be informed by the Preston Model.

This book is essential reading for those interested in regional and national policy, economic democracy and alternative economic and political ideas.

Julian Manley is a researcher in the Centre for Citizenship and Community at the University of Central Lancashire, and ex-chair and founding member of the Preston Cooperative Development Network.

Philip B. Whyman is professor of economics and co-director of the Lancashire Centre for Business and Management Research (LCBME) at the University of Central Lancashire.

The Preston Model and Community Wealth Building

Creating a Socio-economic Democracy for the Future

Edited by
Julian Manley and Philip B. Whyman

Routledge
Taylor & Francis Group

LONDON AND NEW YORK

First published 2021
by Routledge
2 Park Square, Milton Park, Abingdon, Oxon OX14 4RN

and by Routledge
605 Third Avenue, New York, NY 10158

Routledge is an imprint of the Taylor & Francis Group, an informa business

© 2021 selection and editorial matter, Julian Manley and Philip B. Whyman; individual chapters, the contributors

The right of Julian Manley and Philip B. Whyman to be identified as the authors of the editorial material, and of the authors for their individual chapters, has been asserted in accordance with sections 77 and 78 of the Copyright, Designs and Patents Act 1988.

All rights reserved. No part of this book may be reprinted or reproduced or utilised in any form or by any electronic, mechanical, or other means, now known or hereafter invented, including photocopying and recording, or in any information storage or retrieval system, without permission in writing from the publishers.

Trademark notice: Product or corporate names may be trademarks or registered trademarks, and are used only for identification and explanation without intent to infringe.

British Library Cataloguing-in-Publication Data
A catalogue record for this book is available from the British Library

Library of Congress Cataloging-in-Publication Data
Names: Manley, Julian, editor. | Whyman, Philip, editor.
Title: The Preston model and community wealth building : creating a socio-economic democracy for the future / edited by Julian Manley and Philip B. Whyman.
Description: Abingdon, Oxon ; New York, NY : Routledge, 2021. | Includes bibliographical references and index.
Identifiers: LCCN 2020054372 (print) | LCCN 2020054373 (ebook) | ISBN 9780367514082 (hardback) | ISBN 9780367514099 (paperback) | ISBN 9781003053736 (ebook)
Subjects: LCSH: Economic development. | Community development. | Urban renewal. | Urban economics. | Equality.
Classification: LCC HD82 .P655 2021 (print) | LCC HD82 (ebook) | DDC 307.1/416--dc23
LC record available at https://lccn.loc.gov/2020054372
LC ebook record available at https://lccn.loc.gov/2020054373

ISBN: 978-0-367-51408-2 (hbk)
ISBN: 978-0-367-51409-9 (pbk)
ISBN: 978-1-003-05373-6 (ebk)

Typeset in Sabon
by Taylor & Francis Books

To 'Prestonians' everywhere

Contents

PART II
Beyond municipalism, beyond Preston: The new socio-economic
democracy   151

Illustrations

Contributors

Dr Mike Aiken is an independent researcher engaged in the European third sector. He holds an MA in social policy (University of Sussex), a PhD (Open University) and has published in *Voluntas, Voluntary Sector Review, Public Management Review*, and *Interface*. Mike has lived in Germany and Mexico where he taught community social work and social policy. His recent research with the Institute for Voluntary Action Research examined advocacy and community assets. He remains active in local campaigns to support health rights for migrants.

Alex Bird is a freelance researcher and co-operative activist, and a founder member of the Consultancy Coop. He is a Member of the Institute of Economic Development (IED) and a Fellow of the RSA. He is Chair of Banc Cambria, the emerging co-operative bank for Wales, and an active member of Union Co-ops UK. He was Chair of Cardiff YMCA Housing Association until 2019 and has served as a Board member of Wales Co-op Centre and Co-ops UK. He was the founding secretary of the Cross-Party Group on Co-ops at the Welsh Senedd and has been a worker co-op member for four decades. He has contributed to research reports for the Co-operative College, Co-operatives UK and the TUC which looked at co-operative solutions to the disadvantages experienced by the self-employed and has contributed to the CECOP working group on this subject.

Michael Brookes is the professor of HRM as well as Leader of the Management of People Research Group at the University of Southern Denmark, and research associate at Nelson Mandela University. His research interests include employment relations, international and comparative HRM and community wealth building, with the central strand connecting all aspects of this research being to explore the relationship between national institutional configurations and their impact upon behaviour at the firm, community and individual levels.

Pat Conaty is a member of the Consultancy Co-op in Wales and the Solidarity Economy Association. He has worked freelance for the past 10 years as Associate of Co-operatives UK with a strategic focus with the Co-operative College since 2016 on Union Co-op solutions for precarious workers. His work at the Birmingham Settlement and New Economics Foundation in the 1990s led to development funding for the establishment of the Community Development Finance movement – including pioneering ones he co-founded in Birmingham, London, and rural regions. With Community Finance Solutions at the University of Salford he co-led development work to establish the Community Land Trust (CLT) national demonstration project and the founding of the National CLT Network. He is co-author of *The Resilience Imperative: Co-operative Transitions to a Steady-state Economy* (2012) and *Commons Sense: Co-operative Place making* (2016).

Unai Elorza is an industrial engineer currently working as a lecturer and researcher within the Department of Mechanical Engineering and Industrial Production at Mondragon Unibertsitatea (University). He has a Master's in mechanical systems engineering from Cranfield University (UK) and a PhD in psychology from the University of the Basque Country / Euskal Herriko Unibertsitatea. Dr Elorza previously worked in an automotive component manufacturing company for several years. His main research interest is to help manufacturing companies maximise wellbeing, motivation (engagement), and organisational performance.

Michael Farrelly is a senior lecturer in English language studies at the University of Hull, UK, where he teaches critical discourse analysis. His research applies critical discourse analysis to politics and policy. He is currently researching language, climate change and the environment. His book *Discourse and Democracy* is published by Routledge, and he is co-editor of a second book, *Critical Policy Discourse Analysis* published by Edward Elgar, which showcases methods for critically analysing policy texts.

Alaine Garmendia is a lecturer and researcher at the faculty of engineering of Mondragon Unibertsitatea inside the Department of Innovation, Organisational Model and Strategic HR Management. Alaine defended her PhD in the strategic HRM field in November 2019 and she currently focuses her activity on researching the relationship between high-involvement (participatory) work systems, employee well-being and organisational performance. Her mixed education background combining an engineering degree with a PhD in social sciences has provided her a very enriched perspective that she loves to transmit to students and put into practice with practitioners encouraging them to make changes in the way organisations are structured and managed.

Mick McKeown is professor of democratic mental health, School of Nursing, University of Central Lancashire and trade union activist with Unison, playing a role in union strategising on professional nursing. He has taken a lead in arguing the case for trade union solidarity and alliances with service user/survivor groupings and is active in promoting union interests in co-operative solutions linked to organising. Mick sees union renewal as inextricably linked to aspirations for workplace democracy and views unions as key within wider systems of community action, civic engagement, and fair economic regeneration. He is a board member of Preston Cooperative Development Network and a member of Union Co-ops UK.

Anita Mangan is senior lecturer in organisation studies in the School of Management, University of Bristol. Her research focuses on co-operatives, credit unions and union co-ops, volunteering processes and community activism, with an emphasis on issues of identity and subjectivity, power, and control. She is particularly interested in how alternative forms of organising are silenced or delegitimised in mainstream accounts of business (be it in education, government debate or the media) and how what is considered alternative varies from country to country. Much of her community-based research has been on interdisciplinary projects with colleagues from a broad range of disciplines in the humanities and social sciences. Her research has been funded by the Arts and Humanities Research Council's Connected Communities programme, the Daiwa Anglo-Japanese Foundation and HEFCE. She has published in journals such as *Sociology, Human Relations, Organisation*, and *Management Learning*.

Julian Manley was social innovation manager in the Centre for SME Development, and currently works in the Centre for Citizenship and Community at the University of Central Lancashire, Preston. He was the first chair of the Preston Cooperative Development Network and has a long-standing research interest in the development of the Preston Model. He is often invited to give presentations and lectures about the various aspects of the Preston Model, nationally and internationally. Manley's research combines a psychosocial approach through a Deleuzian lens. He is also a director on the boards of the Climate Psychology Alliance and the Centre for Social Dreaming. His most recent publication on the Preston Model (with Mike Aiken) applies a social dreaming perspective to the development of the Preston Model and similar strategies elsewhere: 'A Socio-economic System for Affect: Dreaming of Co-operative relationships and affect in Bermuda, Preston and Mondragón' (*Organisational and Social Dynamics*, 20.2).

Jonathan Michie is professor of innovation & knowledge exchange, director of the Department for Continuing Education, and president of Kellogg College at the University of Oxford. He is also chair of the Universities Association for Lifelong Learning, an 'interdisciplinary' member of the Management and Business Panel for the Research Excellence Framework (REF2021), and managing editor of the International Review of Applied Economics. Jonathan was previously professor of management and director of the Business School at the University of Birmingham; the Sainsbury Professor of Management and head of the School of Management and Organisational Psychology at Birkbeck University of London; university lecturer at the Judge Business School, University of Cambridge, and fellow and director of studies in Economics at Robinson College; and an expert to the European Commission in Brussels.

Dr Christopher Nicholas is a researcher and lecturer in economics and business strategy at Hertfordshire Business School, University of Hertfordshire. His primary research area is in community and regional economics with a focus on spatial linkages. He also has interests in economic geography, deprivation and social capital.

Michael Alden Peck co-founded and serves as executive director of the non-profit 1worker1vote movement (www.1worker1vote) advancing hybrid model, shared ownership enterprises, ecosystems and culture to 'Build Back Fairer' starting with unionised, worker-owned co-operative businesses. Michael serves as the American Sustainable Business Council board secretary (www.asbcouncil.org) and on the Blue Green Alliance corporate advisory board (www.bluegreenalliance.org). For two decades (1999–2019), Michael served as USA & Canada international delegate for Mondragon Corporation, the world's largest industrial co-operative ecosystem (www.mondragon-corporation.com). Michael founded a mission-driven consulting company – MAPA Group (1994–2019), served as an officer in the US Navy, worked on Capitol Hill for the Senate Majority Leader and then for several multinationals including SAIC (1988–94), the nation's largest employee-owned, R&D company at the time with its own internal stock market as a senior vice president for corporate business development. In Q2 2020, Michael co-founded a second company, The Virtuous Cycle Collaboratory (tvc2) worker co-operative, 'flattening the curves through virtuous cycles' to enlarge a more inclusive and mutualism-driven global stakeholder economy.

Dr Ioannis Prinos is a researcher in the Centre for Citizenship and Community, the School of Social Work, Care and Community, in the University of Central Lancashire. His primary research interests seek to combine empirical research and social theory in understanding the socio-dynamics of unequal power relations and their consequences in terms of poverty, marginalisation, and socio-economic inequality, focusing on the role of the voluntary third sector, the co-operative sector and the social welfare state in these processes. This reflects a commitment to striving for a deep understanding of the development of contemporary urban society and economy and their unequal outcomes, alongside an explicit engagement with public policy; particularly social policy and the challenges it faces. By extension, this often entails the exposure of policy 'myths' and critique of the inadequacy of both current conceptualisations and applied policy solutions, as well as the critical reflection of innovative community development projects such as the Preston Model.

Julie Ridley is reader in applied social sciences, School of Social Work, Care and Community, University of Central Lancashire. She is also a director of the Centre for Citizenship and Community, an applied research centre at UCLan focusing on the complexities of engaging communities whilst also promoting the development of community capital. As director of studies she supervises PhD students researching youth loneliness and coastal communities, connected communities and disability, and other subjects applying participatory methodologies. Julie has managed Connected Communities projects in Preston, involving diverse community members as researchers and continues involvement in local community organising. She is active in the Broadgate and Hartington Community Connectors Group to increase connections between neighbours and sees the potential of connected communities for co-operative development (and vice versa). Julie is a director of Preston Cooperative Development Network and is part of the leadership team for developing the Preston chapter of Citizens UK.

Cilla Ross is the principal of the Co-operative College, UK, and works in higher, community, and adult education. She has led interdisciplinary blended learning and research initiatives internationally and is currently exploring a co-operative university, a union co-op, and is associated with the Greater Manchester Co-operative Commission. She is also exploring new ways of thinking about co-operative learning for livelihoods and decent work. Cilla was a Commissioner on the Centenary Commission on Adult Education in 2019 (www.centenarycommission.org) and has recently been appointed to a 3-year Honorary Professorship in Co-operative Education at the University of Nottingham, UK. A recent publication is *Reclaiming the University for the Public Good: Experiments and Futures in Co-operative Higher Education* (Palgrave).

Anita Sharma is an experienced senior research fellow with a PhD in sociology, and several years' experience of interdisciplinary, collaborative researching within social science faculties and business schools. Her background combines communication studies, film and television studies and cultural studies/sociology. Her expertise lies in qualitative research and she has worked on several externally-funded research projects relating to her areas of interest in race/ethnicity, identity, poverty, work and employment, inequality and disadvantage, retirement and ageing.

Simon Taylor researched union co-ops for his master's dissertation in international labour and trade union studies from Ruskin College, and is a trade union activist seconded full time to union duties in a large local authority. Simon is a co-author of the *Union Co-op Manifesto*. He believes the Manifesto should be of interest to anyone concerned about the democratic deficit prevalent in mainstream economic models, and with trade union renewal strategies.

Tracy Walsh is a visiting lecturer in the Business School, University of Hertfordshire. She is a founder member of the RED Learning Coop: Research, Education and Development, which works with trade unions, NGOs, social enterprises, charities, community groups and the co-operative movement, to develop critically reflective radical pedagogy (www.redlearning.coop). Tracy represented RED on the Interim Academic Board of the Cooperative University Project (www.co-op.ac.uk/pages/category/co-operative-university).

Philip B. Whyman is professor of economics and co-director of the Lan... Centre for Business and Management Research (LCBME) at the University of Central Lancashire. He is the author of fifteen research monographs, editor of a further six books and has had in excess of fifty papers published in learned journals. His main research interests lie in economic policy, European economics and the implications of Brexit, the significance of alternative forms of ownership and local economic development (including the Preston Model). He has acted as advisor and been commissioned to produce research for government departments and parliamentary authorities, local authorities and local enterprise partnerships (LEPs), business organisations and trade unions. He is also principal investigator for an ongoing project examining the impact of the Preston Model upon specific sectors within Lancashire, funded by the Creative Industries Policy and Evidence Centre (PEC), led by the National Endowment for Science, Technology and the Arts (NESTA).

Sarah Wolfe is a doctoral candidate at the University of Hertfordshire, studying wage markup in labour unions representing dispersed gig economy workers. Holds a master of science in organisational leadership specialising in international management from Colorado State University and a bachelor of arts in anthropology from the University of Colorado. Former managing director of Spectrum Talent Solutions, a diversity and inclusion consultancy. She has held a number of public speaking engagements including at the University of Colorado and Front Range Community College. In addition to consulting within the public and private sectors, she has provided technical assistance to the United Nations International Day of Women and Girls in STEM. She has published in the journal *Gender, Work & Organization* as well as *Maize Magazine*.

Susan Wright is professor of educational anthropology and co-director of the Centre for Higher Education Futures (CHEF) http://edu.au.dk/forskning/cen tre-for-higher-education-futures at the Danish School of Education, Aarhus University. She studies people's participation in large-scale processes of transformation, working with concepts of audit culture, governance, contestation, and the anthropology of policy. She has researched university reforms for over 30 years in the UK and Denmark. She coordinated the EU ITN project on Universities in the Knowledge Economy (UNIKE) in Europe and the Asia-Pacific Rim. Informing all her work are insights gained from studies of political transformation in Iran before and after the Islamic Revolution. She co-edits the journal *LATISS (Learning and Teaching: International Journal of Higher Education in the Social Sciences)* and the book series 'Higher Education in Critical Perspective: Practices and Policies' (Berghahn). Her latest book (co-authored with Stephen Carney, John Benedicto Krejsler, Gritt Bykærholm Nielsen, and Jakob Williams Ørberg) is *Enacting the University: Danish University Reform in an Ethnographic Perspective* (Springer, 2020).

The 'Preston Model' was Preston's answer to austerity, government cuts, and the 2008 failure of the economic system in England, with northern towns and cities hit especially hard. In the case of Preston, the situation hit home with the abandonment of the £700 million Tithebarn regeneration project in 2011. Along with like-minded colleagues in Preston City Council, I began to attempt a different way of approaching local economic and social problems. We began with the premise that there was already considerable wealth in Preston, but the problem was that it was leaking out of the economy. What if we could retain some of that local wealth and significantly advance a more democratic economy?

Instead of primarily concentrating on inward investment, we started to encourage local investment. Our Anchor Institutions – those major spenders and employers in Preston who are 'anchored' in the community, come rain or shine – began spending more and more locally, with spectacular results: Anchor Institution spend in Preston increased from 5% to 18.2%, an increase of £74,750,857, and in the Lancashire region from 39% to 79.2%, an increase of £199,688,679. But we didn't stop there. Our vision is to transform the local economy on many levels. The public pension fund we are part of is investing pension funds in the city, we are expanding worker-owned co-operatives in partnership with the University of Central Lancashire and Mondragón through our own Preston Cooperative Development Network, establishing a North West Community Bank, and creating a Preston Cooperative Education Centre to support the creation and development of worker-owned businesses. All of these projects work together to create the Preston Model.

These pillars, which follow the idea of the framework in Mondragón, are further supported by a series of progressive policies implemented by the Council in Preston. Examples include, promoting the real living wage, municipal ownership, insourcing, establishing a vehicle to directly deliver local authority housing again and working with the University of Central Lancashire to establish a Civic Drone Centre. There are even new explorations around Lancashire's first Community Land Trust and how we may create district and community energy networks.

The success we have enjoyed in Preston is being noticed in other parts of the UK, and has also become a significant part of national Labour Party policy decisions. There are instances of community wealth building ideas catching on in places such as Islington and Haringey Council looking to insource services; the Welsh Assembly supporting a Welsh Community Bank; Plymouth and Oxford committing of doubling the co-operative economy, with similar work in North Ayrshire; and a commitment to establishing municipally owned energy companies in Hackney and Birmingham, to give just a few examples.

There are also international case studies in Tanzania, in Sydney, Australia, Cincinnati, and New York, USA, as well as 'new municipal' ventures that work along similar lines, in cities such as Barcelona. All in all, the values and principles of the Preston Model are spawning in many different places where people and communities are eager to establish alternative and better ways of living. At the time of writing, Preston, like many other parts of the world, is gripped in the COVID-19 pandemic. The economic future of our city is looking troubled, but I hope that initiatives like the Preston Model, built out of austerity and crisis, will help us to 'build back better'.

After seven years or so of the development of the Preston Model, the time is right for a review of its progress and hopes and aspirations for the future. This book provides a very welcome contribution to this reflection, and is the first book to review the Preston Model from an academic perspective. It comes at a time when I, too, am reflecting on our achievements and challenges, soon to be published under the title *How to Paint Your Town Red* (Repeater). I hope that my own forthcoming book, co-written as an example of how community wealth building was introduced in Preston and how it is expanding nationally and internationally, and this book that you hold in your hands, can provide a complete and up-to-date vision of what the Preston Model is and how it might develop in the future, for the benefit of communities in Preston and, indeed, in the rest of the UK and internationally.

In this book, Julian Manley, who has been working closely with me in supporting the development of the Preston Model, and colleague Phil Whyman, have collected chapters that focus on the Preston Model on the one hand, but also on some of the more transferable aspects of the work in Preston. It includes international contributions, from Mondragón and the USA, as well as welcome discussions about the part that education and community can play in a socio-economic reboot of the way we live. The chapters cover the range of the ambitions of the Preston Model, from economic perspectives, through to studies of language and social issues. As such, the book goes a long way to addressing the complexity of the Preston Model and what it represents for the future of our communities around the world. I commend this book to all of us who are striving for a better, richer society based on social justice and democracy for all.

Matthew Brown
Leader, Preston City Council
Senior Fellow for the Promotion of Community Wealth Building with The
Democracy Collaborative

Acknowledgements

Work on the Preston Model has been on-going since 2012, and from then until now, there have been so many people who have contributed to the build-up of the story and therefore to this book that these acknowledgements will never be able to name them all nor do their contributions justice. We apologise in advance for any omissions.

Those actors and stakeholders who helped to develop the Preston Model include the Councillors and officers of Preston City Council. Preston City Council has funded some of the research that has gone into this book, as well as other elements of the Preston Model. To them all, we owe our thanks, and especially to Cllrs Matthew Brown, Martyn Rawlinson, and Debbie Shannon, all of whom provided an initial impetus. In recent times, Cllr Freddie Bailey has continued to bear the torch for Preston City Council. Council officers have played an important part since the beginning, in particular Derek Whyte, without whom many aspects of the Preston Model may never have seen the light of day. Rachel Stringfellow currently takes the weight of the project on her shoulders for the Council. Our thanks to them all.

The people of Preston and its institutions have joined in collaboration at different times and in different ways. We are grateful to the contributions of the Anchor Institutions – especially Gateway Housing Association and Preston's College – and the businesses, co-ops, and voluntary organisations that make up the Preston Panorama, including The Larder co-op, The Birley art studios, Link Psychology Cooperative, The PDF co-op, NW Cabs co-op, TAS Partnership, The Preston Vocational Centre, Let's Grow Preston, and others too numerous to mention.

The Preston Cooperative Development Network continues to play a crucial part in the development of the co-operative aspects of the Preston Model: Gareth Nash, Bob Cannell, Gordon Benson, Gillian Oliver, Aniela Bylinski, Mark Porter and Gaynor Wood have all contributed practically and conceptually to its development.

Mick McKeown and Michael Peck (1Worker1Vote, USA) have provided inspiration in bucketloads and have developed, with colleagues, the union co-op model that will be applied in Preston.

Andrew Birchall continues to be a tireless activist for co-operation and social justice. We are grateful for his commitment, energy, and dedication to democracy.

Thanks to the team at the Cooperative College in Manchester and the members of the Interim Academic Board for the Cooperative University project, in particular Cilla Ross, principal of the college, whose leadership provides motivation and encouragement to all.

We would like to thank our colleagues and friends in Mondragón who have been so generous with their time and advice: Mikel Lezamiz, who was the first from Mondragón to visit Preston, Ander Etxeberria, who welcomed us to Mondragón, Yolanda Lekuona, who helped to fund some of our research, Zigor Ezpeleta, Jon Altuna, Javier Santos, Eva Alejo, Ibon Zugasti, and Marta Boixados, among others: Eskerrik asko!

The University of Central Lancashire has been supportive throughout. In particular, we thank Professor Sue Smith, who funded a secondment for one of the editors of this volume (Manley) to pursue the research around the Preston Model. Our colleagues in the Centre for SME Development have been hugely supportive, in particular Alison Hitchen, the centre manager. Many colleagues in various faculties and schools across the university have provided insights and conversations that have contributed to the on-going debate. Among them, Dr Julie Ridley and Professor David Morris, whose work with Preston communities and community links to the Preston Model has also been funded by the Council.

The Open Society Foundations, the Creative Industries Policy and Evidence Centre (PEC), and National Endowment for Science, Technology and the Arts (NESTA) are currently funding some of the research included in this edition, as well as other aspects of the Preston Model project. We are deeply grateful to them for this support.

We thank our publisher, Routledge, and in particular our commissioning editor, Andy Humphries, for the flexibility and encouragement in the publication of this book, which has faced some unusual delays and hurdles during the current COVID-19 pandemic. Thank you for your co-operative patience!

Finally, and certainly not least, we wish to thank our families for their forbearance during the hours we have spent pulling this book together.

Any remaining errors or omissions we gladly attribute to each other.

Preston
November 2020

Introduction

The Preston Model: let's keep it complex

Julian Manley and Philip B. Whyman

Introduction

This book comes at a time when the public is being exhorted to 'build back better' from the ruins of the coronavirus pandemic. 'Build back better' could also be a description of the motivations behind the emergence of the array of developments that constitute the Preston Model. Another motivation connects one slogan with another: 'build back better' and 'take back control', which is a way the Leader of Preston City Council and one of the prime shakers and movers of the Preston Model, Cllr Matthew Brown, has sometimes described the Preston Model (Chakrabortty 2018). In both cases, when applied to the Preston Model, the slogans resonate with a public desire to reconstruct and be empowered to do so, but perhaps not in the ways that the slogans were intended. 'Build back better' is promoted by the UK Government as a means of rebuilding the capitalist economy (Sharma 2020), and 'take back control' is, of course, the famous Brexit campaign battle cry.

In the context of the Preston Model, the city of Preston is taking back control of its own resources, economy, sense of identity and pride, so weakened by the operation of an orthodox form of capitalism – aided and abetted by the Thatcherite monetarist experiment, which undermined a significant swathe of manufacturing industry across the north of England. Jobs, economic vitality, future prospects, and even on occasion hope itself seemed to have been removed from the local community. With this, the north–south divide also became apparent, and those responsible for this economic decline have been located in the popular mind with having headquarters in London and the south of England, and with global corporate ramifications that are far removed from the realities of people and life in Preston. It is this same system that offered an inward investment package to Preston known as the Tithebarn project, which collapsed as a result of that same system's failure in the form of the 2008 financial crash (BBC 2011). From that moment onwards, instead of bringing in investment from outside, the focus has been on tapping, increasing and retaining the local wealth that already exists in Preston.

In the course of this 'taking back control', the Preston Model is emerging as a design to build back better. However this 'better' is not a reference to a return to the systems that have failed Preston, but rather to build a system that has social and economic ambitions of system change and transformation. Above all, therefore, the Preston Model is an aspiration for change that makes a difference to people's lives in Preston. This is why there is a two-pronged emphasis on the economic and the social:

- To increase economic wealth and create a more equitable share of that wealth (for example, efforts to increase local procurement from anchor institutions, a push for the widespread adoption of the living wage).
- To promote democracy and co-operative values and principles at work that will eventually make a difference to communities in Preston (for example, the focus on the development of worker-owned co-operatives that adhere to co-operative principles).

This book attempts to respond to both the social and the economic aspects of the Preston Model, and we include chapters on both in this book. Section 1 considers the Preston Model as a system of change, while Section 2 contemplates the relevance of related change in other contexts. As such, the book is transdisciplinary in its approach.

Social aspects are approached from a Deleuzian perspective by Manley (Chapter 1), where change is interpreted as a movement from hierarchies to democratic 'rhizomatic' structures, and from a sociological angle by Prinos (Chapter 2), who brings out the voices of Prestonians. The language and discourse of the Preston Model is discussed by Farrelly (Chapter 5), as an important and yet often overlooked element of both understanding and broadening the appeal of the approach. The focus upon communities as the fulcrum of the Preston Model is emphasised by Ridley (Chapter 4). This discussion of community in Preston and the later discussion of social enterprises by Aiken (Chapter 10), expand the understanding of co-operative to mean 'co-operation' as a whole, binding together communities and social enterprises in a single vision, an important aspect of the Preston Model. Although part of the overall strategy in Preston is about creating co-operative businesses, the Preston Model also includes an overarching desire and ambition for a sense of mutual support and co-operation that goes beyond co-operative businesses. This 'beyond' calls for a direction of transformation that requires planning, education and training. Wright and Manley write about the central importance of education in Mondragón, Bilbao, and through to the development of the Preston Model (Chapter 3), and the transformative potential of citizen (adult) education is amplified by Michie in a more general context in Chapter 13.

The economics of the Preston Model and economic democratisation more widely, are discussed in the two chapters by Whyman. Chapter 8 provides an in-depth study of the economics of the Preston Model, outlining the fundamental aspects of the approach before evaluating the conclusions which can be reasonably drawn at this early stage in the evolution of the Preston Model. Chapter 9 considers the Preston Model within the broader context of economic democracy theory and the accompanying academic literature. The intention is to highlight those areas where gains are most likely to be made, potential weaknesses identified and insights gleaned as to how the Preston Model might be extended or refined in the future. The transformational potential of the Preston Model is debated by Bird et al. (Chapter 6), who explore the part that democracy and trade unions play in the model; a theme that is picked up by Peck (Chapter 11), as a voice of activism from the United States, that makes the case for unionised participation in co-operative models as being another way of 'building back better'. This is followed by Elorza and Garmendia, who warn the reader against idealisation of and lazy assumptions about the co-operative model as a means of social change (Chapter 12). The transferability of the economic case in Preston is discussed by Brookes et al. (Chapter 7) who discuss to what extent the economic success of Preston can be made transferable to other sites in the UK, in this case Hertfordshire.

As editors, we provide an overview and conclusion to the book, followed by an appendix that collects references to the many articles that have been written about the Preston Model and have appeared in media outlets in the last five years or so.

A caveat

Depending on any person's ideology, opinion or attitude, focus, work responsibilities and position, status in community and commitment to movements, voluntary work, business or entrepreneurship, and a myriad of angles, prejudices and adopted stances and definitions of selfhood and neighbourhood, it is possible to see the Preston Model as a whole as a manifestation of any one or more of such positions. It can be a radical left policy associated with the now defunct 'Corbynism' (Economist 2017), which persists post-Corbyn (Brown forthcoming; Hatherley 2020); or an rebirth of the co-operative movement from the mid-nineteenth century; a celebration of worker co-operativism as practised in Mondragón (www.mondragon-corporation.com/en/about-us); a leaf taken from the book of the Cleveland Model (www.evgoh.com/about-us); and an example of new municipalism, among other possibilities, and has indeed been seen as all of these things. Equally, an approach vested in the regeneration of local communities could dovetail with a post-Brexit industrial strategy that might prove rather attractive to the current Conservative government. This in itself demonstrates its inherent complexity.

The Preston Model is additionally often perceived in terms of its constituent parts, rather than a holistic approach. For example, very often, it is identified as a project for increasing local procurement through harnessing the economic potential of anchor institutions, mainly because this aspect of the Model was developed in the very beginning of the project and where achievements so far have been greatest (O'Neil 2016; CLES 2019). This is a simplification that also speaks to a perceived reductionist 'scientific' cognitive rational need to fragment, categorise, and classify, as opposed to embracing the constituent parts of the Model as a single entity and observe its development in all its interrelated-ness and complexity. Farrelly, in Chapter 5 of this edition, discusses this very problem of the reduction of complexity in terms of discourse. Like all complex systems, the Preston Model defies straightforward accounts. Indeed, what it is today it will not be tomorrow.

Complexities of this nature, or at least the acknowledgement, (but not the clear perception), of the possible existence of such complexities, are anti-paradigmatic standpoints that are similar to the positions taken by philosophers such as Morton (where complexity is defined as a 'hyperobject' that cannot be perceived through its very complexity, and yet touches people all the time) (Morton 2013), or systems thinkers such as Capra, who weave systems from the natural sciences to the social sciences in webs of increasing complexity. In fact, the more complex they are, the more living these systems become (Capra 2002). We see the Preston Model in these systemic terms, when taken at a distance, and the system that constitutes the Model is 'living', in the sense that it is in many respects a self-organising system of people which is in process of growth, not just because it is unfinished business, but because its process of self-organising and growth is part of its very (in)definition.

The model

Notwithstanding the above, we will proceed to provide a snapshot of the Preston Model as we interpret it at the time of writing (Figure 0.1). In this representation of the Preston Model as an ecosystem, the City of Preston takes position as the centre of the hub in recognition of the fact that the system is a human one, without which there would be no model. This is not as obvious as it might initially seem. It might be possible, for example, to conceive of Preston City Council in their role as political and social leaders in the Preston Model, to be placed in the centre, governing the model from the base of a national Labour Party aspiring to govern the nation.

Indeed, the reference to 'Corbynism' in relation to the Preston Model would seem to corroborate that (Manley 2018). However, the relationship between the Labour Party and other stakeholders in Preston is one of partnership and community between the various anchor institutions and many other community players and activists. The political identity of the Preston Model in this sense has often been played down, and the strategies that form part of the Model have often been referred to as 'common sense', rather than progressive or socialist action. Russell and Milburn argue that socialist action *is* or can be transformed into 'common sense' behaviour as a flip side to Thatcherite behaviour change:

> After more than forty years of social conditioning within the socio-eco-nomic infrastructure of neoliberalism, we need to start consciously envi-sioning and promulgating a new common sense, designing institutions that work to inculcate and disseminate a different everyday understanding of what constitutes rational behaviour.
>
> (Russell and Milburn 2018, p. 50)

The Preston Model Ecosystem Design

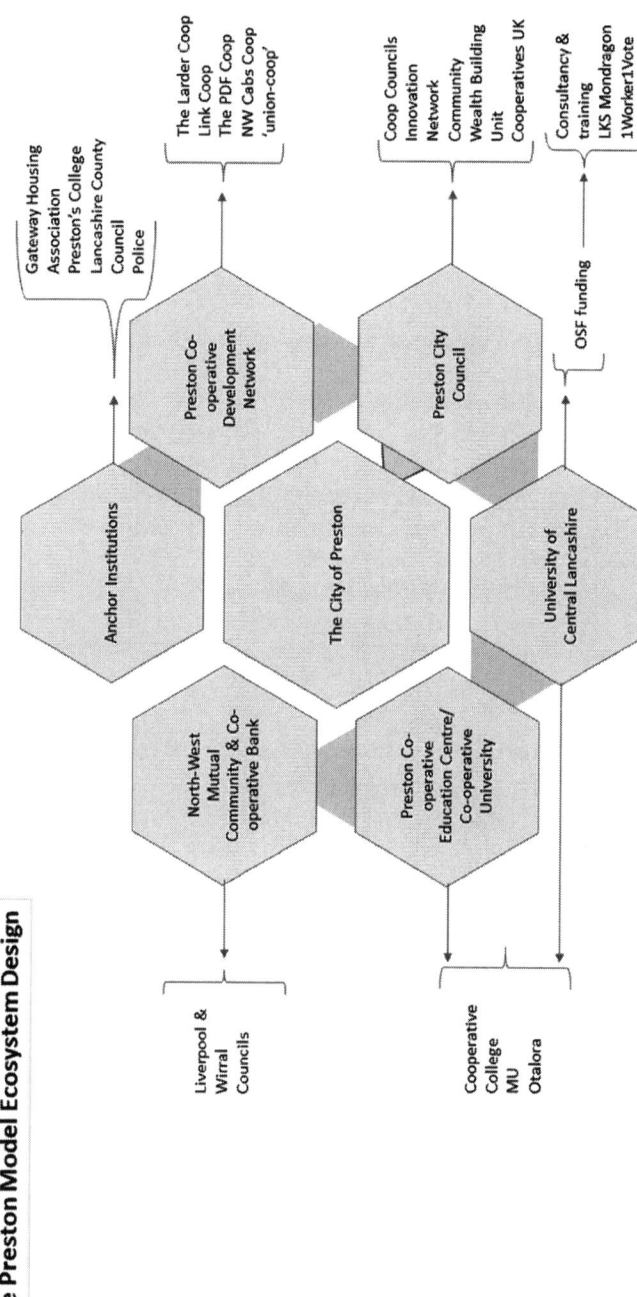

Figure 0.1 Snapshot of the Preston Model
Source: Julian Manley

In this way, the Preston Model as a strategy has something in common with so-called 'new municipalism', (Russell 2019; Thompson forthcoming; Davies 2021). This ties in with Russell's assertion that:

> These new municipalist initiatives *must not* be understood simply as left political parties looking to implement progressive policies at the municipal scale. Engagement with institutions and elections should be understood as a component of broader strategic approaches, rather than the defining feature of the new municipalism.
>
> (Russell 2019, p. 997; Russell's italics)

Similarly, Thompson (forthcoming) emphasises defining new municipalism as 'rupturing' traditional party politics.

The ecosystem in Figure 0.1, therefore, places the city of Preston in the centre, rather than Preston City Council. Nevertheless, it is also true that the Council has been visible and instrumental in the development of the Model. Unlike Barcelona, for example, with a new municipal movement taking office from the roots of activism (Davies 2021), the Preston Model has emerged from traditional party politics, albeit in its more radical manifestation. For the Preston Model, then, there is a strong link between the City Council and the City of Preston, as demonstrated in Figure 0.1.

This does not mean that the version of 'new municipalism' in Preston is 'managed', as categorised by Thompson, where he makes a distinction between three kinds of municipalism, 'platform', 'autonomist' and 'managed'. Certainly, the Preston Model is not managed in the sense that the work in Cleveland was managed, which was very much a top-down effort where Ted Howard and the Cleveland Foundation designed and launched the entire project, including all the negotiations with the anchor institutions and the specific design templates of the three worker-owned co-operatives that have a specific mission to supply the anchors, as well as a large investment of capital. As Prinos, in this book (Chapter 2) explains, there is certainly an element of managed transition in Preston, but at the same time there are also feelings of a social movement in development. The Manley and Froggett (2016) report to Preston City Council particularly emphasised the co-operative readiness of Preston-based organisations independently of the Council's projects. Moreover, the first co-operative developed under the Preston Model umbrella, a café and food education hub called The Larder, was not designed to serve an anchor institution, but designed itself from its own roots in community activism. Other co-operative businesses created as part of the Preston Model include a digital co-operative, created by students and staff from the University of Central Lancashire (UCLan), and a taxi co-operative created largely by cab drivers of British Asian/Asian descent, neither of which were designed to serve an anchor institution in the way the Evergreen co-operatives in Cleveland were designed. In fact, these examples are closer to the description by Thompson et al. (2020) of the actors in the Preston Model as being 'activist entrepreneurs' (p. 1178).

The 'management' of the Preston Model is often limited to facilitating a framework for the emergence of opportunities that are captured 'bottom-up'. Thompson's 'managed' version of municipalism is based on a strategy that aims to regenerate the local economy. Again, although this is partly true in Preston, it misses the fact that the Preston Model is just as interested in regenerating democracy and community as in promoting the economy, as Ridley's chapter in this book (Chapter 4) testifies. As is often the trap when complex movements or systems are classified in this way, it turns out that the reality is rather more complex. For Thompson, the Mayor of Barcelona, Ada Colau's view of her version of municipalism, 'platform municipalism', as an 'agora' contrasts with the Preston Model's 'temple' pursuit of change, with the 'temple' indicating top-down management, while the 'agora' indicates a social space of democratic debate and generation from community activism-up. However, this is a simplification, as Manley (Chapter 1), Prinos (Chapter 2), Ridley (Chapter 4) and Bird et al. (Chapter 6) discuss from their different perspectives. Manley's chapter explains the 'rhizomatic', flat structure of the Preston Model and the importance of shared affect; Prinos provides a DNA of Preston citizens' views of the model; Ridley discusses the importance of community engagement; Bird et al. discuss the development of democracy through the co-designing of a union–co-op collaboration for Preston.

Returning to Figure 0.1, the Preston Model includes the other important stakeholders in the design, which is a 'design' mostly in the sense that it exists as ideas that are mostly suggestive rather than prescriptive in nature. Some of the structure is more established than others and the constituent parts are in various stages of development. Importantly, the role of Preston City Council is closely linked to the University and the Preston Cooperative Development Network (PCDN).

The PCDN was created as a result of a Preston City Council funded research report carried out by the University (Manley and Froggett 2016). The creation of the PCDN emerged, therefore from a PCC/UCLan partnership, and collaboration between the three has led to external funding from the Open Society Foundations (www.opensocietyfoundations.org) (OSF) to further the development of the Preston Model. Although this funding includes start-up funds for worker-owned co-operatives, there is also funding available for training and consultancy from Mondragón that brings the ecosystem experience of Mondragón and Bilbao to Preston, and the 1Worker1Vote organisation in the United States (http://1worker1vote.org), that provides support for the union–co-op work that is described in Bird et al.'s chapter in this book. Peck (Chapter 11) describes some of the aspects of the development of the union–co-op in the United States and shows how the Preston project is not confined to the 'local', but is as much a community of practice as it is a community of place, which is not always noted in discussion of the Preston Model.

The possibility of transferability of the Preston Model is discussed in the case study by Brookes et al. In Chapter 7, giving further indications of the model as a community of practice, where the design, such as it is, is moulded and adapted to a different place according to the needs and requirements of that place. In other words, the Preston Model is not a templated design to be applied to place, but rather an aspiration to practice based on firmly held but loosely structured, beliefs with their roots in 'common sense' rather than ideology. It is worth noting, for example in this context, that the early champions of the co-operative in Preston were as much of Liberal Democrat origin as they were a Labour Party policy design.

An emphasis of the thinking behind the Preston Model is on education and training, represented in Figure 0.1 by UCLan and the Preston Cooperative Education Centre (PCEC), and the OSF funding supports the development of the education centre. The Education Centre speaks to the ambition in Preston for a socio-economic transformation that is sustainable and embedded in future developments. The Mondragón experience places a huge emphasis on education and on encouraging a co-operative culture through education at all levels, and, as Wright and Manley demonstrate in their chapter, (Chapter 3), education and training, from Mondragón to Preston is a fundamental part of the sustainable development of change. It has always been clear since the publication of the report recommendations (Manley and Froggett 2016) that education needed to be an essential aspect of the model, especially with regards the dissemination and awareness building of what co-operatives and co-operation are in a place like Preston which shares with the rest of the UK a relative public ignorance of the idea of co-operatives as businesses that might have a significant role to play in the economy.

Education in the Preston Model includes a range of education and training ranging from practical and skills-based learning to degree level education in collaboration with the Cooperative College in Manchester. It includes training and work that will lead to co-operative businesses and an incubation of those businesses. It also includes potential partnerships between the university's Centre for SME Development and its incubation hub, Propeller, and FE providers in Preston. Michie in Chapter 13 of this book further discusses the value of adult education in the context of the desire to establish a strong, autonomous basis for people's lives with relevance to a city like Preston, where governance emerges from self-governance rather than imposition. This is an important observation, since adult education has very often been squeezed by a lack of financial support, amidst the commodification of the education system. Yet, the insight – that citizens and workers need a sufficient level of knowledge and skills to make the most of the opportunities provided by initiatives such as the Preston Model – is a central feature of most discussion relating to economic democracy across different time periods and national settings, as noted by Whyman (Chapter 9). Preston has existing local resources that could facilitate this broader citizen education. It is blessed with two further education colleges and a large university, all anchor institutions, as well as other training centres, such as the Preston Vocational Centre, which is affiliated to Community Gateway Housing Association, another anchor institution, and provides training in construction skills for young people of school age. As anchor institutions, all of these educational offers combine with the future PCEC to offer a strong basis for change in Preston within the framework of the Preston Model.

The final piece of the jigsaw in Figure 0.1 is the development of a bank for Preston. In collaboration with Wirral and Liverpool Councils a mutual society, North West Mutual Ltd, has been registered with the Financial Conduct Authority, and aims to serve Preston and the region in the near future. The mission of the future bank is described as the following:

- the creation of a bank to serve the everyday financial needs of ordinary people, local community groups and small and medium sized companies
- help redress regional inequalities, make financial inclusion the norm, build and build community wealth
- significantly increase the proportion of bank lending going to the 'real' (non-financialised) economy and SMEs instead of the financial economy
- build regional economic resilience, and
- bring about a revitalisation of customer service, relationship banking and mutual trust.(Preston City Council 2020)

The Bank, as in the other pieces of the Model depicted in Figure 0.1, is envisioned as an integral part of a holistic approach to the socio-economic transformation that constitutes the Preston Model as a whole, that is to say, 'increasing the amount of procurement spend within Preston, promoting the real living wage, expanding worker ownership' (Preston City Council 2020).

The Preston Model is, then, a complex mix of policies, ambitions, current developments and future dreams, an unusual hotchpotch of semi-related developments that loosely hang together and build up their momentum through a combination of blue sky thinking and 'management' and a determination to make the most of whatever can be made to succeed at any given moment and in collaboration with a wide range of local actors.

Tracing the progress of the Preston Model

The timeline in Figure 0.2 shows the main developmental moments of the Preston Model. Tracing these events, it can be seen, as indicated above, how the model emerged (and is still emerging) from a combination of 'management', top-down and bottom-up, and good ideas and responses to fortune/misfortune. Serendipity plays its part, especially because until the moment of writing this Introduction, resources have been scarce and stakeholders in the model have had to rely on creative ideas and the making the most of any arising opportunity. What the timeline also demonstrates is the gradual, organic nature of the growth of the Preston Model, in contrast (as an example) to the meticulously planned design of the Cleveland Foundation in the creation of the Evergreen co-operatives.

The story begins with the demise of the inward investment programme known as the Tithebarn Project, which was intended to develop the city centre,

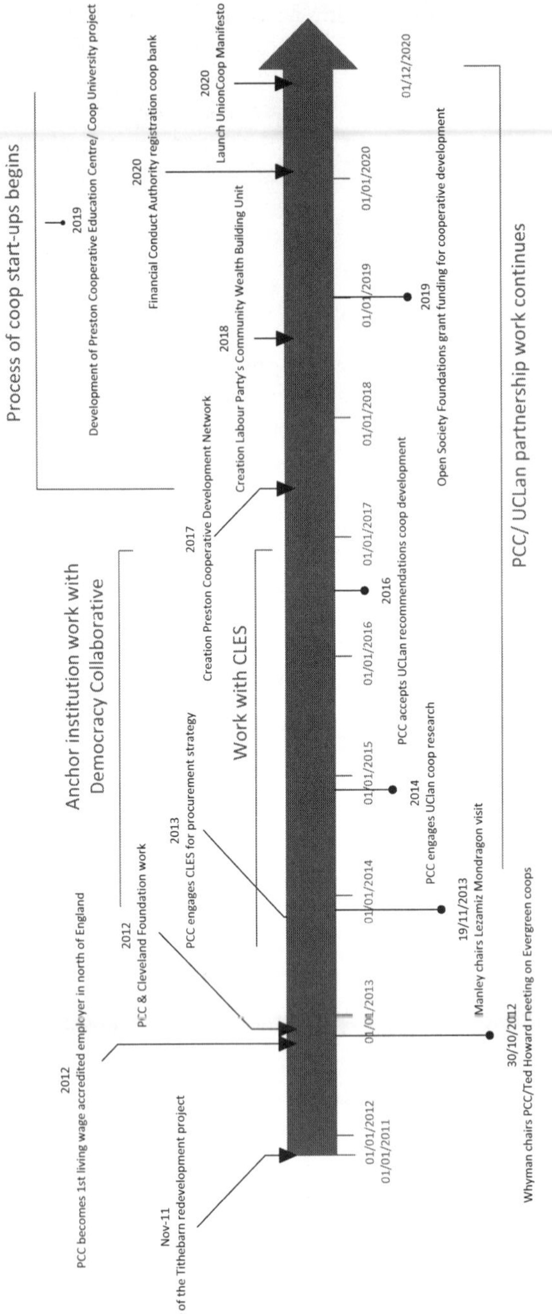

Figure 0.2 Timeline of the Preston Model
Source: Julian Manley

including new cinemas, shops and a redesign of the city centre, and, most importantly, a commitment from John Lewis to build a flagship store as part of the project. It was the withdrawal of John Lewis that provoked the collapse of the project in 2011. The collapse of the project was also symbolic of the collapse of inward investment both as a physical reality and as a sign of the dependence and lack of empowerment that a place like Preston has when relying on investment from outside. From this disaster were sown the seeds of the Preston Model, with Cllr Matthew Brown engaging on a mission to find alternatives to traditional forms of regeneration.

In 2012, Preston City Council became the first local authority to introduce the living wage, and in the course of 2012–13, Brown began to make contacts with the Cleveland Foundation, whose Evergreen co-operatives project appeared to provide some potential alternative to ways of running a local economy. At the end of 2012, Philip Whyman, co-editor of this book, chaired a meeting where Ted Howard from Cleveland gave a talk to City Council members and others about the Evergreen co-operatives. In 2013, Julian Manley, this book's other co-editor, organised a series of seminars, talks, and classes from a senior representative of the Mondragon Cooperative Corporation, Mikel Lezamiz, to discuss and inform the public, including Council representatives about the co-operative work in Mondragón. At this meeting, Manley forged a working relationship with Cllr Brown that has endured throughout the development of the Model.

From this moment, the Preston Model took two complementary paths, one with the Council in partnership with the Centre for Local Economic Strategies (CLES) to investigate the leakage of procurement spend outside Preston by anchor institutions in Preston, and the other through the Council's partnership with the University of Central Lancashire (UCLan) to investigate the potential for the development of co-operatives in Preston as part of an alternative economy. The former strand led to a transformation of the spending of local anchor institutions in Preston, with spending in Preston increasing from 5% of anchor institution spend in 2013 to 18.2% in 2017, and in the Lancashire region as a whole, from 39% to 79.2%. The latter led to the pivotal report to the Council (Manley and Froggett 2016) that recommended co-operative development in Preston, accepted by the Council and resulting in the creation of the Preston Cooperative Development Network in 2017. In 2018, the first worker-owned co-operative, the Larder, was created with the support of the PCDN and Preston City Council.

Meanwhile, in early 2018, the Labour Party created a Community Wealth Building Unit in order to channel lessons from the Preston Model to other local authorities in the UK. This followed an intensive period of talks and presentations by Brown and Manley between 2017-to the present, and visits to Preston by influential politicians such as John McDonnell and Ed Miliband, turning the Preston Model into a national and even an international Model.

In 2019 the Open Society Foundations awarded funding to the Preston project partnered by Preston City Council, the University of Central Lancashire and the

Preston Cooperative Development Network. The funding provides start-up support for 10 worker-owned co-operatives, including a Preston Cooperative Education Centre, training and consultancy from Mondragón and 1Worker1Vote in the USA, as well as project resources and an evaluation team from UCLan. This development period ends in March 2022 and includes significant additional investment from the City Council and the University, including dedicated time to the project allotted to Council officers, Councillors and UCLan staff.

In 2020, a Project Committee was set up to advise on the project 'Designing a Co-operative Entrepreneurship Initiative for Preston', in collaboration with Mondragón. It is hoped that this will lead to further Preston Model project design as projected by Preston City Council with future funding for city centre projects including the possibility of housing the various elements of the Preston Model project under one roof.

Also in 2020 the Financial Conduct Authority approved the registration of the proposed community and co-operative bank for Preston, (created in Preston with the support of Wirral and Liverpool Councils), which will have a mission of supporting all aspects of the Preston Model, providing loans and financial support that the major banks would be reluctant to give.

Later in 2020, *Union Co-ops UK: A Manifesto for Decent Work* (discussed by Bird et al. in Chapter 6), was launched in collaboration with the Preston Cooperative Development Network to support the commitment as part of the Preston Model, to include trade union participation in co-operative development.

Simplicity out of complexity

The Preston Model is, therefore, simultaneously both complex and yet has an innate simplicity. It is a straightforward argument to make that there are areas of the country that have missed out on much of the prosperity and investment resources taken for granted by core regions, and that this is not only damaging to these areas, but to the whole of the country, as its economic performance is sub-optimal as a result. This is, in essence, the argument made by former Chancellor Osborne, when he advocated the rebalancing of the UK economy, and underpins the Northern Powerhouse project. But it goes further than that. Where local communities wish to take back greater control over their lives, they need a new approach to economic development – one that places local communities at the heart of what is to be achieved, and identified as the key resource in bringing about social and economic change. Citizen empowerment is essential, suitably facilitated through educational opportunities, as any claim that local communities are indeed taking back control requires the authentic local voice to be at the heart of any change. Depending upon how this is handled, this could be narrow and self-defeating, or enriching and transformative – not just for the local people immediately involved, but more broadly. That is the essence of democracy. It can be used to level up all citizens or focus more narrowly upon certain segmented interest groups. Yet, it is certainly the case, that there are many marginalised and left behind communities, in the UK and across the globe, who have taken particular interest in the potential of initiatives like the Preston Model to inspire them to consider different development paths.

Achieving these simple objectives, however, is more complicated. The absence of a dominant policy organisation – which in the case of Preston would be the City Council as a left-wing Labour Party group, but that prefers to share policy decisions with other stakeholders in Preston – implies that initiatives have to be at least partly negotiated among different stakeholder groups and implementation is dependent upon their continued commitment. In one sense, enacting initiatives is more difficult, and yet the absence of dominant institutional actors does increase the possibility for a truly bottom-up approach, where democratic participation becomes a necessity as well as a desired feature of the Preston Model. In terms of transferability from Preston to other parts of the UK, different areas will have different approaches by virtue of the differences or distinctiveness of their individual local voices. While it is true that ensuring the authentic presence of local voices must be common to both the Preston Model and others that follow Preston's lead, paradoxically it is also the reason why different areas will diverge in their interpretation and implementation of a Preston Model-type approach. The importance of local voices resides in a vision of participatory democracy taking precedence over the representational democracy of elected Councillors. Similarly, this will inevitably imply that different areas and their communities, interested in implementing a Preston Model-type approach, will take different decisions and design their own set of distinct actions. To that extent, the Preston Model is less a formulaic structure that can be imposed upon communities in different circumstances, than an inspiration to those local actors to do it for themselves.

It is the hope of the editors, shared by the contributors of all of the chapters contained within this book, that we have successfully captured a flavour of the different aspects that, when combined, are manifested in the form of the Preston Model. Hopefully we have transmitted something of the authentic local voice in our description of the development of the approach, thus capturing the interrelationship between simplicity and complexity. Moreover, we hope that this book has successfully evaluated the achievements realised to date, in the light of the existing academic literature, to place the Preston Model into a broader context. In these unprecedented, difficult, and unstable times, we hope that the reader will find this book both instructive and thought provoking. Our final wish is that you enjoy the material contained within this volume and that it sparks in you new ideas of how we can truly build back better.

References

BBC (2011) Preston Tithebarn scheme abandoned after John Lewis withdraws. Retrieved from www.bbc.co.uk/news/uk-england-lancashire-15571764) accessed 03. 11. 20.

Brown, M. (Forthcoming) *How to Paint Your Town Red*. London: Repeater.

Capra, F. (2002) *The Hidden Connections*. London: Flamingo.

CLES (2019) How we built community wealth in Preston. Retrieved from https://cles.org.uk/tag/the-preston-model (accessed 03. 11. 20).

Chakrabortty, A. (2018) In 2011 Preston hit rock bottom. Then it took back control. *The Guardian*. Retrieved from www.theguardian.com/commentisfree/2018/jan/31/preston-hit-rock-bottom-took-back-control (accessed 01. 10. 20).

Davies, J.S. (2021) *Between Realism and Revolt: Governing Cities in the Crisis of Neoliberal Globalism*. Bristol: Bristol University Press.

Economist (2017) Preston, Jeremy Corbyn's model town: how one city became an unlikely laboratory for Corbynomics. *The Economist*. Retrieved from www.economist.com/britain/2017/10/19/preston-jeremy-corbyns-model-town (accessed 03. 11. 20).

Hatherley, O. (2020) *Red Metropolis: Socialism and the Government of London*. London: Repeater.

Manley, J. and Froggett, L. (2016) *Cooperative activity in Preston*. Preston: University of Central Lancashire. Retrieved from http://clok.uclan.ac.uk/14526/1/Cooperative%20activity%20PrestonREPORT%20copy.pdf (accessed 03. 11. 20).

Manley, J. (2018) Preston changed its fortunes with 'Corbynomics' – now other cities are doing the same. *The Conversation*. Retrieved from https://theconversation.com/preston-changed-its-fortunes-with-corbynomics-now-other-cities-are-doing-the-same-106293 (accessed 03. 11. 20).

Morton, T. (2013) *Hyperobjects: Philosophy and Ecology After the End of the World*. Minneapolis, MN: University of Minneapolis Press.

O'Neil, M. (2016) The road to socialism is the A59: the Preston model. *Renewal* 24(2): 69–78.

Preston City Council (2020) North West councils partner up for Community Bank. Retrieved from www.preston.gov.uk/article/2498/North-West-Councils-partner-up-for-Community-Bank (accessed 31. 10. 20).

Russell, B. (2019) Beyond the local trap: new municipalism and the rise of the fearless cities. *Antipode*, 51(3), pp. 989–1010.

Russell, B. and Milburn, K. (2018) What can an institution do? Towards public-common partnerships and a new common-sense. *Renewal*, 26(4), pp. 45–55.

Sharma, A. (2020) *Let's build back better*. Keynote address at the Let's Build Back Better event, hosted by the British High Commission, Wellington. Retrieved from www.gov.uk/government/speeches/lets-build-back-better (accessed 01. 11. 12).

Thompson, M. (forthcoming) What's so new about new municipalism? *Progress in Human Geography*, online first. Retrieved from https://journals.sagepub.com/doi/full/10.1177/0309132520909480 (accessed 03. 11. 20).

Thompson, M., Nowak, V., Southern, A., Davies, J. and Furmedge, P. (2020) Re-grounding the city with Polanyi: from urban entrepreneurialism to entrepreneurial municipalism. *Environment and Planning A: Economy and Space*, 52(6), pp. 1171–1194.

Part I
The Preston Model

1   The Preston Model: from top-down to rhizomatic-up

How the Preston Model challenges the system

Julian Manley

Introduction

The 'Preston Model' is not really a model at all, in the sense that there is no finally defined and complete framework that can easily be referred to and identified as such.

This is probably a frustrating way to begin a chapter on the Preston Model, but it actually points to the underlying strength of the socio-economic changes that have been taking place in Preston since 2012/2013. This strength is rooted in its autopoietic flexibility and responsiveness, in its potential to allow for movement, change and adaptation to circumstances, needs and requirements as they appear, so that ideologies and fixed ideas or templates for change do not impede its progress. This has sometimes been recognised before. For example, in the Centre for Local Economic Strategy's (CLES) report on the Preston Model, they say that 'we must see what has happened in Preston as an example of the benefits brought by restless innovation and creativity' as opposed to a 'model' that can be easily transferred elsewhere (CLES, 2019: 25). In a sense, however, the CLES report does the opposite of what it says, by providing what looks remarkably like a 'model', with guidance as to how to achieve success through a series of tried and tested steps towards 'community wealth building', which, dubbed as such, can be made transferable to other places. Instead of this, the Preston Model is a hotchpotch of more or less progressive ideas, none of them completely new, thrown into a cauldron of desire for pro-active and positive change where change once seemed impossible. It combines pragmatic approaches to wealth building, for example by encouraging increased local spending by 'anchor institutions, with an enigmatic sense of wanting to live and work differently. This latter 'sense' comes close to Raymond's 'structures of feeling' (Matthews, 2001), with 'structure' in the case of the Preston Model being the 'system' that is changing, and 'feeling' denoting a quality of unknown but positive force. This is how one respondent from a Preston anchor institution puts it:

> I believe that regardless of how it will develop, from what I understand I would describe it [the Preston Model] as an effort to present an alternative to neoliberalism; and also in theory at least to these massive issues that we have

in Britain and honestly all over the world with support for the vulnerable, the environment, the insecurity young people so ... all these things; that's a tall order but I think kind of like the MeToo movement these are efforts that broadly speaking try to address these huge inequalities in our society.

(Interviewee A, anchor institution 1, Preston)

Above all, what this quotation expresses is a desire for social and ethical justice as a priority over bald economic targets. In terms of system change, these socio-ethical desires are couched in the language of a movement (compared to '#MeToo') and an undefined system change (alternative to neoliberalism). Although it is true that the speaker also refers to young people's insecurity and inequalities in society, which would suggest providing improved economic possibilities for the young and a more equal distribution of wealth, the tone and emphasis of this response evokes a social and cultural reaction over an economic imperative. Indeed, it is this very emphasis that is likely to characterise the emergence of many of the different aspects identified with the Preston Model. After all, one of the most striking developments in Preston has been the huge increase in local procurement from the various anchor institutions. As is now reasonably well known, local spend in the Preston and Lancashire region has dramatically increased since 2013 (Manley 2018), but it is certainly not obvious why the people responsible for this increase in these institutions would have been bothered to make these changes on such a large scale. Certainly, there must have been little economic advantage in doing so, and some extra avoidable effort. Instead of a primary focus on the economy, employees close to procurement activities in the Preston anchor institutions appear to be drawn to social value in a vague but aspirational manner that speaks to a system or structure of feeling:

In my opinion people feel that there is an opportunity with the Preston Model for the city and they area to improve its economy and community without necessarily knowing much about the Preston Model; and the same goes for some people in anchors, willing to try and find new ways to add social value to the ways they do business.

(Interviewee B, anchor institution 2, Preston)

Significantly, in this quotation, the speaker indicates how it is possible to improve both economy *and* community without knowing much about the Preston Model. It would seem that in this case, then, the Preston Model is not a 'model' as such but more similar to an aspiration for social justice that might suggest different ways of doing business. This different way is identified as 'social value' and it is not difficult to imagine that this is implicitly contrasted to the other way of doing business in the neoliberal fashion denounced by Interviewee A, above. Although this period of change in Preston coincides with the Public Services (Social Value) Act 2012, which encourages local authorities to pay greater attention to local stakeholders when considering procurement, there are indications that in Preston the response to social value and the consideration of the effects of changes in procurement towards greater wealth generation and retention in Preston, run deeper and beyond a reaction to law and the guidance of central government. Many of the anchor institutions appear to be directly responding to the agency and empowerment that is provided by a small shift in perspective that makes the good that emerges from the attention given to social value coveted, valuable and worth pursuing. In particular, such changes can be felt and noted by buyer and supplier in immediate ways that can then be associated to abstract notions such as pride and hope. From this perspective, for example, it is right and just to recognise that a local supplier will have a much reduced carbon footprint compared to an international corporation. A local supplier will provide local quality jobs as a result of increased procurement. These are not primarily economic considerations, even though there may be some economic benefits in the longer term. These are social and ethical considerations. Indeed, although they work in a neoliberal context, they shift that context from its purest manifestation that focuses uniquely on price and value for money. In this way, it is the people inside the anchor institutions who are making small but significant changes to satisfy a sense of what is right and good for themselves and the people around them, rather than according to the rules and norms of the economic market. It is not that the latter is ignored or rejected, however. This is not a revolution against the system or a battle of ideologies (even if some of the political actors would themselves see it in those terms). It is characterised more by a sense of what it is to be human and what has often been characterised by stakeholders in Preston as 'common sense'.

One of the most fascinating aspects of the Preston Model is precisely this self-organising, relatively unplanned development where change emerges through the very haecceity of the untapped and hidden existence of human interconnectivity that creates a web of hope that deep in the very makeup of human being in relationship with each other. It maybe comes close to the emerging awareness of the importance of human co-operation and altruism as qualities innate to social relationships, as suggested in Rutger Bregman's new publication Humankind (Bregman, 2020). The Preston Model was born in 2012 from adversity and despair (Manley 2018; Chakrabortty 2018), and Bregman identifies the need to re-evaluate human endeavour especially in the light of multiple crises as a need for friendliness, co-operation and hope. In doing so, Bregman emphasises how such qualities are natural in humankind, and therefore available for nurturing. Bregman's book promises to provide continuing evidence of the growing sense of system change that the Preston Model is anticipating, as I have discussed elsewhere with reference to Preston, Bermuda, and Mondragón (Manley and Aiken, 2020).

Beginnings

The Preston Model has been linked to developments in Cleveland Ohio (Sheffield 2017), and it is in Cleveland via Ted Howard and the Democracy Collaborative that the idea of using anchor institutions – large, wealthy institutions that are 'anchored' to place, such as a hospital, for example – to generate more local spending was first devised and later adopted by Preston City Council's

Labour Party administration, under the guidance of Cllr Matthew Brown. However, the design of the strategy that used anchor institutions in Cleveland differs in a very significant manner from events developing in Preston. In Cleveland, Howard and colleagues in the Cleveland Foundation and Democracy Collaborative were able to design the entire formula and apply the whole project as a top-down initiative, from a blank slate beginning to the final outcome. Lacking the philanthropy and design capabilities available in the United States, actors and stakeholders in Preston have had to rely on any available help and a good dose of goodwill and creativity. The Council cleverly exploited the possibilities of the EU's URBACT project,[1] bringing together anchor institutions and local businesses to discuss ways of changing local procurement habits. The Council embarked on a spend analysis (2013–2017), which enabled stakeholders, including the anchor institutions, to understand exactly how much wealth was leaving the local area and how much of this could be repatriated. The City Council, along with its think tank partner, CLES, visited the local anchor institutions to propose a vision and options for increasing local wealth, and changes in spending were initiated. However, the Council's role was more one of suggestion, encouragement, and persuasion rather than a detailed strategy along the lines of the work in Cleveland. Instead of negotiating a whole package with anchor institutions, as in Cleveland (for example working with the hospital to ensure a client for the Evergreen Laundry co-operative), anchors in Preston have used their own initiatives, following discussions with the Council, to increase local procurement. The work in Preston to create local worker-owned co-operatives (bound in a single 'package' in the Cleveland example) is only loosely linked to the anchors' changing procurement habits, and the idea that these – anchors and co-operative development – can become strongly connected in a practical way, while a distinct possibility, is secondary to the development of the Preston Model ethos that has its own impetus. In Preston, the spirit of co-operation (Manley and Froggett, 2016) and the desire for change has been an underlying but vital factor in the transformations taking place. This is what is meant by Andrew Ridehalgh, Procurement Manager of Preston City Council, when he says:

> ... not only has 'spend analysis' enabled us to develop an evidence base; it has also enabled us to work together more effectively, to develop a common vision, to understand the Preston business base, and most importantly change the culture of procurement.
>
> (Quoted in Baqueriza-Jackson, 2019)

This is where the bottom-up story of Preston slowly becomes apparent.

Common sense and ownership

The so-called 'Preston Model' consists of at least the following initiatives ('at least' because a new as yet unforeseen or incipient initiative may emerge at any moment):

1 Stimulating local procurement of anchor institutions (including Lancashire County Council, University of Central Lancashire, Preston's College, Cardinal Newman College, Community Gateway Housing Association, Lancashire Constabulary), thereby increasing the generation and retention of local wealth.

2 A programme of development of co-operative businesses, especially worker-owned (centralised in the work of the Preston Co-operative Development Network (PCDN)), creating high quality jobs and encouraging the adoption of democratic principles in the workplace and in community.

3 A very pro-active encouragement of the adoption of the living wage in Preston, encouraging inclusivity and equity.

4 The on-going development of a community and co-operative bank for Preston and the immediate region in the NW of England, ensuring that future local businesses, such as SMEs and co-operatives have access to financial support that normal High Street banks would be reluctant to back.

5 An open-minded and pro-community approach to the use of Council buildings, such as, for example, the collaboration with fine arts graduates from the University, creating artists' studios in the centre of the city (The Birley), encouraging the activation of an arts and cultural hub for Preston.

6 A growing partnership with the University, both from an economic perspective – such as in encouraging local procurement and collaborating on the development of the University campus to be shared with the citizens of Preston – and in partnership with the University's Centre for SME Development within Innovation and Enterprise, encouraging the development of networks of SMEs and a more significant encouragement for graduates to create new businesses for Preston. Work with the University includes growing research and evaluation programmes to encourage the development of co-operatives and communities in Preston.

7 Work towards the development of a Preston Co-operative Education Centre, as part of the Co-operative University project in partnership with the Co-operative College in Manchester.

As time goes on, it seems that these different initiatives begin to coalesce and take on the form of design, but it is a design that begins to make sense through its own emergence as opposed to grand plan. In fact, there is a lot of 'letting go' involved in these developments, the opposite of a strategy or plan that has been designed *a priori*, which is more often associated with urban regeneration plans, especially the traditional plans that inject inward investment into a town or city. As the council's website rightly proclaims:

> Some of this approach is about the council letting go of its controlling role, which is not always easy. But it does allow us to open up opportunities for other elements of civic society to have much more control over their own agendas, whether those be single issue or neighbourhood focused.
>
> (Preston City Council 2020)

Of particular interest in this respect is how Cllr Brown has frequently referred to the Preston Model as being about 'taking back control', and this has been taken up by others (e.g. Chakrabortty, 2018; Watkins, 2018; Jones 2020), taking the Brexit slogan and turning this into a shout for local democracy. In this case, 'taking back control' is the same as letting go of control, meaning that the Preston Model is precisely about 'control' finding its way to communities of stakeholders who self-organise developments and improvements to their lives. In other words, communities and the people who populate them ('communities' here being multi-tiered examples of communities of place, interest and practice) are empowered to take responsibility for what directly matters to them. This is not where the emphasis may be in many urban regeneration schemes that have been focussed on the physical environment linked to efforts to improve the local economy, such as the Tithebarne project (BBC, 2011), which was the failed urban regeneration scheme that kick started the change of approach to improvements for Preston from 2012 onwards.

Although urban regeneration schemes in theory need to attend to social needs as well as environmental and economic imperatives (Tallon, 2010), there may be difficulties in understanding the meaning of 'social' in the context of urban regeneration, where the project is very much centred and controlled by governing authorities and investors. Hausner (1993: 526, quoted in Tallon, 2010: 5) has 'emphasised the inherent weaknesses of approaches to regeneration that are "short term, fragmented, ad hoc and project-based without an overall strategic framework for city-wide development"'. Some of what Hausner pointed to in this context was the need for urban regeneration projects to include a far greater empowerment of local communities, and he recommended 'the decentralisation of responsibility to local communities' and 'the further strengthening of local civic renewal partnerships' (Hausner, 1993: 529).

In Preston, as if by a sort of guided chance and by way of a series of half-planned directions, there is a sense of transformation of communities in the direction of empowerment and participation. Why this has come about and how it is sustained are important questions, not only in order to maintain the development in Preston, but also to consider the potential for the transferability of the Preston Model elsewhere.

As has already been indicated, the beginnings of the Preston Model came about by chance, or 'bad luck turned good' (i.e. the collapse of the Tithebarne project and consequently the impossibility of a renewed project for inward investment at a time of austerity). While many places might have fallen into passivity in the face of such a challenge, Matthew Brown, at a time when the late Peter Rankin was Leader, began leading a change of attitude towards local development, based around a set of concepts that could generally be understood and supported without too much difficulty by most people. These ideas have been referred to by many in Preston as 'common sense', even though Brown is politically identified as belonging to the radical left. Themes broadly relate to local democracy, tapping local wealth, creating a living wage and quality employment, tackling inequality and deprivation, and none of these ideas are in themselves controversial. Neither are they particularly politically left leaning. The ambiguity behind the political position of these ideas has meant that despite the political identification of the project with 'Corbynomics' (Manley, 2018), and elements of the Labour Party seeking solutions to the party's crisis after the 2019 election (Jones, 2020), many people are able to embrace the Preston Model as 'common sense'. To a certain extent, the ideas can be acceptable to a range of political opinions. For example, with reservations, politicians from the Liberal Democrat and the Conservative parties in Preston are able to uncontroversially show interest in the ideas:

> I think what is very interesting as a whole, is that the Preston Model sort of breeds innovation … the Preston Model is different, it's new, it's possibly unique in some ways, it's influencing the people.
>
> > (Interviewee C, Lib Dem)

> It is a way for chief economic players in the area to help the local economy, at least to a degree; but I wonder how viable this strategy is going forward, especially if it becomes the foremost economic tool in play.
>
> > (Interviewee D, Conservative)

A Liberal Democrat think piece is able to reference the Preston Model:

> The Liberal Democrats are a party with a strong local government base that has pioneered localism and community politics, but at the same time we are hampered by working within one of world's most centralised democracies. The Preston approach could provide more room for manoeuvre in straitened times. On the other hand it's arguably a form of protectionism that raises the familiar localism vs liberalism tensions.
>
> > (Liberal Democrat Voice, 2020)

This is not too surprising, since the co-operative principles that underlie the Preston Model are actually not essentially uniquely left-wing principles. Let us not forget that even Ronald Reagan was able to view co-operatives in a positive light.

> I can't help but believe that in the future we will see in the United States and throughout the western world an increasing trend toward the next logical step, employee ownership. It is a path that befits a free people. Walter Reuther was one of the first major labor leaders to advocate that management and labor shift away from battling over wage and benefit levels to a cooperative effort aimed at sharing in the ownership of the new wealth being produced.
>
> > (Reagan, 1987)

As has been noted elsewhere, the concept of co-operative businesses, which forms the value base for the Preston Model (Manley and Froggett, 2016), can 'provide alternative economic models that "cut across ideological lines – especially at the local level, where practicality, not rhetoric, is what counts in distressed communities"' (Rowe et al. 2017, quoting Alperovitz et al., 2010). This shows how on a personal, individual level, when party politics takes a backstage, there is a possibility for a form of general consensus that is reminiscent of the present social and civil consensus, on a national scale, that, for example, the National Health Service is worth maintaining. There is something about people ownership, even in this example, with references to *the* health service now being frequently referred to as *'our* NHS'. Similarly, with the Preston Model, criticism has been muted, limited to accusations that wealth is not being created but simply relocated, tantamount to protectionism, and that the Preston Model's economic strategy leaves Preston vulnerable to economic downturns by concentrating on one strategy only. This has not significantly damaged the common sensical feel of the core ideas and continued development of the Model.

Rhizomatic-up

These relatively unplanned paths and strategies that have been labelled 'Preston Model' have been strangely successful, 'strangely' because in many ways, this would appear to run counter to the rigorously planned and constructed strategies that are normally defined as worth pursuing, often resembling a logic model leading to concrete outcomes. In fact, the unravelling and re-ravelling of the Preston Model as it goes along its way resembles more a pattern of nomadic theory, as defined by Rosi Braidotti, taking her cue from the pioneering work of Deleuze and Guattari (Braidotti, 2011). The key to Braidotti's nomadic theory is the non-linearity of thought that is embraced as potentially leading to more creative thinking through chance encounter, a 'zigzagging' something that is 'not concept-driven' (Braidotti 2013: 164). It is a 'zigzag' that conducts itself as a Deleuzian rhizome (Deleuze and Guattari, 1988: 3–26), where events emerge at different moments anywhere in a system of interconnectivity, where complexity is maintained, not reduced. Unlike the work in Cleveland, developments have been unplanned. That is not to say that there has not been much thought and work that has gone into Preston, just that each development has creatively been augmented by another, in an *almost* ad hoc fashion. And rather than this being a weakness, it is its strength.

In this context, it is interesting to note how Deleuzian scholar De Landa brings out the affinity between economies of agglomeration, co-operatives and Deleuzian assemblages and the meaning of 'production' in ways that similarly resonate with the Preston Model:

> [T]he same distinction [the dichotomy 'market/anti-market'] applies to production: it's the difference between economies of scale and economies of agglomeration. That is, between oligopolies using managed prices, routinized labour, hierarchical structure, vertical integration etc. and networks

of small producers using market prices, skilled labour, decentralized structure and functional complementarities.

(De Landa et al., 2005: 80)

This tendency to favour local markets and small producers is exactly mirrored in the example of the renovation of the central market in Preston. This is an example of a practical application of Prestonian desire, which is recognisable as holding the ethos of the Preston Model. In this instance – as opposed to the failed inward investment of the Tithebarne project of 2011 (BBC, 2011) – the City Council funds a local construction company, who are then able to employ more local workers to complete the job. The reconstruction of the market was completed in 2018, and was awarded the Royal Town Planning Institute's top regional award for planning excellence. The market now houses local market stalls, producers and businesses. In doing so, the Council has acted to open up a space for local civic pride and development, but what it has not done is injected a market project from a top level-down plan by bringing in a major store from outside the city which is fruit of a master plan to revive the economy, in the traditional style of inward investment (such as the prospect of the arrival of a John Lewis superstore in the Tithebarne project).

Certainly, the market renovation is paid for by the council, but its eventual success will depend on the small-scale producers from Preston who both populate the businesses and the Prestonians who use these services. It is not dependent on the logic of an economy of scale of a national superstore investment. Rather, it is an encouragement to develop something similar to De Landa's 'networks of small producers using market prices, skilled labour, decentralised structure and functional complementarities' (BBC, 2011). In this sense, it is 'up to the people' to make the market project succeed. Furthermore, the way this is organised is through a relatively unplanned accumulation of businesses, who desire to set up, and who react directly to the custom of local people. It is therefore largely self-organising and rhizomatic, in the Deleuzian sense of the word, with market stalls appearing and disappearing according to the desire or 'affect' of the footfall.

This resonates with De Landa's identification of 'self-organization' as a 'pre-capitalist market, a collective entity arising from the decentralized interaction of many buyers and sellers, with no central "decider" coordinating the whole process' (De Landa, 1997: 17). In many ways, it seems that what was a 'pre-capitalist market' may soon look more like a 'post-capitalist' market, as indicated by the plethora of recent publications seeking to define an economic and social future of a post-growth society, ranging from Raworth's 'doughnut economics' to Trebeck and Williams's 'economics of arrival' (Raworth, 2017; Trebeck and Williams, 2019), and many more.

In true rhizomatic fashion, the effects of one success further ripple into other successes and improvements in Preston that may not initially be necessarily directly identified as 'Preston Model', but which nevertheless form part of the whole. This effect can be equated with what De Landa would call ungoverned, emergent properties of the assemblage, the assemblage being the undefined or constantly redefined 'Preston Model'. Although it may not be possible to causally link some of the parts of the assemblage together, they are nevertheless part of the same assemblage and conjunction of parts, joined through affective knowledge as a kind of second sense. An example of this is how the same local constructor that was contracted for the market renovations is later given the job, by Lancashire County Council (not Preston City Council, normally identified with the Preston Model), of improving and refurbishing the bus station, an iconic listed building in the centre of Preston. So successful is this renovation that further recognition is highlighted in the award of the Royal Institute of British Architects 2019 National Award (RIBA, 2019).

The co-operative as a rhizome

The 'rhizomatic economy' as described above is best served by a business that itself is non-hierarchical, non-linear, more democratic and more tending towards a recognition of affect (or humanity in the sense of 'humanity at work', the Mondragón co-operative movement's motto). This explains why the Preston Model does not stop with the generation and retention of local wealth through work with the anchor institutions, but includes a commitment to the development of co-operative businesses. John Protevi, in conversation with De Landa, suggests that worker-owned co-operatives would have been attractive to Deleuze and Guattari, making the link between Deleuzian concepts and co-operative ventures:

> I suspect Deleuze and Guattari would have a pretty strong predilection for worker co-operatives over absentee-owner firms, although they would also say we need to investigate the life affirming or life-denying aspects of particular concrete assemblages, and ask whether in fact this or that worker cooperative (whether a centralized economy of scale operation or a networked economy of agglomeration operation) produces better and larger sets of affects than this or that absentee-owner firm.
>
> (De Landa et al., 2005: 82–83)

The connection made between worker-owned co-operatives and Deleuzian affect is particularly relevant to the way the Preston Model is being built from bottom-up, and rhizomatic-up: 'bottom-up', because, there is a relatively hands-off approach from the political and economic forces in Preston; and 'rhizomatic-up' because as a result of the light touch top-down approach adopted by the City Council and other actors, development is less vertical and more spread out in a web-like fashion, depending to some extent on goodwill or 'affect' that bind together the relationships that constitute the network. Parts of this network are explicit, as in the constitution of the Preston Co-operative Development Network – itself the result of a university study and collaboration with Preston City Council (Manley and Froggett, 2016) – tasked with providing a relational basis for co-operative development in Preston; and parts are organic and self-organising, such as the coincidence of needs and desires that led to the development of the Birley art studios. In this case (Manley and Froggett, 2016: 18 19), the City Council had empty offices in a prime central location and there happened to be a group of University graduates looking for spaces to practice. Combined with these circumstances, there was a willingness to find solutions both from the University and City Council, leading to the establishment of the art studios in the city centre. Although not formally a co-operative, the Birley studios exist to serve the community, and co-operative values fit naturally into their modus operandi.

Later developments have used a similar strategy, but with a greater emphasis on the desirability of new organisations embracing worker ownership. The Larder co-op is an example, where Council property is leased out to a local business – a cafe, food academy and catering service – providing locally sourced and ethically focused food services for Preston. In terms of 'relationships of affect', to use Deleuzian terminology, the Larder was able to support vulnerable people during the Coronavirus pandemic and lockdown in ways that prioritised civic pride, duty, solidarity, care and compassion for the community, and locally recognised as 'community heroes' (Podio, 2020) for this work. This is an example of the 'better and larger sets of affects' elicited by Protevi above.

Democracy and citizenship

The multiplicity of networked relationships that go towards making up the 'Preston Model' are, as indicated above, both pre- and post-capitalist. These developing networks, and therefore the Preston Model itself, appear to be an emergent desire in the making, similar to a return to a Deleuzian 'social machine' which was dismantled by capitalism (Deleuze and Guattari, 2004: 155). The desire for social transformation in Preston (and elsewhere, through the community wealth building project that has been spreading to other towns and cities in the UK) has become more powerful than the capitalist need for 'technical production' (Deleuze and Guattari, 2004: 155). The relational, collective and co-operative feel of the Preston Model is what creates a kind of 'group fantasy' that 'plugs desire into the socius' (Deleuze and Guattari, 2004: 157). This leads to what Holland calls a 'group allegiance' and a 'nomad citizenship' (Holland, 2006: 202), where being a participating citizen in Preston becomes more intense than any 'master allegiance' to the State. Perhaps this partly explains why the Preston version of the Labour Party was able to triumph in the 2019 general election, while other Labour strongholds in the area became Conservative. By following the logic of 'nomad citizenship', that is to say, a citizenship that moves from recognition of the self as a national self, to that of a more personally defined sense of self, then it becomes possible to come closer to the spirit ('group fantasy') of the Preston Model. In Holland's words:

> Developing multiple allegiances to social groups 'beneath' the level of the state would extend the benefits and responsibilities of citizenship

throughout social life, would in effect dissolve the boundaries separating the state and electoral politics from civil society, and would ideally encourage the growth of smaller-scale participatory democracy in numerous venues to accompany – and eventually to supplant – the large scale representative system we have now.

(Holland, 2006: 202–203)

As one interviewee in Preston explained, to encourage participatory democracy in the workplace is to encourage it elsewhere, where it becomes a defining criterion of citizenship made manifest in the 'numerous venues' described above:

It doesn't stop at the boundaries of the workplace. So, once more people are more democratically engaged in this one important path of life which is their work, it would be daft not to think that they wouldn't either apply those values and principles in other parts of the life or seek opportunities to apply those principles.

(Interviewee E, Preston Co-operative Development Network)

In terms of a rhizomatic approach, the sense here is not that participatory democracy in the workplace causes or leads to the application of democratic values and principles in community; rather that the former is likely to transfer some of its practice into another zone of a nomadic citizen's life in a natural and unassuming fashion.

A moving conclusion

The Preston Model fits tidily into what Foucault called a history of thought, as opposed to a history of ideas, that is to say part of a shared flow of thinking and emergence from that thinking, not a project that has been conceived of as an idea, and then applied to a situation. This is the way Foucault puts it:

The history of ideas involves the analysis of a notion from its birth, through its development, and in the setting of other ideas which constitute its context. The history of thought is the analysis of the way an unproblematic field of experience, or a set of practices, which were accepted without question, which were familiar and 'silent', out of discussion and debate, incites new reactions, and induces a crisis in the previously silent behaviour, habits, practices, and institutions.

(Foucault, 2001: 74)

There is no grand idea or theory behind the Preston Model. Instead, there is something more powerful: a sweeping tide of thought which is closer to a 'structure of feeling', as famously coined by Raymond Williams. The exact definition of Williams's coinage has been the source of some debate which has sometimes been oppositional to the deliberate vagueness of the term as conceived by Williams himself. This is not a debate that I have the space to enter into here (for an interesting summary, see Highmore, 2016). It is relevant, however, to Foucault's understanding of history as thought, where the uncertainty of definition is a means of embracing a greater whole before sub-dividing such a grander scheme into different parts that subsequently lose the meaning of the original whole. This is surely what Williams meant when striving to understand a work of art as whole structures of feeling, as opposed to its definable parts:

> When one has measured the work against the separable parts ... there yet remains some element for which there is no external counterpart. This element, I believe, is what I have named the *structure of feeling* of a period, and it is only realizable through experience of the work of art itself, as a whole.
>
> (Quoted in Highmore, 2016: 149)

Williams's definition of structures of feeling was not restricted to artworks; however, maybe it is actually not so absurd to view the Preston Model as a work of art, something created intuitively and as a result of a series of responses to flows of thought that were triggered by the emergency of austerity, precisely when there were no more ideas left to play with. This is a 'moving conclusion' in the sense that such a development for Preston is both inspiring and constantly shifting, just like the desires and affects of the Deleuzian rhizome exist in their own self-contained flux, an eternal network of moving patterns of interconnectivity and meaning.

Acknowledgement

I am grateful to Dr Ioannis Prinos for undertaking all the interviews which are the source of the quoted extracts in this chapter.

Note

1 URBACT is the 'European Territorial Cooperation programme aiming to foster sustainable integrated urban development in cities across Europe. It is an instrument of the Cohesion Policy, co-financed by the European Regional Development Fund, the 28 Member States, Norway & Switzerland' (https://urbact.eu/urbact-glance).

References

Alperovitz, G., Williamson, T., and Howard, T. (2010) The Cleveland Model. Retrieved from www.thenation.com/article/cleveland-model. Accessed 16 May 2020.

Baqueriza-Jackson, M. (2019) Making Spend Matter. Retrieved from https://urbact.eu/making-spend-matter. Accessed 10 May 2020.

BBC (2011) Preston Tithebarn Scheme Abandoned after John Lewis Withdraws. Retrieved from www.bbc.co.uk/news/uk-england-lancashire-15571764. Accessed 10 May 2020.

Braidotti, R. (2011) *Nomadic Theory. The Portable Rosi Braidotti.* New York: Columbia University Press.

Braidotti, R. (2013) *The Posthuman.* Cambridge: Polity Press.

Bregman, R. (2020) *Humankind. A Hopeful History.* London: Bloomsbury.

Chakrabortty, A. (2018) In 2011 Preston Hit Rock Bottom. Then it Took Back Control. Retrieved from www.theguardian.com/commentisfree/2018/jan/31/preston-hit-rock-bottom-took-back-control. Accessed 10 May 2020.

CLES (2019) How We Built Community Wealth in Preston. Retrieved from https://cles.org.uk/wp-content/uploads/2019/07/CLES_Preston-Document_WEB-AW.pdf. Accessed 4 May 2020.

De Landa, M. (1997) *A Thousand Years of Nonlinear History.* New York: Zone.

De Landa, M., Protevi, J. and Thanem, T. (2005) Deleuzian Interrogations: A Conversation with Manuel De Landa and John Protevi. *Tamara: Journal of Critical Postmodern Organization Science,* 3(4): 65–88.

Deleuze, G. and Guattari, F. (1988) *A Thousand Plateaus.* London: Continuum.

Deleuze, G. and Guattari, F. (2004) *Anti-Oedipus.* London: Continuum.

Democracy Collaborative (2020) About the Democracy Collective. Retrieved from https://democracycollaborative.org/about. Accessed 28 October 2020.

Foucault, M. (2001) *Fearless Speech.* Los Angeles, CA: Semiotext(e).

Hausner, V.A. (1993) The Future of Urban Development. *Royal Society of Arts Journal,* 141(5441): 523–533.

Highmore, B. (2016) Formations of Feelings, Constellations of Things. *Cultural Studies Review,* 22 (1): 144–167.

Holland, E.W. (2006) Nomad Citizenship and Global Democracy. In M. Fuglsang and B. Meier Sørensen (eds), *Deleuze and the Social,* 191–207. Edinburgh: Edinburgh University Press.

Jones, P. (2020) Look to Preston for an Answer to Labour's – and Britain's – Woes. Retrieved from www.theguardian.com/commentisfree/2020/jan/13/preston-labour-woes-localism-brexit. Accessed 10 May 2020.

Liberal Democrat Voice (2020) The Preston Model – a Blueprint for Local Liberalism? www.libdemvoice.org/the-preston-model-a-blueprint-for-local-liberalism-64266.html. Accessed 10 May 2020.

Manley, J. (2018) Preston Changed its Fortunes with 'Corbynomics' – Now Other Cities Are Doing the Same. Retrieved from https://theconversation.com/preston-changed-its-fortunes-with-corbynomics-now-other-cities-are-doing-the-same-106293. Accessed 10 May 2020.

Manley, J. and Aiken, M. (2020) A Socio-economic System for Affect: Dreaming of Co-operative Relationships and Affect in Bermuda, Preston and Mondragón. *Organisational and Social Dynamics,* 20(2).

Manley, J. and Froggett, L. (2016) Co-operative Activity in Preston. Retrieved from http://clok.uclan.ac.uk/14526/1/Co-operative%20activity%20PrestonREPORT%20copy.pdf. Accessed 16 May 2020.

Matthews, S. (2001) Change and Theory in Raymond Williams's Structure of Feeling. *Pretexts: Literary and Cultural Studies,* 10(2): 179–194.

Podio (2020) Preston's Community Heroes. Retrieved from https://podiomagazine.com/prestons-community-heroes. Accessed 25 May 2020.

Preston City Council (2020) Community Wealth Building in Action. Retrieved from www.preston.gov.uk/article/1338/Community-Wealth-Building-in-action. Accessed 10 May 2020.

Raworth, K. (2017) *Doughnut Economics: Seven Ways to Think Like a 21st-Century Economist*. White Rover Junction, VT: Chelsea Green.

Reagan, R. (1987) President Ronald Reagan's Speech on Project Economic Justice. Transcript of speech presented at the White House, Washington, DC, 3 August. Retrieved from www.cesj.org/about-cesj-in-brief/history-accomplishments/pres-reagans-speech-on-project-economic-justice. Accessed 19 May 2020.

RIBA (2019) Preston Bus Station Refurbishment. Retrieved from www.architecture.com/awards-and-competitions-landing-page/awards/riba-regional-awards/riba-north-west-award-winners/2019/preston-bus-station-refurbishment. Accessed 17 May 2020.

Rowe, J.K., Peredo, A.M., Sullivan, M., and Restakis, J. (2017) Co-operative Development, Policy, and Power in a Period of Contested Neoliberalism: The case of Evergreen Co-operative Corporation in Cleveland, Ohio. *Socialist Studies / Études socialistes*, 12 (1): 54–77.

Sheffield, H. (2017) The Preston Model: UK Takes Lessons in Recovery from Rust-Belt Cleveland. *The Guardian*. Retrieved from www.theguardian.com/cities/2017/apr/11/preston-cleveland-model-lessons-recovery-rust-belt. Accessed 10 May 2020.

Tallon, A. (2010) *Urban Regeneration in the UK*. London: Routledge.

Trebeck, K. and Williams, J. (2019) *The Economics of Arrival: Ideas for a Grown up Economy*.

Watkins, S. (2018) How the Left-Behind Took Back Control in Preston. Retrieved from https://moneyweek.com/487565/how-the-left-behind-took-back-control-in-preston. Accessed 10 May 2020.

2 The Preston Model and co-operative development

A glimpse of transformation through an alternative model of social and economic organisation

Ioannis Prinos

Introduction

The 2008 economic crisis and, at the time of writing, the ongoing COVID-19 virus pandemic, have both stimulated much interest amongst researchers and policy makers in the possibilities of alternative ways to structure the organisation of our society and economy. Organisations, within the public and private spheres are being reconsidered; the interplay between democracy, solidarity, social cohesion, work, and the market economy, are all being rediscovered. They have even prompted discussions on the meaning of previously largely uncontested concepts such as the intrinsic value of growth and economic development, while questioning the very essence of the hierarchical ordering of social values. In this chapter, and drawing from the findings of continuing research, the Preston Model (PM) is presented as an example of such debates leading into concerted action, producing blueprints for novel and diverse paradigms of socio-economic organisation which are worth paying attention to and which enable us to ponder and visualise a different future for our communities.

The Preston Model is a radical 'community wealth building' (CWB) approach that has been applied in the UK city of Preston by the local Labour City Council, harnessing local economic power to enhance growth, overcome austerity and develop a fairer more resilient and democratic local economy (Manley, 2017), through a dynamic partnership of the public and private sectors as well as the civil society and the third sector in the area. With the development of networks of worker-owned co-operatives being pivotal in this endeavour and the involvement of local 'anchor institutions' (major wealth creators, spenders and employers with long-standing historical ties and presence in the area), these policies have recently captured both the academic and the public eye, and represent steps towards a plural ownership of the economy. The goal is to make financial power work for local places by focusing on local investment, creating fair employment and just labour markets, encouraging the progressive and locally focused procurement of goods and services, and developing the socially productive use of land and property, through a reconceptualisation and widening of the access of communities to local public assets.

Nevertheless, the Preston Model can't be seen as solely an economic approach, but as a long-term and holistic social transformation strategy, with potential ramifications beyond local economic indicators (i.e. income, employment, investment, etc.). It touches on issues of culture, democracy, citizenship, organisation, conceptualisations of our role in workplaces, the ways they shape our social relationships and the meaning of co-operation overall. At the same time, it perhaps indicates a still-unformed response to neoliberalism and the current nature of free markets, hinting at a gradual shift to a new, 'post growth', environmentally sustainable, socially cohesive, and resilient socio-economic paradigm founded on co-operativism. As humanity and its dominant conceptualisations and practices are tested as a whole by this global health crisis and the almost certain economic crisis to follow, a closer look at alternative paths for community organisation, economic development, and democratic governance such as the PM, is both academically and socially relevant.

Community wealth building, Mondragon, Cleveland, and the Preston Model

Preston: context

In order to understand the PM and its goals a brief look at its history and main inspiration is warranted. In 2011 a huge 700 million-pound private investment and regeneration scheme for the city of Preston, collapsed leaving Preston bereft of a way forward. This was largely the result of the deep recession, economic decline and uncertainty following the 2008 financial crisis. It prompted Preston City Council (PCC) inspired by the example of Mondragon in the Basque Country and the 'Cleveland Model' in the US, to experiment with a CWB model that aspires to generate more resilient economic growth, democratise the local economy, create social impact, improve co-operation and social cohesion and overall revitalise the city (Manley, 2017). Since 2006, CWB has been emerging as a powerful approach to local economic development, where local economies are reorganised so that wealth is not extracted, but broadly held and income is recirculated (Haskel and Westlake, 2018). In Preston, it started with altering the procurement strategy (focusing on local suppliers) of local anchor institutions, which are PCC, Lancashire County Council (LCC), Community Gateway Association (CGA), the University of Central Lancashire (UCLan), Preston's College, Lancashire Constabulary, and the local NHS Hospital.

The Mondragon example

The first Mondragon co-operative was formed in 1956 in order to regenerate the Basque country in the aftermath of Spain's vicious Civil War, and has evolved since then, into a £12 billion umbrella corporation holding together over 100 worker-owned co-operatives, distributed across finance, retail, IT, and various other industries (Thomas et al., 2017). They take a non-competitive approach within their own ecosystem, providing services to each other in addition to their external clients, with solidarity and the well-being of the workers and the local community being at the core of their operations (Heales et al., 2017).

Further intra-co-operation is evident in an imposed salary ratio between the lowest and highest paid in each co-operative (1:6 to 1:8 compared to the 1:129 average found in FTSE 100 firms), proving its resilience and flexibility during the 2008 financial crisis when resources were shared and employees were shifted as needed between the co-ops, avoiding layoffs (Arando et al., 2010). Finally, democratic practices are entrenched in all co-operatives, with the fundamental 'one person, one vote' rule being applied on all key corporation decisions and the general assembly of workers of every co-operative being the sole body that appoints and recalls managers and directors (Heales et al., 2017).

The 'Cleveland Model'

Cleveland, Ohio is a USA city marked by blue-collar job displacement in the late 20th century. Similarly to Preston, Cleveland's CWB model was born from a search for ways to revitalise a moribund local economy (Alperovitz et al., 2010). In 2005, the Cleveland Foundation, assisted by the Democracy Collaborative research institute, identified a number of local anchor institutions to partner on a CWB program. It took a fresh approach by focusing on the anchor institutions and creating community-based co-operatives that met the identified gaps in the institutions' procurement, achieving good results for deprived communities in the Cleveland area (Howard et al., 2010).

The Preston Model in a nutshell

Perhaps calling the efforts taking place in Preston a 'model' does them a disservice, but simultaneously, this term has afforded them visibility and exposure in the media as people can more easily grasp and relate to a rather complex, dynamic, and still-in-development interconnected web of initiatives. However, the Preston Model is more of a strategy and an approach that adapts to local circumstances, civic culture, and the socio-economic characteristics of an area, rather than a rigid model or a to-do guide that can be applied in exactly the same form anywhere producing the same results. It's not something that is described in some formal manner in an official policy document called 'The Preston Model'. Rather, it is a commitment, by anchor institutions, businesses, organisations, and individuals in Preston, to move in another direction. For many, it's not even an economic model in the strictest sense, but a holistic, transformative vision of a new way of working and a new paradigm of socio-economic organisation.

It has been patiently and collectively developed by changing mindsets, attitudes, and mentalities towards alternate ways an economy can develop and a community can grow in a sustainable manner, by many stakeholders, all bringing different ideas to the table. By fostering a culture of collaboration, Preston has demonstrated a viable alternative to centralisation and tight bureaucratic control, showing how true collaboration comes when senior managers, political leaders, workers and frontline practitioners across anchor institutions all feel a sense of shared ownership, and are able to mould a collective journey based on individual institutional experiences (Todd, 2017).

Impressive economic results are already being produced in Preston and Lancashire. Repeated analysis[1] of anchor institution spending from 2013 to 2018, spend in the Preston economy had increased from £38 million to £111 million. By 2016/17, out of £620 million spent on goods and services by local anchor institutions, 19% was spent in Preston and 81% in Lancashire as a whole. This compares with 5% and 39% in 2013 respectively (reducing drastically the £450 million leakage out of the Lancashire economy). At the same time, unemployment has been reduced from 6.5% in 2014 to 3.1% in 2017 (compared to UK average of 4.6% in 2017), Preston was named 'Most Improved City in the United Kingdom' in 2018 and rose from 143rd to 130th in the Social Mobility Commission Index (out of 324 local authority areas), while in 2018, Preston moved out of the 20% most deprived local authority areas in the UK. The core belief underpinning the PM is that retaining more civic wealth within a locality can boost growth and economic resilience in that particular area, and the aim is to use local assets to develop the economy in ways that have tangible benefits for its citizens, communities, organisations and businesses (Todd, 2017).

Why Preston focuses on worker-owned co-operatives

Worker-owned co-operatives are enjoying a resurgence as a response to new forms of employment associated with work deficits such as lower and irregular earnings, reduced social protection and security coverage, and diminished working conditions (Erdal, 2011; Deller et al., 2009). They are enterprises run and managed by and for the workers who own the capital, vote as equal members on running the business and can stand in for elections of the Board of Directors (Perotin, 2014). They have proven to be sustainable (often with higher survival rates than conventional enterprises), in terms of productivity and job preservation, as well as debt to equity ratio (Thomas et al., 2017); they, can strengthen financial resilience and economic diversity in times of recession (McInroy, 2018; Kurtulus and Kruse, 1999); and they can enhance social cohesion in a local community (Manley & Froggett, 2016). Finally, they have the potential to create a profound impact on the overall well-being of their members and their respective communities in more impactful ways than that of their 'traditional' business counterparts (Corcoran and Wilson, 2010), forming economic frameworks which are 'people-centred, localised, built on social relationships, reduce inequality, and enhance economic democracy, ethical finance, sustainability and resilience' (Webb and Novkovic, 2014: 287–288).

This is why such an 'unconventional' economic framework and guiding values of the co-operative movement are essential for achieving the goals of the

Preston Model. The co-operative ethos with solidarity, equality, democratic participation and social service at its core, lends itself well to this initiative. As Manley (2017: 1) asserts:

> If there are opportunities for making a success of life in Preston, a place where people have a sense of identity and belonging, then social capital is potentially increased; pride of place is enhanced; a sense of citizenship is developed; and democracy becomes relevant and vital.

The Preston Model evolving

Currently, the Preston Model is attempting to move closer to one of its inspirations, Mondragon. Namely, to identify the gaps in the anchor institutions' procurement needs that local supply chains can't cover and create a network of co-ops to do that, while pursuing the foundation for the provision of 'true co-op education' through the creation of the Preston Co-operative Education Centre (PCEC) in the city, (which will be one of these co-operatives). Education is one of the four pillars supporting the Mondragon Co-operative Corporation – with the other three being social welfare and health, finance, and innovation – (Bakaikoa et al., 2004) and is often considered the most important. This is echoed in the words of Mondragon's founder, the priest Jose Maria Arizmendiarrieta, who contends: 'Let's marry work and education, let us keep them tied together in the service of a progressive community, for the good of the people' (Bakaikoa et al., 2004: 67). It's this vision of promoting co-operation at every level between social classes, generations, believers, and non-believers, liberal and Marxists, men and women (Whyte and Whyte, 2014), that the Preston Model tries to develop. In this context, run by staff and students, the PCEC is intended to become an integral part of the overall Preston Model initiative. It is linked to its transformative goals of connecting education, research, culture, community, and economic practice into a holistic strategy for the betterment of local communities on the basis of widespread co-operation.

Seed-funding has been provided by the Open Society Foundations (OSF) for the establishment of ten worker-owned co-operatives (optimally all housed in the same physical space in the city centre). The stakeholders include PCC, UCLan, and the Preston Co-operative Development Network (PCDN), along with outside consultation and training services provided by LKS of the Mondragon Co-operative Corporation, Coops UK, and the US-based 1Worker1Vote organisation; the latter creates shared ownership ecosystems and union co-operatives. Their intention is to strive to transform both the economic and the socio-cultural framework of the city towards a more co-operative paradigm. As this is a project with a strong knowledge-exchange component, a monitoring, evaluation, learning, and research UCLan team is assessing the process and its learning outcomes for the future.

Finally, another essential cog in the PM's continuous development, is a regional community co-operative bank for the North West (Lancashire, Merseyside, and Cumbria), which, it is hoped, will be fully licenced and open its first branch in Preston by 2022. Its main goal is to enable financially excluded local people and businesses to borrow money (access to capital and banking services is one of the foremost problems of co-ops starting up; see Deller et al., 2009). Previous evidence suggests that such banks depend on small deposits; on a sort of 'grassroots acceptance' by the local community (Hein et al., 2005) and can be 'insulated' from the worst effects of wider financial crises, such as the one in 2008 (Gilbert et al., 2013).

Researching the Preston Model through the eyes of its people

At the time of writing, a UCLan research project[2] is investigating the ways people in Preston perceive the PM: its creation, impact, and future prospects. Key research themes include an examination of whether the PM represents a re-thinking of co-operatives and co-operation; the evolving role of anchor institutions; how it differs from other urban regeneration projects; its potential 'transferability' to other areas nationally or internationally; the question of whether it's a leadership project or approximates a social movement; the extent of support in Preston communities for co-operative values and principles and whether this initiative can instigate processes of wider socio-cultural change in the area based on co-operative ethos, solidarity and equality rather than individualism, competition and marketisation; and the model's political aspect influence in its development. The research is still under way, nevertheless, there is sufficient data for some initial insights to be tentatively presented.

Research design and methodology

Focusing on individual perceptions and experiences, this is a purely qualitative research project. The primary methodological tool employed, were semi-structured but open in nature, qualitative interviews. All types of qualitative interviews, sometimes called in-depth or ethnographic interviews, are among the most familiar and effective strategies for collecting qualitative data in social research (Neuman, 2011). The goal is to have two rounds of interviews with approximately 75 participants. The first round is conducted currently, and the findings presented in this chapter are based on these interviews; the second will be conducted towards the end of the project in 2022, when significant developments such as the OSF project and the regional co-operative bank discussed previously will be in 'full bloom', in order to explore any changes in perceptions of the participants.

So far, 53 interviews lasting from 45 to 90 minutes have been conducted. The participants are (mostly) people working or living in Preston or both, with different educational and socio-economic backgrounds, holding professional roles in various levels of the anchor institutions, employees, members, and managers of local organisations and businesses (co-operatives and 'standard'), third sector organisations (TSOs) and community groups, local trade unionists, academics, co-op development consultants, and policy makers, making for a highly diverse sample. The sampling technique used is partly purposive and partly based on 'snowballing'. The existing contacts of the research team have been initially used during the fieldwork, which then introduce the researchers to other prospective respondents, continuing thus, as the data constantly modifies and enriches the research focus, updating what questions need to be asked, what type of knowledge is sought and who could (likely) provide it.

Initial findings

On the issue of how the Preston Model is different from previous projects and initiatives of urban regeneration and economic revitalisation, there was a unanimous agreement that the unique characteristic of the Preston Model, is its local focus and practical commitment to deliver results for the betterment of the lives of people in Preston. Though apparently not directly comparable to the Preston Model, the 'Third Way' and the 'Big Society Agenda' were mentioned. They were portrayed as examples of initiatives that first, were designed by people in central government far removed from the realities of life in the northwest of the UK, and second, they never truly escaped their nature as just political manifestos; public relation strategies and national party agendas, more performative than substantial.

> I think that the biggest difference is that the Preston Model is local; developed by local people for the local community
>
> > (Participant A, anchor institution)

> It's very local and also it's not just promises or intentions; it's a set of tangible policies put into place like paying the living wage and being environmentally responsible as a council or a business
>
> > (Participant B, anchor institution)

> The Big Society came up from London and there wasn't actually anything realised; in the end, nobody could see a difference, much less a positive influence in their lives, while the Preston Model has helped local economy and unemployment is reduced; probably it's not the only cause of that, but if it helped even a little, then that's the real difference right here, for Preston.
>
> > (Participant C, local co-op)

With regards to whether the PM is a social movement with grassroots characteristics or a leadership project and whether it has affected a wider socio-cultural change towards the principles and ethos of co-operativism in Preston, almost none of the participants characterised it as a social movement, or have noticed any wider social change. They have rather attributed its creation, development, and initial success to leadership figures (mainly within PCC); charismatic and inspired individuals 'who brought these ideas, campaigned for them and got other people onboard' (Participant D, Anchor Institution). This latter point, though, hints at the recognition of a collective effort; a partnership needed for the PM to flourish, slowly forming.

This is reinforced by the fact that many respondents recognised the power of its ideas, as well as the potential for it to acquire substantial wider socio-cultural influence, and thus the possibility and potential to become a movement in the future. Almost all of those, regardless of professional role or background and degree of involvement with the development of the Preston Model, made a direct link between the future creation of a social movement and the need to raise awareness of the Preston Model in the broader Preston community. There is an indication here that the beginnings of something broader that can bring people together in a 'transformative alliance' of sorts resembling a social movement is in the works. Even if it lacks concrete political organisation and its goals and the means to acquire them are not yet apparent or even completely agreed-upon. But the potential of the Preston Model to be a catalyst for 'true social change' can best be realised not only by 'educating the people the people on the ground, door to door' (Participant E, Local Co-op) and communicating the model's successes, but primarily by demonstrating the Preston Model's impact on people's daily lives; their income and employment, the ability of the local councils to continue funding much needed social services, etc.

> If people find more and better jobs, see their services improved and their income rise, find housing more affordable, then the Preston Model can be really known I think.
>
> (Participant F, anchor institution)

That is the 'blueprint' that many identified for disassociating the Preston Model from hierarchical understandings and meanings of 'leadership' and major party politics and making something broader, with 'grassroots ownership' of its goals and a communal, shared understanding of its values.

Politics is always a challenging and sensitive subject to research (Maguire and Ball, 1994). Excluding the few interviewees who refused to comment on the political dimension of the Preston Model, its association with politics is an issue that participants, one way or another, are aware of and concerned with. For a part of our sample, what seems to be worrying many respondents is the identification of the Preston Model with the Labour Party and 'Leftist' or 'Corbynist' ideas:[3]

> I can see it becoming more of a problem, I think … it can open these ideas and practices to attacks which are not focused on the model, but on the fact that it is related to Labour politics of Corbyn, or whatever; it unfortunately can become a part of a very toxic environment and discussion and nothing good can come of it.
>
> (Participant F, anchor institution)

The underlying thinking is that the Preston Model, could be 'condemned' in the consciousness of some people just because of its 'leftist' label and political bias, rather because they gave it much thought or found it to be ineffective or unsuccessful in its aims. These participants see the Preston Model as primarily a common sense, effective, working strategy of local economic and community development rather than a political agenda.

Another part of our sample simply accepts that as the major 'driver' – like it or not – of the PM is a Labour city council, its political aspect and nature can't be denied and those who fervently oppose anything 'Labour-related', would and will oppose it regardless.

> Obviously there is a Labour city council in Preston and they are in favour of it (the Preston Model) and so you couldn't have it any other way with the social media culture and such that we have now; people who hate anything Labour will do that with the PM and nothing can be done about that really other than proving in practice that it works.
>
> (Participant G, anchor institution)

It is, therefore, something inevitable and the best answer would be for the Preston Model to demonstrate with its impact its positive economic and social influence.

There is also a third group, which considers the political backing by a major party quite beneficial for the model, usually with the caveat that there could be a Labour central government in place, which could provide resources, political backing, funding, and partnership programmes.

> I wouldn't say there's anything wrong with that. I mean the Preston Model is political to an extent … and it's good that Labour support it; it gains in publicity and resources, more support from London; it's really a good thing; especially if there was a Labour government, I would assume it would gain substantial backing.
>
> (Participant H, local SME)

Finally, there is a fourth group which actually overlaps with all of the above perceptions. These respondents, whether they see the Preston Model as 'Labour thing' and its political elements a blessing or a curse, are worried about its sustainability. That due to this politicisation of the Preston Model mainly stemming from the ways the media have framed the model, there is a possibility that a change of power in PCC could result in the abandonment of the associated practices and policies, as the latter haven't yet been firmly embedded into the working culture of organisations and businesses in Preston; there is no 'failsafe'.

> My only problem with that (the political dimension of the Preston Model) would be how to make sure that it is not just a firecracker; that these efforts continue even with a Tory government or a Tory PCC … the trick is to sustain it and this is something I wouldn't know how to do.
>
> (Participant I, local TSO for the homeless)

With regards to the creation of the Preston Model, there is not much variance in the data. Some participants were unsure, but the vast majority agrees that it has been a congruence of factors in play for Preston. Its macroeconomic make-up, (the presence and economic power of several anchor institutions), its geographical position with good transportation links to major economic hubs such as Manchester and Liverpool, the city development project falling through and acting as a catalyst for more radical solutions, and charismatic figures in PCC, such as Cllr Matthew Brown who promoted the model and campaigned for it getting executives in anchors to sign up, were all mentioned by most interviewees. Still, this overarching perception doesn't really answer the question why something like the Preston Model wasn't first developed in other localities with similar economic characteristics and were in even more dire straits due to years of austerity and public spending cuts. When prompted to elaborate further on that, only 4 participants mentioned that perhaps there is something in the history and cultural identity of Preston which makes it a more 'fertile ground' for innovation.

> I think that Preston is not enormous and that's an advantage for the Preston Model. There's something about the right number, size, and economic power of organisations which can drive it, and then maybe you had the right people in the right place at the right time getting onboard certainly.
>
> (Participant J, anchor institution)

> I think there were several factors, people in the council obviously, but also scale comes definitely into it. There were anchor institutions which have the right size.
>
> (Participant K, local co-op)

> It is possible that with no option for the development of the city centre the council had to do something; to appear proactive and offer a solution and I guess that prompted people to look to alternative models of economic development.
>
> (Participant L, local SME)

> We've always been at the forefront here in Preston with the Preston Guild[4] and the Rochdale Pioneers are just across, so I think there maybe something of this nature here, that has contributed to the Preston Model.
>
> (Participant M, anchor institution)

Furthermore, almost all respondents believe that the Preston Model is transferable at least in some form and definitely its core principles. The dominant perception is that as long as there is some political backing (a dedicated council to drive it forward) and a few 'powerful anchor institutions' committing to it and supporting it to 'get it of the ground' this would be possible.

I don't see why it could not. Obviously not everything will be the same; every area is unique and there are differences, but the ideas of the Preston Model, like the increase of local procurement spend and the use of public assets by the community or paying the living wage and including workers in decision-making, could be applied anywhere.

(Participant N, anchor institution)

I would think that if enough organisations in an area which play a massive role in buying goods and services in the locality sign up for it, it could be possible; especially if there is the political will to support it.

(Participant O, anchor institution)

When talking about organisational change in the anchor institutions involved with the Preston Model, it is not clear whether tangible, demonstrable change has taken place, and even when a respondent says that it has, it is still unclear whether the Preston Model is a symptom of change within organisations / businesses, or a driver. All respondents stated that they haven't noticed any substantial changes in the ways they do their work, their respective departments / services operate, their governance structures, etc. (apart from the change in procurement strategy which is evidently the most well-known feature of the Preston Model).

I don't think there have been any substantial changes here; not in our daily practice at least.

(Participant P, anchor institution)

However, respondents also said that in recent years, they can 'see' or 'feel' an increased willingness of colleagues to think about and / or apply more co-operative practices and incorporate in their daily work more social responsibility and community engagement mentalities:

Because of the influence of the Preston Model, perhaps such issues have become more predominant; there were always thoughts about the local economy, social value, social responsibility, community impact, the environment; like can we do it? I feel the Preston Model, has raised visibility in these things; it has made them more predominant and put a bit more weight behind them.

(Participant Q, anchor institution)

There is definitely more support put into the third sector from the PCC and LCC; more co-operation and links which we can use; the environment for that in Preston has certainly improved.

(Participant R, local community group for well-being)

We now have more opportunities to be really involved in projects in the city; for consultation with the local government and to engage more closely with other organisations and our community in Preston.

(Participant S, anchor institution)

The above indicate a belief and perception that there is a 'more positive climate' for partnerships and collaborations in Preston with organisations more actively seeking to establish channels of co-operation between them, sharing contacts, links, information and even resources and skills on occasion, trying to increase their community engagement output and imprint. This runs contradictory to the earlier line of questioning discussed, where the majority of participants declared not actually having noticed any significant changes. At the same time, to make things even more complex, several respondents from anchors, were also quick to add that this focus on creating a more cohesive, just and co-operative local economy and community that the Preston Model has ushered, is something their organisations have always been doing to a lesser or greater extent.

It seems that there is a strong case of group and organisational identification at play here (Aharpour and Brown, 2002). During the interviews, participants who work in anchor institutions felt as being their representatives to 'the outside' (represented by the researchers) and tried to not only position them within this perceived 'success story' and optimistic narrative of the Preston Model, but actually thought that there is indeed a positive change happening significant enough (even though they couldn't always specify it), to portray these organisations as precursors of the whole thing in some form. And perhaps this optimism, this vague feeling of things 'going better' without being able to describe in detail what and how exactly is going better is, so far, the most striking finding.

Conclusions

The ways various people in Preston within and outside of the anchor institutions, involved in the continuous development of the Preston Model or not at all, perceive it, is, unsurprisingly, a rather mixed bag with abundant contradictions. Nevertheless, one predominant common thread is that apart from the local procurement strategy, knowledge about the Preston Model and especially co-operative development as a whole, the ideas and values 'running under the hood' or its future aims is relatively low even when talking with senior executives of anchors. People in the third sector, in SMEs, academics not in the field of co-op studies and economic development, frontline workers, etc., don't know much, except from a vague impression that PCC is competent, cares about Preston and looks a bit more now into things like social value and environmental sustainability. In addition, expectations and support for the Preston Model are high across the board with almost none of the participants taking an overtly negative stance towards it. But criticism ('I don't think the most vulnerable members of our communities have seen any improvement in their lives' – Participant T, anchor institution), scepticism ('the high street after 6 p. m. in the winter is still a very rough place' – Participant U, local co-op), and somewhat unrealistic expectations ('the intention is excellent but without government support on a national level, I can't see how there will be lasting change in Preston able to overcome big corporate, neoliberalism or austerity – Participant V, local union member) are also present.

Furthermore, the Preston Model is identified as mainly a leadership project, driven by certain committed individuals but with huge potential to become a social movement (if broader awareness with the general public in Preston is raised). Moreover, perceptions of the political dimension of the Preston Model are divided. The dominant view sees this political link as potentially creating problems but also as an unavoidable development and that perhaps the Preston Model would not exist without this political backing. Finally, it is considered different and novel because it is more locally focused and seems to work; it has a tangible, practical side to it that people can understand and relate to, 'made by people in Preston for people in Preston'.

However, this contradiction between a perception indicating a very low awareness of what has been happening in Preston and that nothing really tangible has changed but at the same time the Preston Model is something that works and can improve communities in Preston, reveals some valuable insights for the model and other similar initiatives. For several of the participants, while declaring they haven't seen an actual change taking place in their organisations' practices, governance, and means of working, or any tangible impact of the Preston Model on the city and the community, they still feel that in recent years the realisation that broad socio-economic change and alternative development paths are at least possible, is much more widespread in the area. They seem to perceive the Preston Model as a story; a narrative; a hopeful and optimistic tale and discourse about a fairer society, sustainable economic development, a more resilient and just labour market, and a community with enhanced social cohesion, based on co-operation and solidarity. As it has been shown, respondents without knowing almost anything about co-operatives as well as the practices and policies that have been taking place, nevertheless perceive the Preston Model as a holistic, positive idea and an aspiration for a better future.

This is the paradox that has been fairly evident in multiple occasions during our analysis. Interviewees feeling that things may change or are changing for the better without really being able to put their finger on how exactly or point out specific examples. Respondents, who while insisting that the core values and ideas of co-operativism and the Preston Model haven't gained any substantial perchance within Preston communities in daily life or that their experiences don't reflect the positive macroeconomic results of the PM, talking about 'an atmosphere' and a 'feel' in the city. The Preston Model M is influencing people subtly, enabling them to change their mindsets and subsequently start changing the culture in their organisations and businesses within this transformative vision.

In conclusion, this investigation is still ongoing, and evaluation of the Preston Model's impact will be continuing for years to come. Nevertheless, already transformative processes seem to be taking place in Preston and meaningful social change appears to be on the horizon. Even so, it is important to note that the Preston Model is actually only beginning. The procurement strategy of the anchor institutions has been going on for roughly 5 years. The Mondragon paradigm, with its intersection of education, a co-operative economic model, democratic governance, innovation and a socio-cultural paradigm of solidarity and social security, has taken more than 60 years to be what it is today. In most participants' perception, and in contrast to the reports proving how beneficial the Preston Model has been for the local economy, perhaps it has not done much to eradicate long-standing systemic injustices and inequalities, cultural stereotypes and processes of social marginalisation and exclusion, or invalidate the class divide so apparent with the situation during the COVID-19 pandemic (Van Bavel et al., 2020). Still, this study indicates so far, that in just a tiny fraction of the time it took for Mondragon to evolve, the Preston Model has seemingly achieved to at least inspire; to become an aspiration exposing different people's minds to the possibility of realising an alternate framework of socio-economic organisation, co-operation, and democratic participation. It is a model, seemingly having the potential to capture people's minds and hearts in Preston in this manner, while running contrary to the guiding principles of neoliberal capitalism and market dominance that have been ingrained to us as a sort of natural law. And this is an encouraging thought.

Notes

1 All statistical data provided with regards to the Preston Model's economic performance has been acquired from Demos–PwC (2018).
2 This research project has been approved by UCLan's Research Ethics Committee (Approval No: PSYSOC 498) and the data has been fully anonymised.
3 It should be noted that some interviews happened pre-election and others post-election. Regardless of not being in government, since the Labour Party hasn't changed its positive stance on CWB economic strategies such as the PM, it can be inferred that these views remain the same.
4 Dating back to 1179 the Guild was an organisation of traders, craftsmen and merchants, all with a monopoly trade in the town. Newcomers could only trade or begin a craft with permission from the Guild.

References

Aharpour, S. and Brown, R. (2002), Functions of Group Identification: An Exploratory Analysis, *Revue Internationale de Psychologie Sociale*, 15: 157–186.

Alperovitz, G., Howard, T., and Williamson, T. (2010), The Cleveland Model, *The Nation*, 1 (1): 21–24.

Arando, S., Gago, M., Kato, T., Jones, D.C., and Freundlich, F. (2010), *Assessing Mondragon: Stability & Managed Change in the Face of Globalization*, William Davidson Institute Working Paper 1003, University of Michigan, Ann Arbor, MI.

Bakaikoa, B., Errasti, A., and Begiristain, A. (2004), Governance of the Mondragon Corporacion Cooperativa, *Annals of Public and Cooperative Economics*, 75 (1): 61–87.

Deller, S., Hoyt, A., Hueth, B., and Sundaram-Stukel, R. (2009), Research on the Economic Impact of Cooperatives, *University of Wisconsin Center for Cooperatives*, 231: 232–233.

Demos–PwC. (2018), Good Growth for Cities 2018, retrieved from www.bl.uk/collection-items/demsc-good-growth-for-cities-2018-2018 (accessed 5 November 2020).

Erdal, D. (2011), *Beyond the Corporation: Humanity Working*, Random House, London.

Gilbert, R.A., Meyer, A.P., and Fuchs, J.W. (2013), The Future of Community Banks: Lessons from Banks that Thrived during the Recent Financial Crisis, *Federal Reserve Bank of St. Louis Review*, 95 (2): 115–143.

Haskel, J., and Westlake, S. (2018), *Capitalism without Capital: The Rise of the Intangible Economy*, Princeton University Press, Princeton, NJ.

Heales, C., Hodgson, M., and Rich, H. (2017), *Humanity at Work: Mondragon, a social innovation ecosystem case study*, The Young Foundation, London.

Hein, S.E., Koch, T.W., and MacDonald, S.S. (2005), On the Uniqueness of Community Banks, *Federal Reserve Bank of Atlanta Economic Review*, 90 (2): 15–36.

Hollway, W., and Jefferson, T. (2008), The Free Association Narrative Interview Method, in L.M. Given (ed.), *The Sage Encyclopedia of Qualitative Research Methods*, 296–315, Sage, Thousand Oaks, CA.

Howard, T., Kuri, L., and Lee, I.P. (2010), *The Evergreen Cooperative Initiative of Cleveland, Ohio: Writing the Next Chapter for Ahcnor-Based Redevelopment Initiatives*, white paper prepared for The Neighborhood Funders Group Annual Conference, Minneapolis, MN, retrieved from https://democracycollaborative.org/sites/default/files/downloads/paper-howard-et-al.pdf (accessed 5 November 2020).

Kurtulus, F.A., and Kruse, D.L. (1999), How Did Employee Ownership Firms Weather the Last Two Recessions: Employee Ownership, Employment Stability, and Firm Survival in the United States, 1999–2011, retrieved from https://research.upjohn.org/up_press/241 (accessed 5 November 2020).

Maguire, M. and Ball, S.J. (1994), Researching Politics and the Politics of Research: Recent Qualitative Studies in the UK, *Qualitative Studies in Education*, 7 (3): 269–285.

Manley, J. (2017), Local Democracy with Attitude: The Preston Model and How it Can Reduce Inequality, retrieved from https://blogs.lse.ac.uk/politicsandpolicy/local-democracy-with-attitude-the-preston-model (accessed 5 November 2020).

Manley, J., and Froggett, L. (2016), A Psychosocial Study of Co-operative Culture, retrieved from https://clok.uclan.ac.uk/14526/1/Co-operative%20activity%20PrestonREPORT%20copy.pdf (accessed 5 November 2020).

McInroy, N. (2018), Wealth for All: Building New Local Economies, *Local Economy*, 33 (6): 678–687.

Neuman, W.L. (2011), *Social Research Methods: Qualitative and Quantitative Approaches*, 7th edition, Allyn & Bacon, Boston, MA.

Perotin, V. (2014), What Do We Really Know about Worker Co-operatives?, retrieved from www.uk.coop/sites/default/files/uploads/attachments/worker_co-op_report.pdf (accessed 5 November 2020).

Smith, S.C., and Rothbaum, J. (2013), *Cooperatives in a Global Economy: Key Economic Issues, Recent Trends, and Potential for Development*, IZA Policy Paper 68, Institute for the Study of Labour, Bonn, retrieved from http://ftp.iza.org/pp68.pdf (accessed 5 November 2020).

Thomas, H., and Logan, C. (2017), *Mondragon: An Economic Analysis*, Routledge, London.

Todd, M. (2017), Local Wealth Building: Harnessing the Potential of Anchor Institutions in Preston, retrieved from https://cles.org.uk/blog/local-wealth-building-harnessing-the-potential-of-anchor-institutions-in-preston/ (accessed 5 November 2020).

Van Bavel, J.J., Boggio, P., Capraro, V., Cichocka, A., Cikara, M., Crockett, M., Crum, A., Douglas, K., Druckman, J., Drury, J. and Ellemers, N. (2020), Using Social and Behavioural Science to Support COVID-19 Pandemic Response, *Nature Human Behaviour*, 4 (5): 460–471.

Webb, T., and Novkovic, S. (eds) (2014), *Co-operatives in a Post-growth Era: Creating Co-operative Economics*, Zed Books, London.

Whyte, W.F. and Whyte, K.K. (2014), *Making Mondragon: The Growth and Dynamics of the Worker Cooperative Complex*, Cornell University Press, Ithaca, NY.

3 Co-operative education
From Mondragón and Bilbao to Preston

Susan Wright and Julian Manley

Plans for the socio-economic transformation of Preston – that have come to be known as the 'Preston Model' – have found an important source of inspiration in the co-operative system of the Mondragón area in the Basque Country. In Mondragón, one of the key features of the founders' approach in the 1950s was to forge a tight connection between advancing technical and social education and developing co-operative ways of organising industrial production and services. At each subsequent turn in the local and global economy, new educational approaches have been fostered and used to inform new phases in the co-operatives' development. This chapter will review the relationship between education and co-operative development in Mondragón. It will focus on the formation of the co-operative university of Mondragón and the major revisionings of education that were undertaken in the light of global changes affecting the co-operatives. The chapter will then explore how Mondragon Unibertsitatea (MU) responded to a recent invitation to join a project to use education to regenerate the post-industrial Basque city of Bilbao, including the challenges faced in designing a new humanities degree for the purpose. The chapter highlights some of the positive features of Mondragón's relationship between educational and co-operative development whilst also raising questions about other features that would make up a 'co-operative pedagogy'. We end by discussing how Preston could fruitfully draw on Mondragón's experience, especially in the design of a future co-operative education centre and Co-operative University, in collaboration with the Co-operative College in Manchester.

Mondragón: co-operation through education

The story of Mondragón starts with the arrival of a priest, Don José María Arizmendiarrieta, to a small industrial town within a rural valley in 1941. The town had a history of small industries manufacturing metal goods, but by then employment was predominantly in one iron company, Union Cerrajera, that was owned by six families. The region had been strongly Republican during the civil war and 'traitorous reds' were now punished with food shortages, denial of public education and lack of employment or hard and poorly paid work

(Kasmir 1996: 84–97). Most members of the upper classes had moved out of this conflictive environment, leaving an un-unionised working class under the control of the fascist police. The only available technical education was in the Union Cerrajera's apprentice school, with access limited to sons of employees and a few chosen outsiders, amounting to 15% of the eligible boys in the area (Thomas and Logan 1982: 18).

Arizmendiarrieta had attended the seminary at Vitoria, which was exceptional for its two teachers of Basque ethnology and Basque language and literature (Lannon 1979: 36). They countered traditional approaches by developing a pedagogy based on 'investigating' rather than 'learning', including walking, careful observation and experimentation and then induction from the material observed. Their students engaged in studies of a working-class suburb of Bilbao, and a mining area of Vizcaya and examined the 'social question' associated with 'new forms of production, with their concentration of large numbers of workers, and their exacerbation of divisions between workers and bosses' (Lannon 1979: 39). They were influenced by the famous Instituto de Libre Enseñanza,[1] and also gave courses on the missionary movement Catholic Social Action that improved workers' conditions and recognised their human value.

In Mondragón, Arizmendiarrieta responded to the restrictions of the apprentice school by bringing boys, parents and town leaders together, first in establishing a football pitch and league, and then buying and operating a movie theatre (Meek and Woodworth 1990: 510). These activities generated support from 600 citizens and small businesses, who raised funding to build an independent technical school. The school started in 1943 with 5 teachers and 20 students. Training in technical skills to yield a better standard of living was combined with 'social and spiritual' education that explored how to value labour and achieve a just society and economic order (Meek and Woodworth 1990: 511). The aim was to create technicians and future leaders of firms with a sense of social responsibility valuing all human beings.

Arizmendiarrieta perceived no division between what it is to be human and the knowledge to be gained through education, a connection that became crucial to the Mondragón project. This perspective persists today in the Mondragón Corporation's motto 'Humanity at Work'. In Arizmendiarrieta's words, 'Human beings are made human through education. Civilization progresses at an increasing pace only through formative and educative action along the searching path for human and social values' (Arizmendiarrieta 2013: 46), and 'It has been said that cooperativism is an economic movement that uses the methods of education. This definition can also be modified to affirm that cooperativism is an educational movement that uses the methods of economics' (Arizmendiarrieta 2013: 52).

Whilst focusing on the moral and social education of students at the technical school, Arizmendiarrieta not only prioritised people over profits, but also saw them as a lever towards creating citizen self-government and greater social justice (Gabilondo et al. 2012: 171). He was able to search out laws that enabled those who worked with him to set up organisations that reflected the social and economic principles they aimed to enact. The technical institute was restricted by its attachment to the church, making it ineligible for state educational funds. In 1948, Arizmendiarrieta found an ancient statute that enabled the institute to be reformed as a League for Education and Culture, with a General Assembly that gave parents, citizens who paid dues, and teachers, business sponsors and government authorities the right to elect members of a Supervisory Board. The institute made all information, including financial accounts, available in a form understandable by the members. This organisational form gave the institute legitimacy and government funding and was a prototype for what later became co-operative organising.

By 1958 the school had 170 students and needed bigger premises. Arizmendiarrieta insisted that what became the 'Escuela Politécnica Profesional' (EPP) be big enough for 1000 students. By then, new levels of education had been added. Eleven members of the first class of 20 had taken evening classes at EPP that were accredited by the University of Zaragoza. In 1947 they achieved the highest technical qualification as professional engineers (Meek and Woodworth 1990: 514).

Five graduates from the first class used the same method as Arizmendiarrieta himself had deployed to set up the football club: they talked to townspeople about how to put into practice the priest's ideas about prioritising labour as first among the factors of production. According to Whyte and Whyte (1988: 34) 100 people pledged the enormous sum of 11 million pesetas to enable the five men to buy a bankrupt firm in 1956, which they called ULGOR, an acronym created from the initials of their names. They gradually worked out an innovative organisational form, and in 1959 ULGOR was incorporated as a worker co-operative (Meek and Woodworth 1990: 517). Others followed. In 1959, Arizmendiarrieta worked out how to set up a co-operative bank so that the co-operatives could raise credit without being dependent on commercial banks. The EPP was reorganised as a second order co-operative, serving the industrial co-operatives, with three constituencies, parents and students, faculty, and the enterprises that contributed to its budget. In 1965 Arizmendiarrieta prepared the statutes of a student-worker co-operative called Alecoop where students could earn money to pay their fees whilst translating their lessons into practical experience. Within 6 months, Alecoop had nearly repaid all its start-up loan. By the 1990s it had expanded to 600 students making prefabricated electrical installations for schools, robotics, information systems and alternative energy uses (Meek and Woodworth 1990: 520–521).

According to Meek and Woodworth, education played an essential role in what became called 'the co-operative experience of Mondragón', where *experiencia* means both experiment and experience and conveys the process on which they embarked. It is important to underline that what Arizmendiarrieta meant by 'education' consisted of this pedagogy of experience, what he called education's 'broader meaning; by virtue of a certain knowledge, a certain experience' (Arizmendiarrieta 2013: 46). The education had three dimensions: Technical education for developing products that were cutting edge and would sell; ideological education for instilling values about human dignity through labour, worker ownership and democracy; and the combination of the first two into organisational forms, in which workers could understand their co-operative's operations and finances and participate in decision making.

Competitiveness and the formation of Mondragon University

At certain moments in Mondragón, the educational institutions have changed to meet economic challenges. By the 1990s, there were over 100 industrial worker-owned co-operatives in four divisions – industry, finance, distribution and knowledge – with one major worker-consumer co-operative (Eroski). The co-operatives were committed to solidarity among themselves. For example, they contributed a portion of their annual surplus to secondary co-operatives, notably the co-operative bank, Caja Laboral (founded in 1959). Through inter-co-operation, they developed common bodies of governance and participatory decision-making, homogenised labour norms and created systems for distributing surplus. In addition, they developed methods for relocating members between co-operatives to avoid redundancies and used their collective resources for education and innovation, or to weather market downturns (Gabilondo et al. 2012: 171–174). In 1987, the co-operatives formed a superstructual body, the Mondragón Co-operative Group, and in 1991, they formed the Mondragón Co-operative Corporation (MCC), to establish Mondragon's policy, regulations, and management of the funds.

This strategic approach was needed because Mondragón co-operatives were facing challenges to their competitiveness. Many were suppliers of components to large automobile brands and when the latter set up branches abroad, the suppliers relocated too. Whereas multinationals were moving production to profit from cheaper labour, the co-operatives engaged in international expansion with the opposite aim: they tried to sustain their global competitiveness in order to generate more employment in the Basque region. A nucleus of around 25 industrial co-operatives pursued a strategy of direct investment – joint ventures, greenfield investment and acquisitions – and transformed themselves into what Errasti et al. (2017: 183) call 'coopitalist multinationals'. The latest figures for Mondragón describe it as consisting of 96 co-operatives with 141 production plants in 37 countries, and sales in 150 (Mondragon Corporation 2020b).

If globalisation was one way to sustain competitiveness, the other was research and innovation. Whereas Mondragon had relied on vocational and then technical training, now they needed a university with specialised masters programmes and PhDs so they could set up their own research and innovation groups in collaboration with the co-operatives to increase their competitiveness. To achieve this, the Mondragon Corporation invested €1 million and brought together the existing educational institutions to form the faculties of Mondragon University (MU). The polytechnic school (EPP) became the Faculty of Engineering. A business school that had been set up to assist in establishing new co-operatives in the 1960s

(Enpresagintza S.Coop) became the Faculty of Business Studies. A teacher training school that was established in 1976 under the supervision of the Pontifical University of Salamanca (HUHEZI S.Coop) became transformed into the Faculty of Education and Humanities. Each faculty was itself a co-operative and the university became a co-operative of co-operatives. This expansion has continued recently, with the creation in 2011 of the Faculty of Gastronomic and Culinary Sciences at San Sebastián, demonstrating both the success and the essential quality of the MU, firmly rooted in the traditions of the Mondragón experience: an education with a constant emphasis on practical application and innovation to sustain the competitiveness of the Mondragón co-operatives.

The University has become closely allied to, but still independent from other relevant co-operatives: Alecop (allied to Business Studies), Saiolan (innovation and entrepreneurship education for new businesses, allied to Humanities and Education), and the three Innovation and Development Research Centres (Ikerlan, Lortek, and Ideko). Links to the Management Leadership and Training Centre of Otalora, are discussed below. The Humanities Faculty also established the LANKI Institute of Co-operative Research in 2001 to foster co-operative identity, practice and organisation in Mondragon and abroad. Their research focuses on the Mondragon co-operative experience and the co-operative movement in general, social and solidarity economics, and social innovation and self-empowerment. As in the other faculties, there is a strong emphasis on practical outcomes, in this case the development of co-operative education, participation in co-operative governance, organisational change, community development and social transformation.

Research in 2011 (Wright et al. 2011) detailed the multiple structured interactions between the Faculty of Engineering, for example, and their surrounding society, and how this made them responsive to the research and knowledge transfer needs of co-operatives and other companies. Students' final year projects were based in companies and were important for networking between companies and the university. Tutors would visit their students in the company three times, and the company mentors attended the students' defence examination at the university. Together they assessed the students on both technical and transversal skills, and lecturers reported back to the faculty not only the companies' assessment of students' educational strengths and weaknesses but also what they had gleaned about the company's future direction and likely educational and research needs. New research opportunities would be discussed in an interdisciplinary commission before making an offer to the company. Sometimes a company would sponsor a PhD related to their business needs or invest in a long-term collaboration between their research and development unit, the university and one of Mondragon Co-operative Corporation's development centres (Wright et al. 2011: 52–53). Every four years the educational programmes were evaluated and revised, drawing on these networks, a survey of companies and company-partners on the faculty's governing board.

One of the Faculty of Engineering's early evaluations of its relations with companies had found that although companies were satisfied with graduates' technical knowledge, students did not have the skills needed to work in contemporary industry (Wright et al. 2011: 52). This led to a project to develop an educational model suited to the needs of a globalising economy, which started in engineering but came to encompass the whole university. This initiative benefitted from Spanish legal reforms that enabled universities to participate in the Bologna Process, which aimed to align higher education systems across Europe and facilitate international mobility and exchange. Ultimately an integrated European Higher Education Area was intended to be a model other world regions would follow and to expand Europe's global trade in higher education. The Spanish legislative changes made it possible for MU to award its own bachelor, masters and research degrees, and design its own programmes and curriculum. Most importantly, as a secondary co-operative, partly funded by the Mondragon Co-operative Corporation, these changes enabled MU to fulfil its remit of working closely with the globalising co-operatives and assisting their development through research and teaching.

In developing its educational model to meet the needs of industry, MU used the EU's 1996 Delors Report as a framework for a fairly standardised set of competences and transversal skills: team-work, effective communication, problem solving, leadership, decision making, global vision and learning to learn. Launched in 2004 and called Mendeberri ('New Century'), this programme allowed Mondragon Unibertsitatea an almost automatic adaptation to the European Higher Education Area, becoming the first Basque university and one of the first in the state to adapt to the new requirements of Europe (Mondragon University 2019) Mendeberri had a wide influence on teaching, learning and evaluation processes. It projected the range of competences promoted throughout Europe at that time as necessary for workers in a globalised economy.

The Fagor shock and a new phase of education

The Mondragón co-operatives' strategy for global competitiveness was in some ways very successful. In 2009, the Mondragón group as a whole accounted for 3.5% of the Basque Country's GDP and 7.1% of its industrial GDP, creating a total added value of €2.284 billion (Gabilondo et al. 2012: 167). In 2008, Mondragón employed more than ninety thousand people (ibid). But the financial crash in 2008 revealed the dangers inherent in some aspects of the internationalisation strategy, as exemplified especially in the eventual demise of the domestic appliance producer, Fagor Electrodomésticos (FE). On the one hand, the failure of FE was a failure of internal management, but on the other hand, it brought to a head some underlying difficulties and the need for Mondragón co-operatives to find a way of joining the global market without losing their sense of identity as co-operatives (Errasti et al. 2003; Flecha and Ngai 2014).

Faced with competing multinationals entering the Spanish market, FE had acquired local and foreign non-co-operative firms abroad. In 2005, with the aim of increasing its share of the French market, FE invested €165 million for an 88% share of the French competitor Brandt Électroménager, which was large as FE itself.

By 2007, FE employed around eleven thousand workers in its eighteen production plants and its sales topped €1.8 billion. However, the expected synergies with the French firm were slow to materialise, and the financial crash burst the Spanish housing bubble, provoking a sharp drop in sales of white goods. By 2013 FE had experienced a 40% drop in turnover, halved its labour force and its factories were working at 80% capacity (Errasti et al. 2017: 187–189).[2] FE made a recovery plan that was backed by a loan of €300 million from Mondragon Co-operative Corporation and a unanimous decision by all the other 120 co-operatives to devote 1% of their salaries to rescue Fagor. When the planned results were not achieved and FE's decline was compromising the viability of other co-operatives, finally in 2013 the General Assembly of the Mondragón Co-operative Corporation decided to allow this flagship of the Mondragón movement to fail. Where this failure would have been an unmitigated disaster for a standard business, in Mondragón, inter-co-operative solidarity kicked in: none of the remaining 2,000 Basque workers were made redundant and all were relocated to other companies, took early retirement or entered education so as to gain skills and take on new roles in other co-operatives. There was a deep analysis of the multiple reasons for the failure. FE's inter-nationalisation strategy was the opposite of its competitors'. Whereas FE tried to keep jobs in the Basque country and invested in other European production units, competitors maintained their profitability in a declining European market by out-sourcing production to cheaper countries. In addition, although FE had halved its workforce and outsourced its production, the management was deemed not to have implemented radical adjustment measures as comprehensively or quickly as required (Errasti et al. 2017: 194). Another argument was that FE's technology and organisation of production were insufficiently innovative in a fast-changing environment, and as a result there had been a danger of FE pulling down the whole co-operative system. However, there were strong protests and demonstrations and 900 members of FE who had lost their assets in the co-operative took the Mondragón Co-operative Corporation to court because it had failed to demonstrate sufficient solidarity. The case was dismissed as each co-operative is sovereign and members, as the owners, are responsible for taking their own decisions. However, the case clearly revealed divergent perceptions and interpretations of co-operative values and principles. Many of the FE worker-members accused the Mondragon group of treating them in the same way as any capitalist business.

In a satirical poster of a spoof advertisement for a washing machine created by the workers during the crisis, the washing machine indicators for the wash cycle are displayed with the words 'Without responsibility'; 'No clarity' (play on the Spanish for 'rinse'); 'Noise free'; 'Shameless'; 'Without dignity'; 'Without justice', and the product label attached to the machine is marked '0% social responsibility'. The door of the washing machine is satirically advertised as having the quality of 'rapid closure', and the washing machine guarantees at the bottom of the poster are the logos belonging to the pillars of the Mondragón system: the MCC itself, the bank and the welfare system. The poster is making a sophisticated complaint that the co-operative culture of Mondragón is failing itself.

The closure of FE brought to a head the argument that 'direct, personal and essentially vital solidarity had been giving way to bureaucratically administered solidarity' and the 'technological drift' of recent years meant that co-operativism was losing its motivational vision, so that solidarity and self-management, the two foundations of the co-operative experience, were losing force (Gabilondo et al. 2012: 181, 183–184). The year before FE's failure, the Mondragon co-operative congress had already defined the need to revitalise their values and principles. In 2014, the congress reinforced the commitment to inter-co-operative solidarity and the idea of co-operative culture, and strengthened measures to manage any crisis-hit co-operatives that needed collective support in future (Errasti et al. 2017: 193). The 2017 congress further endorsed this with a commitment to (1) co-operative values, (2) social transformation, and (3) new financial systems. This strategy for future resilience was reflected in an emphasis on the idea that an 'excellent firm' had to both strongly exhibit co-operative values and principles, and also be profitable; that there was a need for the worker-owner to fully accept the responsibility of ownership and take on the attitude of a manager, not just that of an employee; and a focus on flexibility and adaptability in an environment of unpredictable change. This became central to changes in co-operative 'culture' – as the co-operatives looked beyond the post-Fagor shock.[3] They found expression in two major educational visions for the future of Mondragón – training at Otalora in 'co-operative values', and at MU, a new 'Mendeberri 2025' to educate people capable of navigating an uncertain world.

Otalora and the support for co-operative values and principles

Otalora, the Centre for Management and Co-operative Development in Mondragón, began offering training courses in 1984 to post-graduates, combining post-graduate studies with work-placements, using the traditional Mondragón approach. At the same time, there were the beginnings of a management training programme for members sitting on the various Governing, Social and Management Councils of the co-operatives. By 1988, the current version of Otalora was constituted, and the curriculum includes a series of educational programmes on 'co-operative culture' that respond to the demands of the 2017 congress for developing 'co-operative values'. In partnership with Unai Elorza and colleagues at MU, Otalora has developed an educational programme to tackle the perceived deficit or erosion of co-operative values in Mondragón. Although the entirety of the Otalora catalogue offers training from a co-operative perspective (including programmes in Leadership and Teamwork, Co-operative Education, Management Development, Dissemination of the Co-operative Experience, and Self Development), there has been much recent focus on the Cultural Development courses. While the courses are intended to cater for the development of co-operative values, they are often couched in general organisational terms, demonstrating, once again, the Mondragón tendency to be 'business-like' and 'pragmatic' in its approach, and possibly a tendency to be implicit rather than explicit about Mondragón's co-operative mission. For example, the courses use Barrett's seven 'levels of consciousness' (designed to be an organisational alternative to Maslow's hugely influential 'hierarchy of needs') rather than on Mondragón's co-operative principles, which remain implicit in much of the work. Barrett's 'values' are: *service, making a difference, internal cohesion, transformation, self-esteem, relationships*, and *survival*. Barret's ideal cultural balance is located midway in this list (i.e. at the level of transformation, the pivotal point that provides the balance between personal survival and service to the community). Behind such a list are values that are indeed important to co-operative working. For example, 'Making a difference' is defined by Barrett as 'Actualizing your sense of purpose by cooperating with others for mutual benefit and fulfilment' (Barrett 2020). Nevertheless, it is interesting to note how co-operative values and principles are only implicit in these programmes.

Mendeberri 2025

MU had begun to revitalise its educational project after the 2008 financial crisis and in the light of changes in society. These moves were catalysed by the Fagor shock and the rectorate involved all the faculties in a process of renewing the university's 'educational model' and rethinking 'the student of the future'. The new model, 'Mendeberri 2025' was launched in 2019. In his presentation, the vice-rector, Jon Altuna, emphasised that the model was based on the future challenges faced by companies and institutions in a society characterised by constant change. As he put it:

> The university must respond to the needs of the companies, institutions and society in which it is located, and even anticipate them to become, through their graduates, an active agent of that change, and more in a society like the current one, in constant transformation
>
> (Mondragon University 2019).

The biggest change in Mendeberri 2025 was a move away from acquisition of a standard set of competences to focus on the personal development of each individual student. As Altuna put it, Mendeberri 2025 'puts the accent not only on the training of future professionals but also on their human and citizen development'. As the context for future students was no longer just different work environments, but also uncertain futures for 'society and the world in a broad sense', the educational model is 'flexible and personalized, and designed so that graduates respond as professionals and people to an uncertain but exciting future, and constant changes' (Mondragon University 2019). The video presentation of Mendeberri 2025 explains that the model of personal development has six axes. First, as a *'citizen of the world'* it is important to 'feel connected to the world we wish to know' and work out how to participate within it. To do that, the second is *'identity and personal objectives'*: 'looking inside oneself' getting to know one's possibilities for improvement, set personal goals and 'actively pursue them to achieve an increasingly free and independent identity'. This in turn enables people 'to develop from a personal to a collective level', in short, to become a '*co-operative person*' who 'puts the common good before the individual good and works for social transformation for the sake of justice and dignity of the people'. Being a citizen of the world requires becoming a '*multicommunicator*' able to work in different cultures, languages, technologies and media, one who takes a proactive approach as an '*active learner*' and is capable of adapting to new and uncertain contexts as a '*flexible learner*'. The new educational model is based on student-centred, active methodologies and 'real-life projects and challenges', and focuses on individual mentoring to help the student integrate these six axes in their 'personal academic itinerary' (Mondragon University 2019). The resulting graduate is intended to use these six main characteristics to proactively foster co-operative values in an ever-changing future society.

In this model, Mondragon retains the relational and human in its educational approach and does not just aim for the practical application of competences in successful worker-owned industrial co-operatives. This speaks to the founder's original aim for the values of co-operativism to spread from the companies into society. The promotional video that accompanies the web page description of Mendeberri 2025, also uses 'inspirational' quotations from Nelson Mandela and Malcolm X, to demonstrate Mondragon's effort to move forward into the new world of 2025, while keeping a watchful eye on its past (Mondragon University 2018a). One of the tests of the flexibility and adaptability of this framework to uncertain futures will be in its translation, along with the Mondragon experience as a whole, to an entirely new context, Bilbao.

Translation to Bilbao

From the early 2000s, Mondragon University increasingly received invitations from other parts of the Basque country to set up branch campuses and share their success in professional training, industrial research and innovation and social revitalisation. Mainly other rural-industrial areas sought such collaboration but in 2013 the Mayor of Bilbao asked MU to contribute to innovation in the city. In contrast to Mondragón's small towns and rural roots, Bilbao is the largest industrial city in the Basque Country and based in another province. MU was given a building opposite the city hall and established an 'Innovation Factory' a 'crazy idea' of generating 1000 social entrepreneurs, 400 enterprise students and 50 start-ups (Jon Altuna, personal communication, 17 September 2020).[4] Seven years later it was a great success, with international visitors seeking to copy it. MU had won the trust of city hall and was invited to participate in the next stage of the city's revitalisation. They looked to MU, along with all the universities in its own region, to help make the largest remaining industrial site, the island of Zorrotzaurre in the River Nervión, into a knowledge industry hub. Rather than focusing on the future forms of industrial production associated with robotics, artificial intelligence, smart technology and 5G interconnectivity, they sought to specialise in the new support services demanded by so-called 'Industry 4.0', Zaha Hadid Architects created a masterplan for this knowledge-intense site embedded in a 'truly global city' (Guardo 2019). MU collaborated on a successful EU bid to establish a 'European Advanced Service Factory' (AS Fabrik).[5] On one site, Bachelor programmes in technology, business, data analytics and digital humanities will be brought together to create a 'truly interdisciplinary environment' focused on inter-co-operative and interdisciplinary research and innovation projects with companies. This venture is girded with high expectations where education becomes akin to social transformation. The invitation to come and 'revive Bilbao' gives MU a strategic opportunity to become more central to the initiatives of the whole three-province Basque autonomous community. It is an invitation to expand the educational initiatives, political influence, and development potential of Mondragon's solidarity socio-economic model that is continually under threat from a world order of neoliberal capitalism.

Despite admitting that they do not have the intimate knowledge of a large urban society, which is so important for the way they work in their own context, MU's Humanities Faculty decided to take on the financial, reputational, and intellectual challenge of moving into this urban space and developing a new Global Digital Humanities BA degree. The move and commitment reflect MU's philosophy of engaging with education for the purposes of real co-operative change. A conference called 'UniverCity: Educating for and with the City' brought together faculty members, city planners, commercial and cultural organisations and foreign educators (including Wright) to discuss how they were translating their experience of co-operative education into the new context of Bilbao. This raised three main issues involved in developing co-operative education 'with and for' any new site.

The first issue was the care with which MU faculty members were seeking to understand the way Bilbao and its future were imagined. The conference began with a tour by the professor of Basque studies, Joseba Zulaika, who explained how the governing and cultural classes have reimagined the city. In the late 1800s, Bilbao became a city of heavy industry, with mining, the export of iron ore, 20% of the world's steel production, extensive docks and ship building (Zulaika 2014: 104–105). The Franco dictatorship was marked by social and political conflict, as some of the city's industrial and banking elite supported the regime, putting financial gain above democratic principles. Others were solidly opposed. From the end of that era to the early 1990s, heavy industry closed and buildings became derelict, 37% of the industrial jobs were gone and unemployment was above 20% (Zulaika 2014: 104–105). What had been a city based on industrial capitalism had turned into 'the ruins of a broken cosmos' (Zulaika 2014: 109).

In the 1990s, the city's industrial dereliction was transformed into a centre of culture with the franchise for a branch of New York's Guggenheim Museum. In the context of Bilbao, on the site of the derelict docks, the new Guggenheim museum's undulating torsions in thin titanium and Serra's permanent exhibition of massive torqued and elliptical steel plates that glide into ever transforming relations to each other, suggested that in a post-industrial era, the challenge is to conceptualise the unstable positioning of the individual in relation to a world that is continually flowing and twisting into new shapes. This chimes with Mendeberri 2025, which sees students as having continually to try and grasp the contours of an unpredictable and fast-changing world and reflexively work out how to position themselves within it. The MU faculty presented Mendeberri 2025 as a way to engage with Bilbao's symbolic landscape.

A second issue discussed by the MU faculty, was how to establish relations between the university and local stakeholders, a vital feature of the way MU works. The new BA degree has been designed in a way that clearly addresses the city planners' focus on Industry 4.0 services, as the website explains:

> Digitalization has accelerated the globalization process. We live in an inter-connected and interdependent world that is changing constantly and rapidly. Companies and institutions are forced to widen their horizons and function on the international stage. For this purpose, they require more and more information about cultural, economic, and social trends as well as…people trained in these areas who know how to manage in intercultural contexts.
>
> (Mondragon University 2018b)

The website emphasises that their model of education goes beyond classroom walls, has no exams or traditional classes, and instead connects with the community and the needs of its citizens. To do this, the methodology is 'active and based on challenges', working with stakeholders and taking internships and projects at digital and global firms. The new degree programme is aiming to draw on MU's experience of working closely with enterprises and tailoring education to their needs for skills and competences. The conference discussed how the Global Digital Humanities programme could engage 'with and for' different sectors of the population who had diverse visions of the future. Ideas included Paul Mullins's contemporary archaeology restoring the history of the African American community displaced by a university campus (Mullins 2016), Susan Hyatt's action research on universities' relationships to surrounding communities (Hyatt 2015), Keri Facer's 'learning in the city' (Facer et al. 2019), and Jan Masschelein's 'pedagogy of attention' aiming for students to understand a city in new ways (Masschelein and Simons 2015).

A third issue concerned how education would support students in developing co-operative enterprises. To the international educators, an explicit account of a co-operative pedagogy seemed to be missing: how will the focus on individual development, with a sense of responsibility and leadership – which are all words also used to define the neoliberal subject – instead come together in a co-operative assemblage? How will students learn to translate these values into the organisational design and dynamics of a co-operative? This echoes one of Arizmendiarrieta's aims to combine technical knowledge and spiritual humanity in the social and economic design of organisations that create citizen self-government and greater social justice.

The MU faculty are imbued with a co-operative sensibility, and able to make collective decisions to use their collective resources for innovation. Those responsible for the new humanities programme had consulted widely, then acted decisively to make things happen. As one of them said, 'We're always doing something new, always entangled in innovation, sometimes failing, and then learning from our mistakes.' While strongly aware of their personal responsibility and working hard for success, there was also an acceptance of failure as something to learn from, and then quickly move on, secure of systems of co-operative solidarity. It seemed this co-operative sensibility was so inherent, it was hard to articulate how the person was formed in this way, let alone set out the features of a co-operative pedagogy. MU's vice rector recently recognised that MU is aware of this issue, but the very embeddedness of co-operative values and principles in Mondragón provides a paradoxical obstacle to its dissemination outside Mondragón's ecosystem:

> For us who have inherited the co-ops, the principles and values are embedded in our everyday activity, which does not imply that we are always 100% complying with them. But at least, they are always present and from time to time we take some time to re-think about them (mainly when it comes to define our strategic plan).
>
> (Jon Altuna, personal communication to Manley)

MU faculty emphasised that the Mondragon experience has to be sensitively adapted to each new context and co-constructed with the people in Bilbao. They avidly resist the idea of a blueprint or model. Yet it would seem important for MU to be able to articulate a 'co-operative bildung' and to explain how co-operative principles and values translate into co-operative designs for students and organisations in Bilbao who are not attuned to co-operative approaches.

Conclusion: from Bilbao to Preston

During its history, Mondragon has gone through successive phases, first in developing co-operative industries for the Spanish market, then focusing on research and innovation to keep globally competitive, and currently moving from a narrow focus on technical competences to highlighting co-operative culture and values. At each phase, education played a central role. Education has been rethought each time the economy has changed, along with ways of imagining what qualities a person needs in a differently constituted world. Now Mondragon faces the challenge of exporting its experience/experiment for the revival of Bilbao. The analysis of Mondragon's translation to Bilbao identified three main points. First, the need for MU to position itself within the imaginary projected by the city's cultural activists and planners about the shape of a post-industrial world and the kind of person needed to navigate it. Second is the importance of working 'with and for' a diversity of other communities with different ideas of desirable futures. Third, the ability to articulate how to develop a 'co-operative bildung' and more socially oriented industry in the face of the dereliction caused by corporate global capitalism. Similar concerns are relevant to Preston, as the university, the City Council and anchor institutions, with the support of the Cooperative College in Manchester, embark on a similar collaborative project to develop a co-operative ethos and more solidary socio-economy in Preston.

As part of the development of the Preston Model, stakeholders under the leadership of the City Council and the University are collaborating with Mondragon to begin work on a co-operative ecosystem that will resonate with that being developed in Bilbao by MU and the Council in Bilbao, in particular the Innovation Factory, known in Bilbao as BBF, as an educational centre that combines learning, entrepreneurship and innovation. This is intended to combine with plans to develop Preston Co-operative Education Centre, which it is hoped will be affiliated to the future Co-operative University, a project under construction from the Co-operative College in Manchester (Shaw 2019; Ross 2019; Neary and Winn 2019). The BBF shares the founding principles of Arizmendiarrieta – to join up economics and education in order to create new work enterprises that generate wealth and employment in an ethical fashion – and brings those principles up to date in an exciting new project that aims to develop co-operative businesses and principles in Bilbao and the surrounding areas. The spirit behind the Preston Model is sympathetic with these ideas, values and principles, and practical measures are currently being developed, alongside actors from Mondragon, to make these developments a reality. The university itself is touched by the development of the Preston Model, as noted in recent media articles (Morgan 2018, 2019). In this way, the education of co-operative principles and values becomes an attitude to be adopted as much as a curriculum to be taught, and this attitude becomes 'contagious' and is beginning to permeate the fabric of Prestonian society. In the course of this process, it is clear that overt and pro-active efforts will have to be made to develop a co-operative mind-set for Preston: what is embedded and taken for granted in Mondragón is still in development in Bilbao and in its infancy in Preston.

Notes

1 See www.thisistherealspain.com/en/latest-news/the-free-institution-of-education-the-r evolution-of-freedom-and-critical-thinking
2 Of Fagor's total workforce of 5,634, only 1,600 were worker members. The subsidiaries were affiliated companies with hired wage-laborers owned by the co-operative and the Mondragon Corporation (Errasti et al. 2017: 193).
3 Notably, they did not focus on how to turn their cultural values into the organisational design of cooperative working, which had been the focus of an earlier period of transformation (Greenwood and González-Santos 1991).
4 See http://bbfaktoria.com/en/what-is-bbf
5 See www.uia-initiative.eu/en/uia-cities/bilbao

References

Areso, I. (2017), Bilbao's Strategic Evolution: The Metamorphosis of the Industrial City, retrieved from www.mascontext.com/issues/30-31-bilbao/bilbaos-strategic-evolutionthe-metamorphosis-of-the-industrial-city (accessed 5 November 2020).

Arizmendiarrieta, J-M. (2013), *Reflections*, Otalora, Mondragón, English translation, retrieved from www.laputaproject.com/images/uploaded/20160626/63602508771906928443448445.pdf (accessed 5 November 2020).

Barrett, R. (2020), The Seven Levels of Personal Consciousness, retrieved from www.valuescentre.com/wp-content/uploads/PDF_Resources/Barrett_Model_Articles/Seven_Levels_of_Personal_Consciousness.pdf (accessed 7 June 2020).

Errasti, A.M., Heras, I., Bakaikoa, B., and Elgoibar, P. (2003), The Internationalisation of Co-operatives: The case of the Mondragón Co-operative Corporation, *Annals of Public and Co-operative Economics*, 74 (4): 553–584.

Errasti, A., Bretos, I., and Nunez, A. (2017), The Viability of Cooperatives: The Fall of the Mondragon Cooperative Fagor, *Review of Radical Political Economics*, 49 (2): 181–197.

Facer, K., Buchczyk, M., Bishop, L., Bolton, H., Haq, Z., Gilbert, J., Thomas, G., Tomico, J., and Wang, X. (2019), Learning in the Cat's Cradle: Weaving Learning Ecologies in the City, in Barnett, R. and Jackson, N. (eds), *Ecologies for Learning and Practice: Emerging Ideas, Sightings, and Possibilities*, Routledge, London.

Flecha, R. and Ngai, P. (2014), The Challenge for Mondragon: Searching for the Co-operative Values in Times of Internationalization, *Organization*, 21 (5): 666–682.

Gabilondo, L.A., Idiakez, A.L., and Tricio, E.P. (2012), Mondragón: The Dilemmas of a Mature Cooperativism, in Harnecker, C.P. (ed.), *Cooperatives and Socialism: A View from Cuba*, Palgrave, London, 167–189.

Greenwood, D.J. and González-Santos, J.L. (1991), *Industrial Democracy as Process: Participatory Action Research in the Fagor Cooperative Group of Mondragón*, Van Gorcum, Assen.

Guardo, J. (2019), *Zorrotzaurre: Past, Present, Future*, presentation to UniverCity: Educating for and with the City, Bilbao, 18–19 December.

Hyatt, S.B. (2015), Using Ethnographic Methods to Understand Universities and Neoliberal Development in North Central Philadelphia, in Hyatt, S.B., Shear, B.W. and Wright, S. (eds), *Learning Under Neoliberalism: Ethnographies of Governance in Higher Education*, Berghahn, New York.

Kasmir, S. (1996), *The Myth of Mondragon*, State University of New York Press, Albany, NY.

Lannon, F. (1979), A Basque Challenge to the Pre-Civil War Spanish Church, *European Studies Review*, 9 (1): 29–48.

Masschelein, J. and Simons, M. (2015), Education in Times of Fast Learning: The Future of the School, *Ethics and Education*, 10 (1): 84–95.

Meek, C.B. and Woodworth, W.P. (1990), Technical Training and Enterprise: Mondragon's Educational System and its Implications for Other Cooperatives, *Economic and Industrial Democracy*, 11 (4): 505–528.

Molina, F. and Miguez, A. (2008), The Origins of Mondragon: Catholic co-operativism and social movement in a Basque valley (1941–59), *Social History*, 33 (3): 284–298.

Mondragon Corporation (2020a) Adding to Multiply. retrieved from www.mondragoncorporation.com/wp-content/uploads/docs/MDGN-pres-CORPORATIVA_EN.pdf (accessed 5 November 2020).

Mondragon Corporation (2020b) About Us, retrieved from www.mondragon-corpora tion.com/en/about-us (accessed 16 November 2020).

Mondragon University (2018a), Educational Model, retrieved from www.mondragon. edu/en/information-of-interest/learning-model (accessed 5 November 2020).

Mondragon University (2018b), Global Digital Humanities, retrieved from www.mondra gon.edu/en/bachelor-degree-global-digital-humanities (accessed 5 November 2020).

Mondragon University (2019), Mondragon Unibertsitatea Presents 'Mendeberri 2025', its Renewed Educational Model, retrieved from www.elperiodicouniversitario.com/en/ news/mondragon-unibertsitatea-presents-mendeberri-2025-its-renewed-educational-model (accessed 5 November 2020).

Morgan, J. (2018), Towns and Universities: UK Labour's New Civic Thinking, *Times Higher Education*, 25 October.

Morgan, J. (2019), Is Cooperation the Antidote to Higher Education's Competitive Anxiety? *Times Higher Education*, 5 December.

Mullins, P. (2016), The Last Holdouts: Community Displacement and Urban Renewal on the IUPUI Campus, retrieved from https://invisibleindianapolis.wordpress.com/ 2016/10/09/the-last-holdouts-community-displacement-and-urban-renewal-on-the-iupui-campus (accessed 5 November 2020).

Neary, M. and Winn, J. (2019), The Co-operative University Now!, in Woodin, T. and Shaw, L. (eds), *Learning for a Co-operative World*, UCL IOE Press, London, 169–186.

Ross, C. (2019), The Nature, Purpose and Place of Co-operative Education in New Times: Learning to know, do, be and live together, in Woodin, T. and Shaw, L. (eds), *Learning for a Co-operative World*, UCL IOE Press, London, 87–102.

Shaw, L. (2019), The Co-operative College and Co-operative Education Internationally, in Woodin, T. and Shaw, L. (eds), *Learning for a Co-operative World*, UCL IOE Press, London, 36–51.

Tomas, H. and Logan, C. (1982), *Mondragon: An Economic Analysis*, Allen and Unwin, London.

Whyte, W.F. and Whyte, K.K. (1988), *Making Mondragon: The Growth and Dynamics of the Worker Cooperative Complex*, ILR Press, Ithaca, NY.

Wright, S., Greenwood, D., and Boden, R. (2011), Report on a Field Visit to Mondragon University: A Cooperative Experience/Experiment, *Learning and Teaching: International Journal for Higher Education in the Social Sciences (LATISS)*, 4 (3): 38–56.

Zulaika, J. (2014), *That Old Bilbao Moon. The Passion and Resurrection of a City*, Centre for Basque Studies, University of Nevada, Reno, NV.

4 Community and co-operatives

A Preston perspective

Julie Ridley

Introduction

This chapter reflects upon the values and principles of co-operatives and by implication, the Preston Model, in relation to community. Making reference to what has been termed the 'Mondragón ecosystem', one of the world's largest industrial co-operative associations (Heales et al., 2017), I show how shared values between people, a strong collective drive and a communitarian impulse to improve life chances and increase equality, underpin co-operative development. Reflecting on the concepts of community and social capital, the chapter draws upon the theory of change behind a body of national and local 'Connected Communities' work conducted by researchers at UCLan's Centre for Citizenship and Community in collaboration with community members (Parsfield et al., 2015). Principles of social capital development are identified as fundamental to the co-operative enterprise (Lizarralde, 2009). The chapter concludes by reflecting on the findings of research undertaken with one community in Preston, and considers the implications for the further development of co-operative initiatives based on the existence of a strong sense of belonging, trust in others and evident community spirit. With reference to this research into community connectedness and belonging (Ridley and Morris, 2018), I reflect on the potential for developing a stronger co-operative culture in Preston's communities, as well as whether, adoption of the Preston Model, could be a force for increasing social and community capital.

Meanings of 'community'

In looking at community alongside co-operatives and the Preston Model, it is first necessary to explore the notion of community, as although a commonly used term, what is understood as community is anything but simple. Theories of community abound and can seem, for instance, in relation to some aspects of modernity and community, to be ideologically opposed (Cohen, 2013; Smith, 2013). The notion of community means different things to different people and groups, in different contexts and time. At its most basic, community denotes a group of people having something in common, though what that is, is itself highly subjective. The importance of building the capacity of communities is espoused by people across the political spectrum: ranging from romanticised ideas of times past, to idealistic notions of solidaristic working-class neighbourhoods, through to a more critical view of community as a 'fig leaf for the socio-economic fractures of capitalism' (Lent and Studdert, 2019: 34).

Although there is limited space here to do justice to the substantial social science literature exploring community and its measurement, of particular import are three main, overlapping ideas: first, the concept of community of place in the sense of people living in a geographical locality; second, the notion of communities of interest, where shared characteristics such as religious beliefs, linguistic or sexual orientation serve to bind people together; and thirdly, the idea of communion, encompassing a sense of attachment (Smith, 2013). This third distinction, identified in the 80s by Wilmott (1986), refers to the 'attachment' or 'spirit' of community that is defined by collective action. The earlier work of Cohen (1985) mainly in rural or island settings, identified what he calls the symbolic boundaries of community and belonging that are closely related to values and identity. This theoretical construct of 'sense of community' refers to the phenomenon of collective experience which has been studied in a variety of contexts and operationalised in terms of four dimensions, that is: needs fulfilment, group membership, influence, and emotional connection (Peterson et al., 2008).

Notably, Lent and Studdert (2019: 34) argue that since 2010 there has been a distinct policy turn towards a 'community paradigm', identifying community as a 'network of individuals collaborating more or less formally to achieve a shared, socially beneficial goal ... mobilised in an ethic of co-operation to pursue wider common good'. The connectedness of individuals' relationship networks helps to further explain or, at least to describe, key aspects of people's experience of community other than to simply define it in relation to a shared locality (Lee and Newby, 1983).

A growing body of research amplifies the importance of social networks and community connections, finding a link between poor social networks and loneliness, particularly for people living in more deprived neighbourhoods (e.g. Kearns et al., 2015a, 2015b). In Marmot's review of health and inequalities, individuals who were socially isolated were between two and five times more likely than those who have strong social ties to die prematurely (SRHIE, 2010), signifying the importance of connected communities. Strong supportive relationships in communities provide a buffer against the worst health outcomes of living in poor and disadvantages areas (Bartley, 2012). All of this speaks of the 'social capital' or benefits to be gained from positive relationships and of supportive social structures that encourage pro-social actions and address inequalities (Claridge, 2004).

Social and community capital

Although some have argued that 'social capital' is a rather 'elastic' term defying consensus (Adler and Kwon, 2002), in this chapter the relevance of the term is in the emphasis placed on the value that social networks hold (Putnam, 2000). This value lies in the opportunities afforded from social networks, and access provided to resources and qualitative attributes such as trust, and community values (Kadushin, 2012; Glanville and Bienenstock, 2009). Fundamentally, it refers to how people interact with each other, the value of social relationships, the bonding of similar individuals, and the bridges created between diverse people, with norms of reciprocity (Dekker and Uslaner, 2001). Support among neighbours can influence personal social capital and positively impact individuals' daily lives (Redshaw and Ingham, 2017). Nyqvist et al. (2016) found that having low social capital, especially in terms of low levels of trust between neighbours, can be a risk factor for loneliness. The results of a multilevel analysis study suggest that daily contact with neighbours is positively related to feelings of not being alone and attachment to one's neighbourhood and thus leads to increased social capital (Seifert, 2020). Other research finds that locality-based social capital is most important for those individuals spending the greatest amount of time in a neighbourhood, which can include less mobile older and disabled people (Hoogerbrugge and Burger, 2018).

Despite its slipperiness as a concept, recent decades have seen a growing policy and practice interest in this notion, especially in how to access and nurture social capital. Founded in communitarian principles and the hypothesis that increasing civic-mindedness contributes to making life better for local people and communities, a major research programme concluded that building structural or community capital generated four types of value or 'dividends': namely, wellbeing; citizenship, capacity, and economic dividends (Parsfield et al., 2015). The resultant theory of change acknowledged that assets within communities can be used to benefit members of these communities. In short, community capital refers to 'the sum of assets including relationships in a community and the value that accrues from these' (Parsfield et al., 2015: 12). A body of Connected Communities work undertaken by the Centre for Citizenship and Community at UCLan continues to demonstrate that community-led action and bespoke interventions can contribute to strengthening local communities and that working in this way can accrue substantial benefits for community members (Wilson and Morris, 2019; Ridley and Morris, 2018; Parsfield et al., 2015). I now turn to considering these notions of community, social networks, social and community capital alongside the ideas surrounding co-operatives.

Co-operatives and community: in the DNA?

As has already been established earlier in this book, but worth briefly revisiting here, co-operatives around the world operate according to a common set of core principles and values now adopted by the International Co-operative Alliance (ICA) and which date back to the first modern co-operative founded in Rochdale, England in 1844 (Vo, 2016). Essentially, a co-operative is a group of people who work together to achieve a joint purpose and have the freedom to govern their own affairs. Co-operatives are based on the values of self-help, self-responsibility, democracy, equality, equity, and solidarity (Parker et al., 2014). These co-operative values enable communities from across the globe to establish good connections between neighbours. Core principles, extended in Mondragon's Industrial Co-operative Association, emphasise the centrality of people centeredness in co-operatives, as well as strong social, ethical and environmental leanings that incorporate ways of relating and being that go far beyond co-operatives as purely an economic model:

> We view innovation today as a collective social endeavour. As a result, the capacity to collaborate is becoming an ever more important attribute, with the person (knowledge) considered as being the most important asset.
>
> (Lizarralde, 2009: 28)

In short, as well as being centrally concerned with inclusion, co-operatives are open and non-discriminating, organise in ways that underline democratic participation, are based on collaborative ways of working and being, and importantly, in the context of this chapter, there is an explicit focus on community. In 1995, a major revision added a seventh core principle: concern for community, which states, 'Co-operatives work for the sustainable development of their communities through policies approved by their members' (International Co-operative Alliance 2020). Several writers have since pointed to the community, as well as economic development potential of co-operatives (see Gertler cited in Vo, 2016). By improving the economic conditions of communities, co-operatives advance broad social aims and achieve social development potential through democratic ideals and a key emphasis on community trust (Majee and Hoyt, 2009). Indeed, the power of co-operatives to address major societal issues including inequalities was highlighted in a United Nations report which stated:

> As the world today faces unstable financial systems, increased insecurity of food supply, growing inequality worldwide, rapid climate change and increased environmental degradation, it is increasingly compelling to consider the model of economic enterprise that cooperatives offer.
>
> (COPAC, 2008: 1)

One of the world's largest industrial co-operative associations, the Mondragon Cooperative Corporation in the Basque Country in northern Spain, set up in the late 1950s in response to widespread hunger and challenging socio-economic needs in the local community, describes itself as 'humanity at work' (Heales et al., 2017). The Mondragon 'solution' developed in response to these socio-economic needs created an organisational culture that to this day places high value on the social drivers of growth and sustainability. Implicit and intrinsic to the Mondragon model are values that underpin its social innovation mission including democracy and participation, and concern for the common good (Heales et al., 2017). Key to the development of Mondragon's co-operatives is

'Auzolan', which translated into English means community work or community-led practice, denoting the ability of the community to not only work together but to achieve things collectively. Importantly, this sense of shared responsibility to 'create social sustainability by generating well-distributed wealth with broad social benefits' (Heales et al., 2017: 8) is seen as fundamental to the success of the Mondragon co-operatives. Some commentators below suggest that this humanistic characteristic, that is, of caring for one's neighbours and the wider good of the community, existed in Mondragon before co-operatives were developed and provided fertile ground for the seeds of co-operation to grow. It is, however, clear from the literature that whilst there is truth in this assertion, co-operatives both increase social connectedness, thus enhancing social and community capital, and have a wider transformational value for communities.

Social and community capital through co-operation

A review of the literature finds that the capacity-focused paradigm of co-operatives ensures that the skills, talents and gifts of local community members are recognised (Wanjare, 2017). Indeed, social relationships and interactions are a 'defining feature of co-operatives' (Manley and Froggett, 2016: 5). The co-operative model makes linkages across different parts of the social economy. For example, Majee and Hoyt (2010) explain how individual growth through involvement in a home-care co-operative extended to members' families as well as the wider community as co-operatives engaged with the wider community membership. In strengthening ties between people (family, friends, neighbours) *within* a group sharing common concerns or interests, co-operatives have developed bonding social capital, while at the same time, developing bridging social capital, encouraging links *between* different social groups and co-operatives (Majee and Hoyt, 2009, 2011).

Co-operative groups often come together based on shared interests and characteristics demonstrating their strength in developing bonding social capital (Majee and Hoyt, 2011). The core principle of co-operation between and among co-operatives, however, serves as an impetus for developing more 'bridging social capital', increasing links and networks between diverse co-operative groups and communities. Furthermore, in bridging social divisions, the co-operative model can be seen to contribute to social cohesion (Dobrohoczki, 2006). Once operational and providing goods and services, co-operatives can serve as an organising vehicle bonding smaller networks into a larger coherent group, facilitating community socio-economic development whilst their collaboration with other co-operatives, and involvement at national, regional and international levels assures broader influence (Majee and Hoyt, 2011). In this way, co-operatives can enhance economic and social goals, for example, in reaching new markets. Collaborative working between villages in India provides further evidence of the bridging capital that can be achieved through co-operatives (Peredo and Chrisman, 2006). In prioritising the conservation of scarce water resources for production and community use, villagers were able to develop a co-operative venture that was not only beneficial for their village but led to the formation of seven other water projects in neighbouring communities, becoming the backbone of prosperous organic farming and oil enterprises.

Transformative value

Some early commentators suggested that it might be difficult to replicate the Mondragon model elsewhere given its unique foundations in solidaristic traits of Basque culture and the challenging socio-economic circumstances of post-war Spain, which offered rich, fertile ground for co-operative development (Bradley and Gelb, 1983). A thread throughout the international literature on co-operatives, however, finds a common emphasis on the wider community and social transformational value of co-operatives across the world. Inherent within systems of democratic control and fair incomes, worker co-operatives emphasise social wellbeing by providing settings where members are recognised as individuals and members of their communities carrying multiple identities, being valued not only as workers but as human beings (Heales et al., 2017; Macpherson, 2013; Lindenfeld, 2003). Furthermore, Majee and Hoyt's (2011) research about co-operatives, has shown how a values-led approach that includes focusing on equality and community, predisposes co-operatives to look for the 'common good'.

Social transformation has been linked to the consensual leadership styles adopted by co-operatives, which minimise social distinctions at work, in public affairs and in interpersonal relations (Thompson, 2014). Several commentators highlight an obvious intersection between co-operative and community development (Thompson, 2014; Erdal, 2012; Phillips, 2012). Focusing on three Italian towns with varying degrees of co-operative activity, Erdal (2012) found that the town with greatest employee ownership scored most positively in all five areas of crime rates, education, health, social environment and social participation. It also scored significantly better than the town with no co-operatives. In addition, people in the town with the greatest number of co-operatives were found to live longer, to have better cardiovascular health and to suffer less from stroke or heart attacks. In another study of food co-operatives, Phillips (2012) found that co-operative development aligned closely with community development through collective efforts to meet the needs not only of co-operative members but of the wider community, broadening access generally to healthy and affordable food.

Being equally motivated by social as economic principles, co-operatives engage in community practices to sustain high levels of community engagement even during adverse market conditions. For instance, Vo (2016: 68) observed among some struggling co-operatives in South America, what she termed a fundamental 'ideological' commitment to community building:

> When I asked managers, administrators, employees, leaders, and members
> of the cooperatives why they sustained community engagement, the

response was always ideological, reflecting an interest not just in themselves, but also in social welfare.

In addition to generating incomes and offering employment to community members, co-operatives actively strengthen their links with communities through, direct investment in social and welfare services including providing education programmes about co-operatives at the community and regional level (Zeuli and Radel, 2005). Strategic investment in broader education and development has enabled co-operatives to meet local community needs (Vo, 2016; Simpson and Rapone, 2000). A Mexican coffee producing co-operative funded secondary school education for young people in mountainous areas alongside community service and sponsorship for further study (Simpson and Rapone, 2000). In another case study of coffee co-operatives in South America, co-operatives supported the health and well-being of the entire community through their investment in educational opportunities and housing, protecting the environment, and through influencing public policies that are conducive to community flourishing (Vo, 2016).

Are connected communities ripe for co-operative development?

So far, this exploration of community and co-operatives has illuminated an intersection of values and principles between these found in the literature. In this final part of the chapter, drawing on Manley and Froggett's (2016) exploration of co-operative groups and organisations in Preston and more extensively on Connected Communities research in one Preston community (Ridley and Morris, 2018), I ponder on the evidence that there is inherent potential for further development of a co-operative culture in Preston's communities. Using co-operative values and principles as the lens through which to view the findings, to what extent does this show a community that is co-operative in the way it sees the world and organises itself? Were the residents of this geographical community demonstrating co-operative values and principles in how they related to each other and their area? The original reasoning behind the project commissioned by Preston City Council arose from Manley and Froggett's (2016) report into co-operative activity in Preston. In that report, they found that co-operative values were overwhelmingly the values that drove community stakeholders, voluntary groups and charities in Preston, even when these groups were ignorant of the formal aspects of co-operativism.

Using a combination of deliberative community engagement methods - including recruiting 20 residents as researchers, surveying over 200 people and holding community feedback events – alongside social network analysis (Borgatti et al., 2017), the Connected Communities study examined health and wellbeing, loneliness, sense of belonging and levels of social and community capital - that is, the resources embedded in individual social networks that are accessed and/or mobilised through these ties (Parsfield et al., 2015). Taking selected findings from the community survey of over 200 residents, which is reported in detail elsewhere (Ridley and Morris, 2018), I explore the ethos of co-operation that was apparent in this community and what the patterns of social connectedness among residents imply for future collaboration. Also, I consider whether this offers an example of a community working co-operatively and finally, how the resultant new community-led organisation showed signs of democratic participation and co-operation.

This case study focuses on a community of place, Broadgate and Hartington/Christchurch situated in the south east of Preston, which is a large part of what is now known as the Riversway (political) ward. Based on 2011 census information for the ward the resident population is 6,351 (ONS, 2016). The mean age of this ward's population is 35 years, and while the majority of its residents are White, over one fifth are of Asian/Asian British background, which is a higher proportion than Preston as a whole or in the North West of England. The most common household tenure is people living in privately rented houses and flats followed by owner occupiers. This locality was selected by Councillors for a study of community cohesion as part of the Preston Model's attention to the less affluent communities in the city, in order to level up opportunities for all of Preston's residents, and eventually making this possible through the creation of equitable co-operative community principles, or even the establishment of co-operative businesses, thereby regenerating the area through using the community's strengths and existing assets. The initial study took place from 2017 to 2018 and was followed up by a brief enquiry into specific co-operative values in the community.

A community with a co-operative ethos

Successful co-operative developments in other countries emerged from geographical areas with strong communitarian values and common bonds between people, sometimes strongly faith based such as, the Mondragon Cooperative Corporation's basis in Catholic social action. The area contrasted with indications from the national Community Life Survey (DCMS, 2020) suggesting that the vitality of community life in the UK has been waning in recent years. Instead, our study found high levels of trust between people, high satisfaction with the area, and a strong sense of belonging indicating an existing foundation of communitarian values and bonds helpful to future co-operative development. Four out of five people found this to be a good place to live and similarly, felt a strong sense of belonging to the area. This contrasted with the findings from the UK Community Life Survey 2019/20 (DCMS, 2020), finding just over half of people nationally felt a sense of belonging to their neighbourhood. However, it did chime well with Manley and Froggett's (2016) report regarding co-operative groups, organisations, and associations in Preston that they found had come together around a shared sense of place and belonging, as well as pride in their communities.

Furthermore, residents in this locality tended to agree that people in the area looked out for each other: almost three quarters (72%) agreed that this was the case, while just 11% disagreed and over three quarters agreed that they will always find someone to help them in the local area. When asked to identify the 'best thing' about living in the area, half gave an answer broadly related to the locality or physical environment. Next most common was a strong sense of community locally, including referring to 'friendly local people' and good neighbours. Related to this, were many positive comments about the diverse, multi-cultural character of the area with 16% of people suggesting that there was nothing stopping people from diverse backgrounds getting on well together despite different backgrounds and a perception that 'people mix well'. The main barrier was that there are few places in the local area where people who have less in common can meet, for instance, those from different faiths or younger and older people.

The more connected people felt to area, the more trusting they were generally of their neighbours. This was a neighbourhood where many people were pre-disposed to engaging with their neighbours if opportunity arose. A significant proportion of residents reported spending time volunteering, in part reflecting active engagement with local faith groups or the local Police and Community Together (PACT) group. In support of the idea of engagement, those who volunteered were the most positive about the area and had the strongest sense of belonging. Significantly, half of survey respondents stated they wanted to volunteer more, indicating valuable community capacity that lies untapped and a common desire for greater connection. In short, high levels of engagement with the local community were associated with social and community con-nectedness as well as greater trust in neighbours.

Existence of small world networks

While the findings from Broadgate and Hartington/Christchurch were indicative of a strong ethos of co-operation within this community, the pattern of rela-tionships between neighbours and organisations reported below suggests there was potential for improving community connectedness and that this could have positive impact on both individual and community health. Manley and Frog-gett's (2016) earlier work had uncovered a healthy commitment to community and local democracy in Preston as well as a desire to work co-operatively for the benefit of various communities. Co-operating groups and organisations were connected to each other in unofficial networks, which were said to repre-sent significant social capital. Connected Communities research in the Broad-gate and Hartington/Christchurch community found patterns of social networks which showed an over reliance on family and friends but also the existence of 'small world' networks based on connections with faith-based institutions in the area: 53% of respondents had a connection with a faith-based organisation which for many was fundamental to their wellbeing and offered a wide range of types of support.

This finding reflects the somewhat unique multi-faith nature of the area and its population – the area has a mosque, four temples (two Hindu, one Sikh, and one Buddhist temple), and a Christian church. It speaks also of an obvious connection between community work and faith work and of the importance placed by many religious faiths on working together for the common good and of actively developing community spirit. Relationships with neighbours in this community were, however, found to be more distant and clearly did not extend to relationships through which support and mutual interests were exchanged and actively shared. Community needs tended to be met in 'silos', that is, universal services such as lunch clubs, youth clubs, exercise classes offered by the various faith organisations were limited in their ability to enhance bridging social capital and develop community capacity. The research concluded that bringing neighbours and others together was vital for increasing engagement and encouraging future collaboration.

An example of a co-operative community?

As in the previous study (Manley and Froggett, 2016), we found compelling evidence of co-operative practices in this area. There was co-operation between residents who volunteered as community researchers; between and across different community organisations through their participation in the Project Steering Group; and with the residents from across the area who were actively engaged as survey respondents and at the community feedback events. This all points to significant potential community capacity which was increased by the Connected Communities approach. It also provides evidence of natural co-operation and collaboration in existence within this community. As one resident reflected:

> I think we are co-operatively working with other groups. Well, we are working co-operatively as our group, and we are hoping to work co-operatively with other groups as well. I think the desire is there.

Another emphasised the importance of working collaboratively for the common good:

> The meaning for me, is working for the greater good of the area, not just for my good, but hopefully contributing to the good of other people.

The general perception that this is a place with 'friendly people', 'good neighbours', where people look out for each other and residents report a desire to increase involvement with neighbours and enhance 'community spirit', all highlight the potential that lies largely untapped. Indeed, there is evidence that as a result of the Connected Communities project both bonding and bridging social capital in this community continued to evolve: individuals and groups have formed an open and inclusive community organisation whose core aim is to bring neighbours closer together and build social connections for the good of the whole community; an event was organised in collaboration with the local primary school offering free food and activities for local families during school holidays; a Big

Lunch event brought over 300 people together over summer 2019; and this year, the group celebrated community during COVID-19 through facilitating street activities involving over 400 neighbours from a range of diverse backgrounds, some collaborating with their neighbours for the first time.

Foundations of democratic participation

In the tradition of their founders, co-operative members believe in the ethical values of honesty, openness, social responsibility and caring for others. The resultant community-led approach from the Connected Communities study was to form a constituted community group in February 2018 to help people to better connect and to bring neighbours closer together. Broadgate Community Connectors Group has five goals – to enhance social connections and communication between neighbours; to support and develop neutral 'bumping into' places for the community; to help to reduce loneliness; to help improve the local environment; and to increase citizenship through volunteering. Membership is open to anyone over 18 years old living in the area or associated with, for example, the local primary school, the church, mosque or temples and includes others who are interested in helping the group achieve its aims.

Similar to the groups and organisations involved in Manley and Froggett's (2016) study, the organisation of this group is democratic and co-operative. For example, principles of open membership, focusing on a community agenda and democratic processes are reflected in what two residents say about the processes within the new community association:

> We all have a say and if we all want to say something we can do. It doesn't matter what you say whether they agree with you or not that is not the point - You get your point across and that is what matters ... everybody is given a voice. They might not like what they're hearing they got a voice and they are entitled to say it, and it gets considered. We are all entitled to our own opinions, we work towards the common good of everyone.

> The process of decision making in the community connectors group is quite good really. There are lots of people that seem to be doing lots of little jobs. It's like when you see other committees it's just one person that does everything; they will talk about it but don't actually do things whereas this group seem to talk about it and actually get things done and work seems to be spread and people use their skills ... Community Connectors action most things after each meeting.

There was then a sense that working co-operatively 'in humanity for everyone's benefit' and instituting democratic processes of listening and involvement were already evident in the resultant community association and how it functions, even though it did not officially constitute itself as a co-operative. Moreover, the group was already demonstrating the core characteristics of community collectives and an understanding of the need to work co-operatively in the community.

Conclusion

Concern for community comes naturally to co-operatives, in other words it is in their DNA. This is explicit in the seventh core principle of community added in 1995, and a growing body of literature showing how co-operatives have increased social capital and transformed communities and societies. The social dimension of growth and sustainability encapsulated in 'Auzolan' or community-led practice, emphasises the importance placed by co-operatives on humanistic values, on working together for the common good. Studies also find that co-operatives increase social connectedness and enhance community as well as social capital. Working to better connect communities and enhance social capital can similarly result in groups focusing on achieving the common good and collaborating and co-operating for the benefit of the community. Examining the social network research findings from a community project in Preston exploring social networks and seeking to increase community capital, finds compelling evidence of one community's co-operative leanings. As one resident commented:

> There is a sense of optimism in Preston. There is a sense in which 'can do' attitude which says, 'We can make a difference' if we do things locally, we don't just have to depend on people coming in from outside. I think there is lots of potential. Bringing people together knowing who their neighbours are increases people's sense of wellbeing and sense of contributing to something locally, which is very important.

Together with the previous study of co-operative groups and organisations in Preston (Manley and Froggett, 2016), this analysis points to the potential for further development of the Preston Model in the future within existing local communities that are already predisposed towards collaboration and working together for the common good. Furthermore, wider adoption of the Preston Model could, of itself, help strengthen collaboration and community capital. The overarching aim of the Preston Model is socio-economic transformation of the City but achieving societal and community changes are equally important. It focuses on economic change based on co-operative principles and values, but at the heart of the Preston Model is change to the way people behave and work together. Some have indeed argued that social innovation practices involve people making change happen together, whatever their backgrounds, and new tools which facilitate democratic participation need to be developed (Heales et al., 2017). This is especially important for those individuals and communities experiencing greatest socio-economic inequality as transformative solutions are most likely to arise from people working together collaboratively. Ultimately, the successful implementation of the Preston Model will depend upon fostering a greater sense of community. Nevertheless, we are left with a chicken and egg question - is successful development of further co-operatives dependent upon how receptive local communities are to co-operative values and principles, or will efforts to further implement the

Preston Model and develop more co-operatives in Preston also serve to build community and strengthen community capacity?

Acknowledgement

In writing this chapter, I acknowledge the work of Hana Patel, a Broadgate community researcher and Research Assistant on co-operatives. Material from Hana's interviews with community members has informed the exploration of co-operative values within a local community.

References

Adler, P.S., and Kwon, S.-W. (2002), Social Capital: Prospects for a New Concept, *The Academy of Management Review*, 27 (1): 17–40.

Bartley, M.P (ed.) (2012), Life Gets under Your Skin, retrieved from www.ucl.ac.uk/ epidemiology-health-care/research/epidemiology-and-public-health/research/international-centre-lifecourse-studies/podcast/how (accessed on 14 October 2020).

Borgatti, S.P., Everett, M.G., and Johnson, J.C. (2017), *Analyzing Social Networks*, Sage, London.

Bradley, K., and Gelb, A. (1983), *Cooperation and Work: The Mondragon Experience*, Heinemann Educational Books, London.

Claridge, T. (2004), Social Capital and Natural Resource Management: An Important Role for Social Capital? Unpublished thesis, University of Queensland, Brisbane, Australia, retrieved from www.socialcapitalresearch.com/literature/definition (accessed on 15 October 2020).

Cohen, A.P. (1985), *The Symbolic Construction of Community*, 1st edition, Routledge, London.

Cohen, A.P. (2013) *The Symbolic Construction of Community*, Tavistock, London.

COPAC (2008), Background Paper on Cooperatives, COPAC Information Note, prepared for the United Nations consultation of UN member states and the cooperative movement on the desirability and feasibility of proclaiming an International Year of Cooperatives 2008, retrieved from www.copac.coop/background-paper-on-cooperatives

Dekker, P., and Uslaner, E.M. (2001), Introduction, In Uslaner, E.M. (ed.), *Social Capital and Participation in Everyday Life*, Routledge, London.

DCMS (2020), Community Life Survey 2019/20, retrieved from www.gov.uk/government/publications/community-life-survey-201920-neighbourhood-and-community/neighbourhood-and-community-community-life-survey-201920 (accessed 12 October 2020).

Dobrohoczki, R. (2006), Cooperatives as Social Policy Means for Creating Social Cohesion in Communities, *Journal of Rural Co-operation*, 34 (2): 135–158.

Erdal, D. (2012), Employee Ownership is Good for your Health, *Journal of Cooperative Thought and Practice*, 1 (1): 3–6.

Glanville, J.L., and Bienenstock, E.J. (2009), A Typology for Understanding the Connections among Different Forms of Social Capital, *American Behavioural Scientist*, 52 (11): 1507–1530.

Heales, C., Hodgson, M., and Rich, H. (2017), *Humanity at Work: Mondragon, a Social Innovation Ecosystem Case Study*, The Young Foundation, London.

Hoogerbrugge, M.M., and Burger, M.J. (2018), Neighborhood-Based Social Capital and Life Satisfaction: The Case of Rotterdam, The Netherlands, *Urban Geography*, 39 (10): 1484–1509.

International Co-operative Alliance (2020), Co-operative Identity, Values and Principles, retrieved from http://ica.coop/en/whats-co-op/co-operative-identity-values-principles (accessed 12 October 2020).

Kadushin, C. (2012), *Understanding Social Networks. Theories, Concepts and Findings*, Oxford University Press, Oxford.

Kearns, A., Whitley, E., Tannahill, C., and Ellaway, A. (2015a), Loneliness, Social Relations and Health and Well-Being in Deprived Communities, *Psychology, Health and Medicine*, 20 (3): 332–344.

Kearns, A., Whitley, E., Tannahill, C., and Ellaway, A. (2015b), Lonesome Town? Is Loneliness Associated with the Residential Environment, Including Housing and Neighbourhood Factors?, *Journal of Community Psychology*, 43 (7): 849–867.

Lee, D., and Newby, H. (1983), *The Problem of Sociology: An Introduction to the Discipline*, Unwin Hyman, London.

Lent, A., and Studdert, J. (2019), *The Community Paradigm. Why Public Services Need Radical Change and How it Can be Achieved*, New Local Government Network, London.

Lindenfeld, F. (2003), Commentary on 'The Organization of Work as a Factor in Social Well-being', *Contemporary Justice Review*, 6 (2): 127–131.

Lizarralde, I. (2009), Cooperatism, Social Capital and Regional Development: The Mondragon Experience, *International Journal of Technology Management and Sustainable Development*, 8 (1): 27–38.

Macpherson, I. (2013), *Cooperatives' Concern for the Community: From Members Towards Local Communities' Interests*, Euricse Working Paper 46/13, retrieved from https://papers.ssrn.com/sol3/papers.cfm?abstract_id=2196031 (accessed 5 November 2020).

Majee, W., and Hoyt, A. (2009), Building Community Trust through Cooperatives: A Case Study of a Worker-Owned Homecare Cooperative, *Journal of Community Practice*, 17 (4): 444–463.

Majee, W., and Hoyt, A. (2010), Are Worker-Owned Cooperatives the Brewing Pots for Social Capital?, *Community Development*, 41 (4): 417–430.

Majee, W., and Hoyt, A. (2011), Cooperatives and Community Development: A Perspective on the Use of Cooperatives in Development, *Journal of Community Practice*, 19 (1): 48–61.

Manley, J., and Froggett, L. (2016), *Co-operative Activity in Preston*, report written for Preston City Council by the Psychosocial Research Unit, UCLan, Preston, retrieved from https://clok.uclan.ac.uk/14526/1/Co-operative%20activity%20PrestonREPORT%20copy.pdf (accessed 5 November 2020).

Nyqvist, F., Victor, C.R., Forsman, A.K., and Cattan, M. (2016), The Association between Social Capital and Loneliness in Different Age Groups: A Population-Based Study in Western Finland, *BMC Public Health*, 16 (542): 1–8.

ONS (2016), Data Tables, retrieved from https://webarchive.nationalarchives.gov.uk/20160105225455/http://www.ons.gov.uk/ons/guide-method/census/2011/census-data/index.html (accessed 12 November 2018).

Parker, M., Cheney, G., Fournier, V., and Land, C. (eds) (2014), *The Routledge Companion to Alternative Organization*, Routledge, London.

Parsfield, M., Morris, D., Bola, M., Knapp, M., Yoshioka, M., and Marc, G. (2015), *Connected Capital: The Value of Connected Communities*, RSA, London.

Peredo, A., and Chrisman, J. (2006), Toward a Theory of Community-Based Enterprise, *Academy of Management Review*, 31 (2): 309–328.

Peterson, N.A., Speer, P.W., and McMillan, D.W. (2008), Validation of a Brief Sense of Community Scale: Confirmation of the Principal Theory of Sense of Community, *Journal of Community Psychology*, 36 (1): 61–73.

Phillips, R. (2012), Food Cooperatives as Community-Level Self-Help and Development, *International Journal of Self Help and Self-Care*, 6 (2): 189–203.

Putnam, R.D. (2000), *Bowling Alone: The Collapse and Revival of American Community*, Simon and Schuster, New York.

Redshaw, S., and Ingham, V. (2017), 'Neighbourhood is if They Come Out and Talk to You': Neighbourly Connections and Bonding Social Capital, *Journal of Sociology*, 54 (4): 557–573.

Ridley, J., and Morris, D. (2018), Preston Connected Communities Project: A Study of the Social and Community Networks of Residents of Broadgate and Hartington, retrieved from https://clok.uclan.ac.uk/26146 (accessed 5 November 2020).

Seifert, A. (2020), Day-to-Day Contact and Help Among Neighbors Measured in the Natural Environment, *Innovation in Aging*, 4 (2): 1–13.

Simpson, C., and Rapone, A. (2000), Community Development from the Ground Up: Social-Justice Coffee, *Human Ecology Review*, 7 (1): 46–57.

Smith, M.K. (2013), Community, retrieved from https://infed.org/mobi/community/ (accessed 12 October 2020).

SRHIE (2010), Fair Society, Healthier Lives: The Marmot Review, retrieved from www.instituteofhealthequity.org/resources-reports/fair-society-healthy-lives-the-marmot-review/fair-society-healthy-lives-the-marmot-review-full-report.pdf (accessed 12 October 2020).

Thompson, S.P. (2014), Is the Mondragon Co-operative Experience a Cultural Exception? The Application of the Mondragon Model in Valencia and Beyond, *Journal of Co-operative Studies*, 47 (3): 19–33.

Vo, S. (2016), Concern for Community: A Case Study of cooperatives in Costa Rica, *Journal of Community Practice*, 24 (1): 56–76.

Wanjare, J. (2017), Social Capital, Asset-Based Capacities and the Worker Co-operative Model, *European Journal of Social Sciences Studies*, 2 (7): 1–14.

Wilmott, P. (1986), *Social Networks: Informal Care and Public Policy*, Policy Studies Institute, London.

Wilson, S., and Morris, D. (2019), *Stronger Together Moorclose: A Connected Communities Research Project in Moorclose, Workington Cumbria (Stage One: Community Research)*, UCLan, West Lakes.

Zeuli, K.A., and Radel, J. (2005), Cooperatives as a Community Development Strategy: Linking Theory and Practice, *Journal of Regional Analysis and Policy, Mid-Continent Regional Science Association*, 35 (1): 1–12.

5 Reimagining local governance in the UK

Understanding public discourse on the Preston model

Michael Farrelly

Introduction

The Preston Model of local economic development seeks to implement policies of community wealth building; it is a deliberate effort to create and implement a new model of local governance in England that simultaneously serves the material, social and health needs of the people of the city and empowers them economically. The Preston Model combines local procurement by anchor institutions, a preference for worker-owned co-operative businesses to 'fill the gaps in the local economy' (Manley, 2017), and the establishment of several strategic partnerships which have responsibility for the development of local procurement and co-operative business. These include a partnership between the University of Central Lancashire (UCLan), the city council and The Preston Co-operative Development Network. The work undertaken under this model has had a clear effect. According to Manley:

> In 2012/13, out of £750m spent on goods and services by six Anchor Institutions, 5% was spent in Preston and 39% in Lancashire as a whole. By 2016/17, out of £620m spent on goods and services by the same Anchor Institutions, 19% was spent in Preston and 81% in Lancashire as a whole.
>
> (Manley, 2017)

Official figures show that the rate of employment, during a period of near recession at a national level, improved in Preston and has bucked the national trend.

The Preston Model has widely been seen as a success. Positive portrayals of the model can be found across the political spectrum of the mainstream print media in the UK: *The Daily Mirror, The Independent, The Guardian, The Times* and *The Telegraph* can all provide examples of praise. Critics have called the model a form of unwelcome 'protectionism' that could not work across UK local authorities. A joint Preston City Council and Centre for Local Economic Strategy (CLES) report, 'How we built community wealth in Preston', gives a baseline understanding of what the model is and what it entails. Key to this understanding, from the perspective taken in this chapter, are the participants in, processes, context and purpose of the model: it sees the model as an instantiation of community wealth building propelled by 'businesses, public and social sector organisations across the UK who are now driving a shift in economic development thinking' (CLES, 2019: 8). However, both the burgeoning scholarship, and the discussion of the Preston Model in the wider public sphere have, as yet, tended to overlook the discourse of the Preston Model – how language is used to conceptualise the model, deliberate and argue over the model, and to communicate its merits – or de-merits – to wider public understanding. This chapter presents an analysis of how proponents and opponents of the Preston Model have represented the model in public media texts.

Based on this analysis, I argue four things. First, that in the texts I analysed, opponents of the Preston Model presented a limited version of the model; all of these texts focussed exclusively on the procurement element of the model and presented businesses in the city as passive recipients of funds rather than active and dynamic 'winners' of contracts. Second, that some proponents of the model also followed this rather limited focus on procurement and, surprisingly, also represented business in the city in a passive way. Third, opponents and proponents with a limited focus excluded reference to citizens, residents, and workers in the city. Fourth, that some proponents of the model engaged in more detail with the model and these texts included more aspects of the model, a wider range of process and participants and provided an example of the most incisive critical engagement of all the texts analysed with potential improvements to the model. The following section describes the Preston Model in more detail and academic approaches to policy discourse. In section 3, I set out the theoretical perspectives taken in this chapter which draw in work in critical discourse analysis and cultural political economy. Section 4 sets out the analytical method for analysing the representation of social actors and social action used in the chapter. I go on to present analysis first of opponents of the Preston Model and then some of its proponents.

The Preston Model and language

The Preston Model puts ideas on 'the foundational economy' (O'Neill, 2016; Heslop et al., 2019) into practice. It has many important elements which are described in detail in a report by the Centre for Local Economic Strategies (CLES). Understanding something of these elements is crucial for our critical analysis of the public discourses about the Preston Model that I examine later in this chapter. First, it describes the overall approach of the Preston Model as a 'community wealth building' approach to local economic development; the importance of this emphasis on development (rather than protection) and the community (rather than local business only) will become clear as a contrast to some of the texts analysed below. Moreover, the purpose of this approach is clearly stated to be that 'local economies are reorganised, so that wealth is not extracted but broadly held and income is recirculated' (CLES, 2019: 8). The approach is realised through five strategies:

- Plural ownership of the economy.
- Making financial power work for local places.
- Fair employment and just labour markets.
- Progressive procurement of goods and services.
- Socially productive use of land and property.

According to CLES, progressive procurement, 'can develop dense local supply chains, SMEs, employee owned businesses, social enterprises and cooperatives and other forms of community business' (CLES, 2019: 9) The intention, importantly, was to identify which 'contracts could be opened up to more [local] competition' and 'not to simply to increase local spend but to identify areas where money was leaking out of the Lancashire economy or being used in socially unproductive ways, and to find ways to recapture this spend to better benefit local workers, employers, and businesses' (CLES, 2019: 12) We shall see that the extent of ambition shown in this approach, and the detail it gives, contrasts starkly to many of the representations of it found in the media texts analysed below.

Furthermore, the range of 'anchor institutions' is important: Preston City Council, Lancashire County Council, Preston's College, Community Gateway, Cardinal Newman College the Office of the Lancashire Police and Crime Commissioner and UCLan. In particular, UCLan adheres to the principles of being an anchor institution in the Preston Model: 'Over the course of the three years to the financial year ending in July 2017, it increased the proportion of this money spent with Preston suppliers from 8% to 21%. In 2016–17, that amounted to £63 million spent with those Preston suppliers' (Morgan, 2018). However, as well as being an anchor institution, UCLan is integral to the development of the model (Morgan, 2019). As reported in the *Times Higher Education*: 'for some goods and services, there are no local suppliers. Filling these gaps is part of the aim of UCLan's support for undergraduates and graduates to work in, and own, cooperatives' (Morgan, 2018). I show below that many of the texts I analysed included very few of these key actors.

How policy is represented in texts is important. In previous work, I have argued that 'analysis of how policy-makers and legislators represent social actors in texts can give valuable insight into their conceptualisation of objects of governance' (Farrelly, 2019a: 147). As an example, I analysed the discourse of 'competition' in UK parliamentary debates on the shift in the governance of its gas industry from state ownership and control to shareholder ownership and the 'control' of 'market discipline'. During the 1980s, 'competition' had become an important trope for the Conservative government and, by 1985, was repeatedly used in reference to the privatisation of British Gas. In those debates 'competition' was almost universally referred to by government ministers without specifying who would compete with whom. 'Consumers' were consistently represented in a 'passive' way – receiving 'benefits' of competition without having to do anything. I argued that the absence of 'competitors' and the passive representation of 'consumers' in the competition discourse predicted observable problems in the contemporary UK gas retail industry: there are few competitors in the gas 'retail' sector and consumers tend not to switch suppliers. This chapter applies the same analytical methods to texts on the Preston Model: does the analysis show significant absences in the discourse?

Understanding discourse in economic policy

For this chapter, I view the language of deliberation and communication of the Preston Model from the perspective of critical discourse analysis (CDA) (Fairclough, 2003; Farrelly, 2019b). In CDA, 'discourse' refers to patterns of language that are typical, or conventional ways of using language in a particular social practice. This can include the types of text typically used in social practice (opinion or news articles, blog posts for examples are typical for practices of public policy debate) and it can include the types of other texts that are referred to – as 'evidence' to support an argument, for example (quotes from politicians, or summaries of research reports). In this chapter, we shall see examples of these types of text and types of evidence but I shall focus mostly on another aspect of discourse: ways of describing and representing policies – specifically, how the Preston Model is described and represented. This includes vocabulary: 'procurement' is more typically used by people involved in local government or the study of local government, whereas 'buying' is more typical of journalists writing about local government, for example. I shall focus, also, on what is included and excluded from these representations of how the Preston Model is framed.

I also draw in the work of cultural political economy (Sum and Jessop, 2013; Jessop, 2010) for a more specific view of how discourse works in practices of economic governance – such as in the Preston Model – and practices which engage in public discussion of how economies are governed. Work in cultural political economy argues that to understand how economies are governed, why some choices lead to failure or why some unlikely decisions are sometimes made, we should take account both of material elements of economies – actual work, resources and conditions, for example – and semiotic, or meaning-making that goes into creating economies. Major functions of discourse are in complexity reduction and in the selection of economic strategies. Complexity reduction is an inevitable aspect of economic governance: 'Because the world cannot be grasped in all its complexity in real-time, actors … must focus selectively on some of its aspects in order to be active participants in that world' (Jessop, 2010: 338).

Decision-makers and commentators must simplify the way they describe and represent economies; the question is: are their simplifications adequate to successful economic governance? Descriptions and representations of economies must also be argued over so that they are selected as a model for economic strategies.

Method of analysis

To analyse the discourse of public deliberation over, and description of, the Preston Model I applied two analytical frameworks which focus on a) the representation of social action and b) the representation of social actors. Doing so, we can critically analyse how the participants in the Preston Model are conceptualised and how the processes in which they are taking part are imagined. The frameworks are taken from Van Leeuwen (2008). In these frameworks social actions – what people do – can be categorised in several ways; for this chapter, I used the following categories:

a   Activated action (representing action as dynamic) or deactivated action (representing action as static).
b   Transactive action (representing action as taking place between two or more people) or non-transactive action (representing action as involving only a single participant).
c   Agentelised action (representing action as being brought about through human agency) or de-agentalised action (representing action as being brought about without human agency).
d   Generalised action (representing sequences or sets of specific actions in an amalgamated form) or specified action (representing component actions of a generalised action).

Social actions that appear in the analysis sections below have been italicised.

Social actors – the people represented as doing things in texts – can, according to Van Leeuwen, also be represented in several ways. For the analysis presented in this chapter I used the following categories:

a   Included social actors or excluded – as we shall see, almost all the texts analysed include Preston City Council but many exclude the citizens or people of the city.
b   Active social actors or passive social actors – again, as we shall see, Preston City Council is often represented as the one doing an action, whereas business is sometimes represented as being passive recipients of the actions of others.
c   Nomination (named) social actors – some business are named, for example, or Categorised (represented by function or identity) – again, as we shall see, in most cases businesses are not named but categorised as 'local business', for example.

Social actors in the examples below are in bold. Analysis of the representation of social action and action can, as I have argued elsewhere (Farrelly, 2019b) give valuable insight into how objects of governance, or in this case an economic policy, are conceptualised. It highlights not just the words used but the perspective from which the Preston Model is understood, deliberated over and communicated to a wider public audience.

The texts analysed in this chapter were collected in two ways. First, from the LexisNexis newspaper database. National newspapers from the UK were searched for the phrase 'Preston Model' from 2008 to 'present'. This found

15 articles. Second, intertextual links – where one of the texts referred to the Preston Model in another text (Farrelly, 2020) to other relevant texts were sought out and used. In total, this gave 20 articles which discussed the Preston Model. Each of these texts was then categorised for its stance on the Preston Model; sections of articles that discussed the Preston Model were identified and these sections were analysed for the inclusion and exclusion of social actors and actions. Social actors were analyses for passive and active participation; social actions for transactive and non-transactive processes. The texts were analysed for the representation of context: social circumstances within which actions and actors were set. The representations were compared with each other and against the descriptions of the model discussed in the literature. This allowed me to critically analyse the textual representation and the implicit conceptualisation of the Preston Model as discussed in the public sphere. In the following sections we shall see critical analysis first, of texts that oppose the Preston Model, then texts that are supportive of the model.

Analysis: opponents of the Preston Model

All of the texts that are in opposition to the Preston Model present this opposition as part of a broader criticism of another issue: of 'protectionism', 'local' procurement, or 'Corbynism'. Two of these texts – the What Works blog on 'Local Procurement' and the Centre for Cities blog on 'protectionism' – have only a passing engagement with the model; the third text – an opinion piece by Daniel Finkelstein in *The Times* – is a little more elaborate than the others. Each presents a limited representation of the participants and process in the model and excludes reference to its purpose and context entirely. First, we shall examine the What Works webpage on 'Local Procurement'. Its brief encounter with the Preston model comes in a text which comes out against 'local' procurement, urging 'considerable caution on the ability of such policies to deliver local economic growth'. In this text Preston is used as an example of what they call 'local procurement':

> Using Preston as an example, *the argument goes* that if **the council** *employs* a Preston construction firm **for a local building project, that firm** is *more likely to source* supplies from **neighbouring businesses,** and their **staff** *will provide* more business for **local cafes and shops.** If **a firm from outside Preston** *wins* the contract – let's say one based in Sheffield – more of their supply chain spending and salaries will be in Sheffield. The economy there *will benefit* instead.
>
> (What Works Centre for Local Economic Growth, 2020)

The processes represented here (italicised) are problematic – the elaborate processes of progressive procurement in Preston that we saw above are reduced to 'employs' and 'more likely to source'. Absent are:

- processes which help to develop the capacity of local firms to tender successfully for contracts;
- development of selection criteria which may specify short supply chains; and
- engagement in local co-operative networks to set up new businesses which could meet procurement needs.

The model does more than 'employ' firms, it develops the capacity of firms across the city; it does not leave it to chance that firms source supplies from neighbouring businesses, it tries to develop supply chains in the city so that its businesses can provide supplies. Absent, too, are the anchor institutions which are part of the progressive procurement aspect of the Preston Model. Finally, this hypothetical example excludes important elements of the real context: high levels of deprivation, unemployment and health inequality; the inclusion of Sheffield as the imagined implicit loser from the Preston Model ignores the actual context in which it is firms based in the more affluent area of London and the South East of England that are the more likely losers of progressive procurement in Preston.

Next, we shall examine the Centre for Cities blog on 'protectionism'. It uses the Preston model as an example of a 'Corbynomics', which it equates with 'protectionism' and the position of Donald Trump:

> Do we stand on the verge of a new trade war? … I'm not talking about **Donald Trump**, steel and whiskey. I'm talking instead about the idea of **councils** *buying* their goods and services locally, an idea that has been dubbed 'Corbynomics' and has **Preston** as its poster child. But the parallels are striking.
>
> In recent years **Preston City Council**, in particular, has been *active in increasing its spend* on **local businesses**, *giving them preference* over suppliers from elsewhere.
>
> (Swinney, 2018)

As with the previous example, the elaborate processes of progressive procurement in Preston that we saw above are reduced to 'buying' and 'active in increasing its spend'; the active development of local business capacity is, again, absent. Importantly, in this case, these processes misrepresent the procurement process in which local businesses do not 'buy' goods locally but go through extensive and auditable decision-making steps; the text excludes the context in which most of the money spent by the anchor institutions still goes out of the local economy. The representation of participants is limited too: Donald Trump, councils, Preston, Preston City Council and local businesses are present but the people of Preston, be that as a citizen, resident, employee, worker or business owner are all absent. In terms of active and passive representation of social actors, the City Council is active, local business is represented as being a passive recipient of the 'spend' as though they have not had to work hard to win contracts. Again, a central pillar of the model, the anchor institutions, are absent. This limited discursive representation of the model disguises the complexity of the changes in Preston in a problematic way; it equates its limited description with protectionism instead of recognising the many efforts that go toward building capacity. It misses the purpose of community wealth building to combat deprivation and unemployment and to create wealth for the people of the city.

Last, in this section on texts that are in opposition to the Preston Model, we shall examine the more elaborate opinion piece by Daniel Finkelstein in *The Times* newspaper. As with the example above, this text is primarily an expression of opposition to the former leader of the Labour Party, Jeremy Corbyn. The Preston Model is given as being emblematic of 'Corbynism':

> The poster child for this idea is **Preston city council**. What is known as the Preston model is *much talked about* in Corbynite circles. **The council** has *embarked* on a strategy of getting **'anchor institutions'** such as **the council itself, local universities** and **the police**, *to buy* from **local business**, some of them co-ops, who will also *invest* locally.
>
> It's inspiring and dynamic but there is an obvious problem as the experiment spreads. What happens when **the next-door council** *keeps* all the money in their area? *All you get* are a load of mini-states *paying more* for their local goods. When this question is asked of **Preston** they simply say 'no one can suggest with any credibility that all of local government, or the local public sector, will swing into action in the same way'. And this works for Preston, but means, logically, it cannot be a model.
>
> (Finkelstein, 2019)

In contrast to the previous examples of oppositional texts, this includes 'anchor institutions' as a group and lists some of them by category (although it also appears to misrepresent the one university, UCLan, and two FE anchor institutions – Preston's College and Cardinal Newman College – as 'universities'). However, there are still key absences in the text: the people of Preston are absent; at the crux of the argument the social actors for whom Preston could be a model are also excluded: 'it cannot be a model' for whom? The major problem in this text is in the social action 'keeps all the money'. As we saw above, the anchor institutions do not spend all of the money at their disposal in their area, as the text implies; nor are local councils the only economic actors spending money. We have also seen that 'paying more' is not 'all you get' from the Preston Model; the article excludes key benefits and beneficiaries of the model: reduced deprivation, reduced unemployment, reduced health inequality among the people of the city.

In this Finkelstein article – the critical questions ('Who will create any new business, though? How will it be financed? Won't whoever provides finance (even if it is the state) want to take some of the control from the co-op?') that ought to probe the model and push it for conceptual clarity fail because its engagement is with an impoverished version of the model; this is a pity because important social actors, actions and circumstances are missing; there is slippage between distinct social actors from one point to the next. Ultimately, the impoverished conceptualisation sets up a straw man. This means that their engagement is too limited to be of value – critique becomes a rhetorical engagement only – it is about who can find the expressions that win rather than who can correctly and accurately engage with the changes the model had brought and thereby deliberate over its merits. This leads to another question – how is it that it is possible to discuss the Preston Model without discussing the protagonists, processes, purposes and wider circumstances?

Analysis: supporters of the Preston Model

My search found twenty articles that were broadly in support of the Preston Model. Of these, half mentioned the Preston Model in passing – that is, the article was clearly about something other than the model but made a passing reference to it in one or two sentences. As we shall see, these passing references had very similar discursive features to those examined in the section above. Half of the supportive articles were primarily about the model, or a particular aspect of it and represented the model in detail. Let us look first at the articles that mention the Preston Model favourably, but in passing. These are articles which appear in a range of mainstream newspapers: *The Telegraph* (1); *The Observer* (1) and *The Guardian* (7) and letters to the Editor which appear also in *The Guardian* (1). In the first text, from *The Telegraph*, includes part of the progressive procurement element of the model:

> We could also expand the so-called Preston model in which **local institutions – the police, universities, NHS trusts** – *pledge to spend* a proportion of their budgets locally.
>
> (Goodhart, 2018)

The action, though, is non-transactive: the pledge to spend does not represent either the participants who bid for the contracts or the business owners and employees who stand to benefit from these contracts.

The second example, from *The Observer*, is likewise limited to the procurement element of the model but is more elaborate than the example above – including as it does transactive social action in which the beneficiaries are included:

> The basic idea is that **big public sector bodies**, such as the **police**, should spend their budgets as far as possible with **local businesses**. In Preston, the £1.6m council food budget was awarded to **local farmers** and **the constabulary's** £600,000 printing contract went to **a Lancashire supplier**. Four years after starting the initiative in 2012, the city council spent an extra £4m a year in its area.
>
> (Lewis, 2017)

These beneficiaries are represented passively, however (contracts were 'awarded to' and 'went to' those businesses). Excluded too, are the employees of those firms who may stand to keep their jobs, or become an employee if the contract leads the firm to expand.

Finally, from *The Guardian*:

> The new Labour party is setting great store by the so-called Preston model, whereby that **city's council** *is boosting* the local economy by *using* its financial clout to help **local business**.
>
> (Harris, 2019)

The representation of social actors here is limited, again, to the procurement element and the inclusion of just the city council and local businesses. Again, local business is not represented actively.

The second group of supportive texts draws on a much richer set of discursive resources in its representation of the Preston Model than critics and the supportive but brief examples shown above. Let us first look are a text from *The People* newspaper:

> The city was in the bottom 20 per cent of deprived areas and life expectancy for its **poorest** was just 66.
>
> Preston had *the second-best improvement* on the Multiple Deprivation Index between 2010 and 2015. And last year it *was named* the best city in the North West to live and work in
>
> (Mudie and Cardy, 2017)

In this first extract, only one social actor is included in the representation: the poorest. What is striking, in comparison with all of the other texts we have seen, is that this category of social actor is absent from the texts which oppose the Preston Model, yet it is one of the most crucial groups of people for understanding the purpose of the model. The article goes on to illustrate one way in which the progressive procurement strategy of the model works to reduce deprivation in the city:

> **Farmers** benefited when **the council** allocated £1.6million of its food budget to be spent locally and **local builder Conlon Construction** won the £2.6million deal for a new market hall, plus a deal to regenerate the bus station.
>
> The firm *was able to take on* **five extra staff** and **three apprentices**, with more jobs being created for **subcontractors**.
>
> (Mudie and Cardy, 2017)

Again, in striking contrast to the opponents, this text includes reference to a type of social actor not seen in the representation of opponents to the model: farmers. Even more striking is that in contrast to oppositional texts that universally represented the model in terms of a generic category of social actors –

local business – this text gives a more specific category, local builder, and specifies that business by name: Conlon Construction. Conlon Construction is represented as being *active* not passive as in each of the oppositional texts: it *won* the £2.6million deal; it was not the recipient of 'spend'. Perhaps most crucially of all, this text demonstrates a mechanism by which progressive procurement strives to work, not explicitly but by the inclusion of *was able to take on* **five extra staff** and **three apprentices** – showing how money spent in this way can lead jobs that did not exist before, implicitly combating the undesirable deprivation in the city.

This richer set of discursive resources is in evidence in different ways across these more expansive supportive texts. These give sometimes more explicit overviews of the mechanisms of the model but, perhaps surprisingly, some of them also level more insightful critical challenge to the model than do its opponents. An example of a more explicit overview of the mechanisms of the model is given in this extract taken from an article by Hazel Sheffield in *The Independent*:

> **Preston council** *is supporting the development* of **new businesses in the city** organised as co-operatives, where *profits are shared* between **workers** rather than **external shareholders** ... **Matthew Brown, Preston council leader,** sees co-ops as one way to *reorganise* power within the economy, *taking it* from **shareholders in the City of London** and *putting it* into the hands of **local workers**.
>
> (Sheffield, 2019)

Here we see named individuals and social actors absent from oppositional texts: workers and shareholders and actions not hinted at in those oppositional texts: supporting development; sharing profits; reorganising power; taking and putting power. Reference to evidence is also a feature of this set of supportive and detailed articles. This from Aditya Chakrabortty writing in *The Guardian* is one such example:

> **The Federation of Small Businesses** has published research by **CLES** showing that for every pound *spent* with **a small or medium-sized firm**, 63p is *respent* locally. That drops to 40p for every pound *given to* **a large or multinational company**.
>
> (Chakrabortty, 2018)

Supportive as Chakrabortty is of the Preston Model, he also levels the most insightful critical challenge to the model than any other seen in the texts examined in this chapter; part of this challenge is to recognise some of the characteristics of people who might not yet have become part of the Preston Model:

> I fully expect some of these ideas to crash and burn. Others need to be improved. Preston hosts an annual carnival, its **taxi drivers** can speak Urdu,

and its shop signs are often in Polski. Yet its new-model economy is, so far, white and male. But as Rawlinson [a Councillor on Preston City Council] argues, more of the same policies will produce more of the same failure.

(Chakrabortty, 2019)

All of the passing representations of the Preston Model, limit their representation to the procurement element of the model and represent local business as passive recipients of this procurement. The contrast with the less detailed articles is stark. Each of these includes a much wider range of participants in the model, shows many more of them as active participants, and includes a fuller range of actors for whom the model takes its purpose: businesses and employees. Most strikingly of all, it is from this more detailed and expansive representation that the most crucial critique of the model comes: Chakrabortty's intervention challenges the protagonists to consider how the model might better serve women, immigrants and people of colour. This critique is, indeed, already being addressed: there is now a BAMME steering group that advises on inclusion and diversity for the Preston Model, and that one of the new co-ops, Taxis NW, is operated largely by taxi drivers of Asian descent.

Conclusion

In this chapter, I presented an analysis of how the Preston Model has been represented in public media texts. Drawing on theories of discourse and political economy taken from critical discourse analysis and cultural political economy, I analysed and compared the representation of social actors and social actions in texts of opponents and supporters of the Preston Model. I argued that opponents of the Preston Model presented a very limited version of the model. Each of these texts focussed exclusively on the procurement element of the model and excluded business and educational development, the co-operative network, promotion of the living wage and the development of a local bank. I argued that some proponents of the model also followed this rather limited focus on procurement and, surprisingly, as with the opponents, presented businesses in the city as passive recipients of funds rather than active and dynamic 'winners' of contracts. Finally, I argued that some proponents of the model engaged in more detail with the model and these texts included more aspects of the model, a wider range of process and participants and, in the case of one of Chakrabortty's articles, provided the most incisive critical engagement of all the texts analysed with potential improvements to the model.

I would draw out two implications from these arguments, the analysis and methods of analysis on which they are based. First, the limited engagement with, and representation of, the Preston Model by its opponents means that the quality of critique is impoverished. This is a pity: matters of public policy, of shifts in economic governance, can benefit through being subjected to high quality, engaged, scrutiny. Second, in dealing with the complexity of real economies, decision-makers must, to a great extent, focus on a simplified version of that economy; good scrutiny can help to point out where they might be oversimplifying and missing important gaps. In the absence of engaged critique from opponents, we need an alternative mode of deliberating over how the model might develop. Focusing on the people and processes and purpose of the community wealth building can guide the development of the model both in Preston and beyond. Opening up the range of social actors and social actions, imagining new participants and processes are engaged in and served by the Preston Model can be a path toward continued democratisation of city economies.

References

Chakrabortty, A. (2018), In 2011 Preston hit rock bottom. Then it took back control, *The Guardian*, retrieved from www.theguardian.com/commentisfree/2018/jan/31/preston-hit-rock-bottom-took-back-control (accessed 16 April 2020).

Chakrabortty, A. (2019), In an era of brutal cuts, one ordinary place has the imagination to fight back, *The Guardian*, retrieved from www.theguardian.com/commentisfree/2019/mar/06/brutal-cuts-fight-back-preston-dragons-den (accessed 16 April 2020).

CLES (2019), How we built community wealth in Preston, retrieved from https://cles.org.uk/publications/how-we-built-community-wealth-in-preston-achievements-and-lessons (accessed 16 April 2020).

Farrelly, M. (2019a), Analysing the representation of social actors: a conceptualisation of objects of governance, in Montessori, N.M., Farrelly, M. and Mulderrig, J. (eds), *Discursive Approaches to Critical Policy Analysis*, Edward Elgar, Cheltenham.

Farrelly, M. (2019b), Critical discourse analysis, in Atkinson, P., Delamont, S., Cernat, A., Sakshaug, J.W. and Williams, R.A. (eds), *SAGE Research Methods Foundations*, Sage, London.

Farrelly, M. (2020), Rethinking intertextuality in CDA, *Critical Discourse Studies*, 17 (4): 359–376.

Farrelly, M., Montesano Montessori, N. and Mulderrig, J. (2019), Concluding remarks on critical policy discourse analysis, in Montesano Montessori, N., Farrelly, M. and Mulderrig, J. (eds), *Critical Policy Discourse Analysis*, Edward Elgar, Cheltenham, 264–270.

Farrelly, M., Montesano Montessori, N., and Mulderrig, J. (2019), *Critical Policy Discourse Analysis*, Edward Elgar, Cheltenham.

Finkelstein, D. (2019), A beginner's guide to life in Corbyn's Britain, *The Times*, 6 February, retrieved from www.thetimes.co.uk/article/a-beginner-s-guide-to-life-in-corbyn-s-britain-gj5jbthzw (accessed 5 November 2020).

Goodhart, D. (2018), Brexit is an opportunity to do things differently – and not just in trade, *The Daily Telegraph*, 7 May, 16.

Harris, J. (2019), Don't Look to National Politics for Hope: You'll find it thriving in local councils, *The Guardian*, 5 May, retrieved from www.theguardian.com/commentisfree/2019/may/05/national-politics-hope-councils-councillors-local-elections (accessed 16 April 2020).

Heslop, J., Morgan, K., and Tomaney, J. (2019), Debating the Foundational Economy, *Renewal: a Journal of Labour Politics*, 27 (2): 5–12.

Jessop, B. (2010), Cultural political economy and critical policy studies, *Critical Policy Studies*, 3 (3–4):336–356.

Lewis, H. (2017), Corbyn had a good week. But are people ready to listen to his ideas?, *The Observer*, 16 April, retrieved from www.theguardian.com/commentisfree/2017/apr/15/corbyn-had-good-week-are-people-ready-to-listen-to-ideas (accessed 16 April 2020).

Manley, J. (2017), Local democracy with attitude: the Preston model and how it can reduce inequality, 23 November, retrieved from https://blogs.lse.ac.uk/politicsandpolicy/local-democracy-with-attitude-the-preston-model/ (accessed 5 January 2020).

Morgan, J. (2018), Towns and universities: UK Labour's new civic thinking, *Times Higher Education*, 25 October, retrieved from www.timeshighereducation.com/news/towns-and-universities-uk-labours-new-civic-thinking (accessed 25 September 2020).

Morgan, J. (2019), Is cooperation the antidote to higher education's competitive anxiety?, *Times Higher Education*, 5 December, retrieved from www.timeshighereducation.com/features/cooperation-antidote-higher-educations-competitive-anxiety (accessed 25 September 2020).

Mudie, K. and Cardy, P. (2017), How one city is beating austerity, *The People*, 5 November, retrieved from www.lexisnexis.co.uk/news-and-media-analysis (accessed 17 November 2020).

Mulderrig, J., Montesano Montessori, N., and Farrelly, M. (2019), Introducing critical policy discourse analysis, in Montesano Montessori, N., Farrelly, M. and Mulderrig, J. (eds), *Critical Policy Discourse Analysis*, Edward Elgar, Cheltenham, 1–22.

O'Neill, M. (2016), The road to socialism is the A59: the Preston Model', *Renewal: a Journal of Labour Politics*, 24 (2): 69–78.

Sheffield, H. (2019), 'We don't need medication, this is what we need…', *The Independent*, 13 April, 44.

Sum, N.-L. and Jessop, B. (2013), *Towards a Cultural Political Economy*, Edward Elgar, Cheltenham.

Swinney, P. (2018), Protectionism is protectionism, whether it's Trump or in Trumpington, Centre for Cities, retrieved from www.centreforcities.org/blog/protectionism-protectionism-whether-trump-trumpington (accessed 12 July 2020).

Van Leeuwen, T. (2008), *Discourse and Practice: New Tools for Critical Discourse Analysis*, Oxford University Press, Oxford.

What Works Centre for Local Economic Growth (2020), Local procurement, retrieved from https://whatworksgrowth.org/resources/local-procurement-1 (accessed 12 July 2020).

6 Together we will stand

Trade unions, cooperatives, and the Preston Model

Alex Bird, Pat Conaty, Anita Mangan, Mick McKeown, Cilla Ross and Simon Taylor

This chapter makes a case for trade union support for a new wave of co-operative development and charts some of the early instances of collaborative working in this regard framed by the Preston Model. We argue for closer affinities between the trade union and co-operative movements in pursuance of mutual interests of renewal and reinvigoration. We believe this represents both a reconnection with important shared heritage and offers crucial openings for deepening the democratic voice of workers and strengthening the connectedness of trade unions to their communities, links which have been sadly denuded in a recent history of decline. As we write amid the turmoil of the COVID-19 emergency and ongoing Brexit negotiations, we suggest that trade union and co-operative alliances offer creative imaginings for a progressive future. We illustrate the somewhat uneasy relationship between union and co-operative movements with reference to the progress of dialogue focused upon addressing problems within the care sector and the potential for a mutually agreeable solution that combines co-operative development with union organising.

Arguably, turmoil in the economy, associated vicissitudes in the labour market and recent decline in trade unions' strength and legitimacy point to a need for innovation in the labour movement. Historically, trade unions have presented an attitude of ambivalence to workers' control as embodied in co-operative forms (Laliberté, 2013) and co-operatives' suspicions of trade unions also need to be acknowledged (Monaco and Pastorelli, 2013). For those with an appreciation of shared heritage, recognising that industrial democracy appears to be, at the very least, implicit in unions' organising mission, antipathies towards co-operative workplaces as a vehicle for worker control seem curiously misplaced. That said, if a more progressive and successful resolution of these tensions is to be attempted, let alone achieved, then demonstrating solidarity and shared interests needs to be a necessary first step. For some, the optimum circumstances would be a sympathetic government looking to the wider labour movement to divine innovatory ideas for regeneration and development with a favourable economic wind behind. Yet, despite most economic and political indicators having been serially against us, perhaps paradoxically the time is opportune for revisiting workers' democracy framed by the co-operative model.[1] Indeed, the social and economic shocks of recent times, not least the COVID-19 crisis and its aftermath, could presage opportunities to renew both the economy and trade unions (Bird et al., 2020a). Local developments such as the Preston Model of Community Wealth Building and other 'new municipalisms' represent unique spaces to forge new organisational forms and practices, even if the 'newness' reflects a substantial historical legacy (McInroy and Calafati, 2017).

Union power, legitimacy, and renewal

Trade unions have long sought to bring about a legitimate means for workers' voice to be heard within, and ultimately gain control of, workplaces. While the legitimacy of any claims for democracy in the workplace need to be stood up on a foundation of authentic internal democracy within the union (Gumbrell-McCormick and Hyman, 2019) external forces and an over-reliance on servicing as opposed to organising have conspired to throw contemporary unions into a crisis of legitimacy (Hyman, 2007; Fiorito and Jarley, 2010). Amid the neoliberal project of deregulation, privatisation and concentration of wealth and power among the few, even non-unionised forums for worker voice have fallen out of fashion and unions can appear to be in retreat from historical objectives for industrial democracy. The desirability of inter-union and trans-national solidarity, co-operation, bargaining and action on the part of unions is undermined by the power of globalised capital to both weaken and circumnavigate the state, diminish job security, and expand numbers of workers in increasingly precarious and unrepresented work. Globalisation, structural shifts in the UK economy and hostile legislation have exacerbated downward membership trends (Anderson et al., 2010), undermining collective bargaining and workplace influence; enfeebling previously strong worker identities (Holgate, 2015; Wills and Simms, 2004).

Recent decades have witnessed a consolidation of neoliberalism despite the sort of shocks which ought to have shattered its internal logic and fatally undermined its foundations. Yet, neoliberalism stumbles on, propped up by an unholy coalition of big business, mass media and a series of governments wedded to the assumed virtues of deregulated markets and diminished workers' rights (Crouch, 2011; Quiggin, 2012). De-industrialisation has produced a servicing economy; with more than three-quarters of UK workers employed in the service sector. Service sector employment is not as simply spatially located as manufacturing and industrial work once was, further complicating union organising.

For decades, overall trade union strength and density has been in decline, with total union members falling from a high-water mark of around 13 million in 1979 to a current figure of 6.44 million (Roper, 2020), with unions insufficiently recruiting younger and ethnic minority workers, arguably most vulnerable to employee discrimination (Holgate, 2004). These sobering numbers hide, however, something of a resurgence in the last three years with membership increasing by around 200,000 since 2017. Unison, the large public service union, claims to be a growing union, with over 114,000 members joining in the previous year (Unison, 2020). Membership growth needs to be seen in net terms, with overall totals the result of overall gains in a context of other losses. Much of the recent growth has involved women joining unions, with 2019 alone seeing 170,000 new women members. Regardless, such examples of union resilience are unevenly spread across the economy, and particular sectors are beset with low membership density and precarious work. Related to this has been the emergence of new unions responding to precarity and new forms of work and employment, which to some extent hark back to older syndicalist forms and reflect a more general turn to defining union identity in terms of organising (Heery, 2015; Simms et al., 2019). Despite a common interest in growing representation, the new and old unions are variously engaged in conflictual or competitive relations, though some collaboration does take place (Meardi et al., 2019).

For some time now, trade unions have acknowledged that representing members via servicing models fails to engage new members. The servicing approach effectively considers the majority of members as consumers of union services, with their representation needs served by a smaller number of activists and paid officials. A detrimental impact upon internal solidarity and social capital has been noted with, in the extreme, union members located in a private relationship to the union with minimal connections to other union members or union democratic structures. Arguably, this resulted in a hollowing out of unions as solidarity organisations into what Nissen and Jarley (2005: 6) have dubbed 'a union of strangers'. Recognising these threats, unions have sought to reverse servicing patterns and shift towards various organising approaches to re-find their purpose, renew their vitality, and re-establish legitimacy (Simms et al., 2013; Murray, 2017; Fiorito and Jarley, 2010; Gall, 2009).

Organising programmes enacted by individual UK trade unions were supported by the TUC establishing an organising academy for activists in 1998 (Simms et al., 2013). Most successful organising aims to re-invent social capital within the union, connecting rank and file members to each other, members to activists, and members and activists to officers and union leadership (Nissen and Jarley, 2005). Innovations include an emphasis on strengthening and building relationships (Hoerr, 1997; O'Halloran, 2006; Saundry and McKeown, 2013) and locating unions more dynamically as community actors with shared social movement interests beyond the workplace (Wills and Simms, 2004; Tattersall, 2010). Thus, organising, although it explicitly involves recruitment and recognises the malaise of singularly focusing on servicing, is neither only about recruitment nor a complete rejection of servicing: recruitment gains will be pyrrhic without more fundamental shifts in union culture and members will still require some degree of servicing, albeit members will also be more autonomously and powerfully engaged within union responses (Reich, 2012; Vandaele, 2020). Recent decades of organising practices have engendered adaptions, involving: organisational strategies for innovation; re-imagining union structures germane to novel representative spaces; expansion of collective action repertoires; and improving connectedness, engaging with a diversity of social actors and interests (Murray, 2017). These strategies can be understood to create 'a larger narrative and practice about the role of unions in society' (Murray, 2017: 11) which may redefine the union as a mobilising structure which seeks to stimulate activism and wider social justice, building a 'movement of movements' (Brecher and Costello, 1990: 331).

Simms et al. (2013) argue that many commentators and protagonists associated with union organising appear confused over what is meant to be achieved: increases in coercive power or enhanced legitimacy? That said, there appears to be substantial consensus that organising is about more than increasing representation; revitalisation and renewal of trade unionism in the workplace and beyond must be the goal. These authors note how matters of democracy have become problematic in debates surrounding union organising. Certain aspects of union structures may be seen as an impediment to the grassroots, democratic mobilisation of resources and activism. Especially if an objective is moving beyond simple representation of members to more ambitious transformations of their workplace or societal relations, union democracy will also often have to be transformed (Carter 2000). Stephen Lerner (2003), activist in the Justice for Janitors campaign, suggests that, particularly in conditions of low density, internal union democracy may be meaningless or an impediment to extending organising and membership to marginalised, exploited and non-unionised workers. Critical allies such as Crosby (2005) bemoan the extent to which matters of democracy have been alternately trivialised and fetishised in union discourses, and while agreeing with the case for improving density at all levels suggests that transformative and democratising objectives are equally important and can go hand in hand with increasing union strength.

Co-operative development in Preston

Out of the ashes of neoliberalism's financial crisis was born the new municipal responses to regional neglect and startling inequalities for a rich western nation. The Preston approach to community wealth building has always considered co-operative enterprises as a key plank of the overall approach. The council commissioned a report into the potential contribution of co-operatives (Manley and Froggett, 2016), complementing encouraging economic and policy analysis from the Centre for Local Economic Solutions (CLES) (Jackson and McInroy, 2015), and advocating establishment of a locus for co-operative development support in the city. Notable figures within Preston City Council (PCC) and other anchor institutions have been inspired by international connections and exchanges between Mondragón in the Basque Country of Spain and similarly disposed allies from further afield, including Cleveland, Cincinnati, and New York in the US.

There have always been co-operatives and co-operative-like organisations in and around Preston. Notably, Gateway, the city's social housing organisation and important anchor institution, emerged from the tradition of housing co-operatives that began in Wales. Indeed co-operatives have been historically important for the economy of Preston since the Rochdale pioneers. For example, Preston Industrial Co-operative Society was established circa 1880 and survived until 1970. In the early part of the twentieth century the Preston Society published an informative magazine, the Preston Co-op Record, describing the range of co-operative activities taking place and produced other literature to coincide with Preston Guilds. The significance of co-operative trade and its social corollaries was reflected in the national Co-operative Congress being held in Preston in 1907. Cultural relevance and an intriguing glimpse of the value placed on education for co-operation is to be found in the fact that a booklet on co-operatives was produced for school children in the town around this time.

PCC supported the start-up of a small artists' CIC, Birley Arts, including providing premises close to the civic buildings. An example of a worker co-operative is The Larder food co-operative, which has a café located opposite the Town Hall and is utilised for informal meetings by councillors, co-operators and community groups. The Larder is more than just a café and is engaged in broader efforts to counteract food poverty; work that has become ever more vital in the midst of the COVID-19 crisis.

The Preston Cooperative Development Network (PCDN) was established to take forward this aspect of the wider Preston Model (Manley, 2018). More recently, the Open Society Foundations awarded a grant to support the establishment of 10 new worker co-operatives, training and consultancy from Mondragón and the USA, project support, and associated evaluation. The Basque Mondragón co-operative ecosystem, while emerging in quite unique circumstances, has been pivotal in inspiring activists and anchor institutions in the formation of the Preston Model, particularly the commitment to co-operative development. In short, the Mondragón system comprises a networked confederation of co-operatives with three key organisational pillars: education, manufacturing and banking, all organised co-operatively. Workers' democratic control is seen as central to delivering a just society, and the primacy afforded to education reflects a foundational ethos to sustain a co-operative culture as a necessary precursor to establishing a successful co-operative economy. Each co-operative is democratically controlled by its worker members and a Social Council also forms part of the governance structure to balance broader worker interests so that, for example, basic worker rights are not eroded by particular strategic or operational decisions. All individual co-operatives are democratically interlinked and subsidiary to an overarching General Council. This allows for attempts to maintain full employment by sharing workforce between co-operatives (Barandiaran and Lezaun, 2017; Morris, 1992; Whyte and Whyte, 2014).

Early developments in Preston include a digital co-op and a black cabs' taxi co-op. There are plans for a co-operative in the construction sector linked to substantial investment in building a new civic cinema. Local health and criminal justice commissioners have also been enthused by the potential for building co-operatives in and out of prisons to provide employment for prisoners and ex-prisoners, with the income and democratic character of the labour process perhaps well suited to nurturing prosocial behaviour and desistance from offending (Weaver & Nicholson 2012, Weaver 2016). This has been stimulated by interest in trailblazing criminal justice social co-operatives established in the Emilia Romagna region of Italy (Thomas, 2004).

One of the ten new OSF funded co-operatives is mandated to be a co-operative education centre for Preston (see Chapter 3). This would provide education on co-operative skills and principles, both on a practical level and theoretical basis and at different levels of attainment to support the development and sustainability of co-operatives, trade union education, and learning for other activists and interested people. The notion of a co-operative education centre is grounded in the Mondragón ecosystem, within which education is paramount, recognising that successful enterprises must be grounded in a co-operative culture. Work is ongoing, supported by the Cooperative College, UCLan staff and community activists to merge these developments with other plans to operate a franchise of a new federated Cooperative University, offering degree level study relevant to co-operatives and modelling a critical and social pedagogy congruent with the act of co-operation.

A manifesto for union cooperatives

A group of UK co-operative developers, academics and union activists, including representation from Unison and PCDN, have come together to draft a manifesto for union cooperatives, launched in July 2020 (Bird et al., 2020b). The union cooperative is a fully unionised, worker co-operative, owned and controlled by the workforce. Worker's control, democracy and equality are built into the model which counters mainstream economic narratives in offering a co-operative solution to inequality and injustice both in and outside the workplace. The governance structure reserves a place for the trade union to represent worker interests alongside the place where worker members manage the business they own.

Pivotal to the manifesto is the clarion call contained with International Labour Organisation Recommendation 193[2] that joint action between trade unions and co-operatives ought to be brought to bear in the achievement of decent work for all. The union cooperative is a worker co-operative that places the trade union at the heart of its governance structure. As in any co-op, the workers are in democratic control and own the business, but the trade union has a formal role to represent worker interests and as a check and balance against worker members acting against established union principles. To the latter extent, the trade union role mirrors somewhat the Social Council aspect of Mondragón co-operatives, which ensures that member decisions are not contrary to the interests of the workforce in the workplace. For example, in case the other workers in management positions get 'beyond themselves' and forget that they are equally worker members in the same organisation. Different international case studies of worker co-ops have been included within the manifesto, to learn the lessons of how best to organise collaborations between the co-operative movement and trade unions.

The manifesto envisages the union cooperative as having the potential to form successful and sustainable organisations in their own right but also to contribute to more transformative social change as credible democratic vehicles for ensuring job security, enhancing terms and conditions, and contributing to local economies rather than extracting from them. The union cooperative approach is informed by ten international co-operative principles, seven belonging to the International Co-operative Alliance (2018) supplemented with three new principles addressing decent work, workers' rights and fair remuneration (Bird, 2015). These ten union co-operative principles form a binding ethical framework and can be summarised as follows:

1   Open and voluntary membership.
2   Democratic member control.
3   Member economic participation.
4   Autonomy and independence.
5   Education, training, and information.
6   Co-operation among co-operatives.
7   Concern for community.
8   Subsidiarity of capital to labour.
9   Solidarity and fairness in wages.
10 Commitment to union cooperative development.

Principles 1–4 bind the co-operative to ideals of democracy, fairness, equality, and autonomy. Anyone within the workforce can be a member and the members are in democratic control of the co-operative. This democratic control is exercised on the basis on one member one vote, this representing a key alternative to the way in which power is distributed in the typical capitalistic business, concentrated in the hands of the wealthiest larger shareholders. Instead, with power equally distributed among members and capital collectively owned, decisions about surplus are made democratically. Thus, in a worker co-operative members can choose whether to invest a surplus to grow the business, return it to the members, set a portion aside in reserve, or allocate to other community activities.

Principles 5–7 commit the union cooperative to positive relationships with other co-operatives and the wider community. Hence, education for all interested stakeholders about the value of and means by which co-operation can be achieved is a central endeavour, as is the desirability of forming a mutually supportive eco-system of networked co-operatives. The commitment to the wider community highlighted in principle seven includes efforts to develop sustainable business practices and, in the case of union cooperatives, addresses matters of union legitimacy. Trade unions can thus improve their public image and appeal to future members by demonstrating that union concerns extend beyond the workplace and workplace issues to broader action on social justice.

Principles 8–10 have been directly inspired by the Mondragon worker co-operatives located in the Basque Country of Spain. These are a crucial supplement to the generic International Cooperative Alliance principles because they explicitly address workers' rights and fair remuneration directly within the co-operative governance system. Subordinating capital to labour consolidates workers' control as opposed to external investors, with decisions being taken at the lowest practical level within the organisation. Flowing from this principle is the understanding that capital is there to serve the interests of the workers in the context of enabling development of the co-operative; not to control them. Worker control and democracy is ensured by the fact that they must own at least 51% of voting shares. Principle nine addresses fair wages and pay structures within the union co-operative, with a commitment to decent pay for decent work. Pay differentials are also important. While top earners' wages might reflect the size and success of the co-operative, flattened ratios between wages at different levels within the union co-operative are expected, and a structure of complete pay parity across the organisation is possible. More usually, there is a commitment to not exceeding a specific ratio, with 12:1 between highest and lower earners being the absolute limit. Lastly, principle 10 supports the development of other union co-operatives by insisting on a minimum 10% levy on pre-tax profits, in cash or kind, for this purpose. Such a commitment potentiates the eventual creation of a supportive eco-system of co-operatives; again inspired by the Mondragon experience.

Recognising the possibilities of union co-operatives offers trade unions a number of potential benefits. A union cooperative does not displace the union, rather it puts unions at the heart of the governance of the co-operative as well as opening up the prospect of a 100% unionised workforce; a form of consensual closed shop. We are advocating union cooperative as one means of organising worker control and workplace democracy, but not necessarily to the exclusion of other worker co-operative models. In general, worker co-operatives offer a range of advantages even if they do not fully realise the union cooperative model. Worker co-operatives have successfully organised workers in sectors typified by precarious work, sectors usually typified by low union penetration and density. They can deliver improved wages and other terms and conditions by eliminating top-slicing by external owners. Management becomes a function not a position of privilege or status, and union cooperatives have flatter salary ranges, some even going for a flat rate of pay for all. Many worker cooperatives that are not full union cooperatives also create openings for unions and ally themselves to the union movement. Ultimately, the democratising turn represented by worker co-operatives can bolster union renewal and organising campaigns, including the revitalisation of links to communities.

The writing and launch of the Manifesto stimulated much interest, including making or rekindling contacts with international trade unionists and co-operators from Europe, the US and Canada. One such constellation of reciprocal interest includes activists and organisers from the American SEIU, 1Worker1Vote, the Welsh Foundational Economy group and allies, and comrades from Kirklees, all engaged in activism regarding co-operatives in the care sector, to which we turn next. This development work and activism need not necessarily manifest itself in the emergence of union co-operatives but there is an undoubted imperative that trade unions and their members working in the sector are thoroughly engaged in the process.

The care sector: ripe for innovation and transformation

Given its uniquely relational character, the care economy is crying out for more sustainable and humane alternatives to the failing private enterprise model. Arguably, a vision for a transformed post-neoliberal society would transplant the logic of profit with a central organising principle of care (Howard, 2020). The care sector is, arguably, an important place to begin to imagine novel and innovatory labour processes and the relationship between unions and co-operatives. Precarity of work in the sector has indeed prompted some trade union engagement with the idea of co-operatives offering a potential solution for decent work (Conaty et al., 2018). The public sector unions were undoubtedly correct to fathom an incipient privatisation tendency in right-wing government policies such as the advancement of mutuals, social enterprises and co-operatives within the taken for granted public domain. UK trade unions have thus implacably opposed anything that smells of privatisation and, wherever possible, sought to bring previously outsourced provision back in-house. The TUC (2010: 18) declared: 'It is our view that through its democratic accountability, unique funding mechanism and long term integrated approach, that the public sector is best placed to provide public services.'

Yet for those on the left interested in workplace democracy and community relations as key aspects of union organising and renewal, an uncritical statism (when the state has been captured by neo-liberalism), with absolute opposition to mutual or co-operative forms of organisation represents a missed opportunity, neglectful of labour movement heritage (Taylor, 2014, 2017) and denying radically improved social solutions. Earlier generations of fruitful intersection between trade union and co-operative movements are reflected in rich expressions of working-class culture such as workers' educational associations, mechanics' institutes, brass bands, arts and theatre, and the deep seated community connectedness of syndicalist forms of organising (Burgmann, 2005).

Trade unions are actually not strangers to relatively recent policy making regarding co-operatives, engaging constructively, for example, in the millennium Co-operative Commission, set up by the Blair government. Interestingly in consideration of potentials afforded presently in a context of UK devolved government, it is worth noting various productive union-co-operative alliances in Wales. Looking back to 1982, the Welsh TUC established the Wales Co-operative Centre (WCC) and both groups have maintained a strong relationship across the intervening decades. With a robust commitment to social and sustainable ends, the WCC has maintained its links with Welsh trade unions helping to realise healthy mutual benefits across the board. There is also a growing membership network, the Social Cooperation Forum, focused upon co-operative developments in the social care sector.

By 2012 the TUC was working with Co-operatives UK to develop a common agenda to defend workers' interests amid ideologically-inspired privatisations stemming from the coalition government. Activists from the both the union and co-operative wings of this dialogue, notably the Worker Co-operative Council, were acutely aware of attendant risks, not least the potential reputational damage of offering even qualified support to an initiative that could result in poor quality business not well placed to deliver either decent work, good quality services or worker democracy. Unsurprisingly, union anxieties coalesced around the dangers of co-operatives representing a stepping stone to investor-led financialisation and privatisation in a public sector the government was committed to shrinking. The main risk in this regard would prove to be erosion of affinities for co-operatives in the eyes of many trade unionists. Nevertheless, this engagement between the union and co-operative movements did prove fruitful and a common statement of best practice for worker co-operatives was produced (Monaco and Pastorelli, 2013).[3]

In recent times unions have not always been central to wider labour movement strategising regarding co-operatives as evidenced in the Greater Manchester Co-operative Commission report of 2020 (GM Commission, 2020) which is strong on community-led and place-based economic development but barely mentions potential or actual trade union contributions and no trade unionists figured among the Commission membership. Conversely, Liverpool City Council with the support of local MPs and the trade union Unison have recently published a policy document addressing insourcing of care (Clarke et al., 2020). Interestingly, this also acknowledges the potential for a plurality of ownership and delivery approaches. Similar work to define alternatives to the failing care economy have been advance by the New Economics Foundation with input from the OSF (Button and Bedford, 2020).

The nature of care work also suggests that the organisational form a co-operative could take might not lend itself to a pure worker or union cooperative, with a need for balancing the democratic voice of multiple stakeholders, including care recipients, families as well as workers. This may arguably be best served by a multi-stakeholder co-operative structure, but such a model could result from hybridisation of the union cooperative approach and, at the very least, involve unions significantly. Furthermore, in a context of inter-connected co-operative development, such as envisioned within the Preston Model or enacted in parts of the US, modelled to some extent on a Mondragón inspired co-operative eco-system, a key role for trade unions thoroughly allied to the local community is the way forward. As we have argued, such linkage of union, workplace and community interests is highly compatible with progressive approaches to organising and social transformation.

Quick and Martin (2020) outline the economic disarray that constitutes the care sector under neoliberalism and urge trade unions to take up the challenge of leading its transformation. This financialised, debt-laden model built upon waves of deregulation and privatisation, makes its profits from a combination of payments provided by the state and exploitation of masses of mainly women, often migrant precarious workers. Despite there being numerous small, family-owned businesses the sector is now dominated by large equity based multi-national firms. On the occasions that such firms have declared bankruptcy, they have had to be bailed out by the state with multi-million-pound rescue packages to save tens of thousands of care recipients and jobs.

Alternative approaches to organising this vital work are urgently needed and could comprise novel mixtures of public sector and co-operative provision to de-financialise and democratise the sector and, crucially, drive up quality (Goodwin et al., 2020; Quick and Martin, 2020). New technology offers distinct opportunities for workers to secure higher wages and better terms and conditions by self-organising their work utilising digital platforms capable of redistributing profits to them rather than private care operators. The US Cooperative Care Homes Associates is an example of a fully unionised worker co-operative, employing over 2000 care workers and 90% owned by women of colour. This co-operative has made common cause with the umbrella organisation 1Worker1Vote, itself formed with the support of the Mondragon Corporation to advance co-operative ecosystems within the US with particular support for union cooperatives. Since 1985 Cooperative Care Homes Associates have improved wages and provided high quality training and development, a rarity in the sector.

On a smaller scale, but with ambitions of growth, community activists in Kirklees have advanced a plan for a local multi-stakeholder domiciliary care co-op to the point of organising a successful community share issue, and these activists are committed to supporting developments in Preston via links between the respective councils and co-operative groups with input from the PCDN. A small grant from the Co-operative Councils' Innovation Network underpins relevant knowledge exchange. The Kirklees business plan includes commitments to improve the terms and conditions of the care workers, but local unions have been relatively absent from the community engagement that has democratically informed the planning.

A care co-operative for Preston?

Efforts to develop a co-operative in the care sector in Preston are at an early stage. Recognising that unions ought to be central to such developments necessitated that early energy was invested in initiating a dialogue with union members, activists and officers largely focused upon the North West Regional office of Unison and local branches within Preston. From the outset, the push to persuade trade unionists of the value of a co-operative approach had a mixed early reception. Despite some knowledgeable and informed support there were also various counter-arguments and resistances; though, as in any large complex bureaucratic organisation, viewpoints are heterogeneous and unevenly spread. The political context in which the early dialogue took place was helpful, coinciding with much positive interest in the Preston Model and a degree of rank-and-file optimism in the Corbyn project within the Labour Party.

Ostensibly, the major public sector unions are committed to public sector ownership models. This is reflected in activism within campaigns such as We

Own It[4] and appreciation for arguments supportive of bringing contracted-out services back in-house made by groups such as the Association for Public Service Excellence (APSE).[5] An ecosystem of co-operatives in a locality could, however, form a route back into the local public sector for some concerns, such as care, if there ever was to be a national shift to state provision of a national care service, in line with another of Unison's campaigning objectives. This would require substantial changes of political will on the national stage, even within the Labour Party, and would have to be legislated for. There would also have to be agreement on the part of members within any new co-operative care enterprises, who may be reluctant to surrender the positive benefits of democratic control in the workplace. In-house management of health, care, and education, for example, has hardly had a glowing track record of empowering workers' voices in neoliberal times; as the union activists, who have often struggled against new public management approaches, been exhausted by seemingly endless disciplinaries and grievance casework, fought horrendous cases of bullying, and faced cycles of impotence and marginalisation within bargaining structures, can attest.

Trade union anxieties about a co-operative specific to the care sector are not only framed by established anti-privatisation policy with its commitment to public ownership and insourcing of previously contracted out services. More nuanced versions of this standpoint recognise that businesses already, and often always having been in the private sector, can be important sites of union campaigning and potential recruitment growth. Problems with market structure and funding shortfalls are also serious hurdles to be overcome. Thus, dialogue in Preston has shifted somewhat from simplistic adherence to insourcing objectives to raise important issues of how to make provision for such matters as workers' pensions across piecemeal development of small-scale co-operative businesses. Union leaders are also quite reasonably nervous of placing precarious and vulnerable members of the care workforce in the front-line of organising in a context where some quite nasty employment practices are endemic. Other points of contention for certain activists have included:

- Attachment to traditional left-inspired partnership approaches to urban and regional regeneration, ideally being informed by Labour Party, union and TUC policy formulations and offering union and Party officials a seat at the table of regeneration boards. That said, such top-down initiatives have always lacked a democratising impulse and have seldom benefited small municipalities such as Preston – indeed, the failure of traditional regeneration and private sector investment was one of the important motivators for the Preston Model in the first place.
- Sectarian objections on both the right and the ultra-left of the union. On the right, a scepticism towards ideas associated with the Corbyn programme and on the left a visceral antipathy to anything which troubles attachment to an arguably simplistic statism.

- Negative experiences with public sector mutuals created in the 1980s and 1990s in waves of local government outsourcing. From a union perspective, these organisations have invariably failed to deliver any meaningful democratic worker voice and have actually eroded union influence and terms and conditions for the workforce. Many were simply a stepping-stone to eventual full-blown privatisations.
- Pointing to the failure of 1970s Bennite worker co-operatives in the private sector; which arguably did not fully democratise decision making, albeit often consolidating hierarchical trade union power. For many, the change of ownership was initiated as the business was in economic crisis, so the future viability was compromised from the start.
- Similar failures of worker buyouts, which to all intents and purposes were management buyouts, with an eventual goal of asset stripping and further sell-off to private concerns. Unions were often indifferent bystanders, led by job protection rather than democratisation imperatives.
- Perceived failings of retail co-ops and the Co-operative Bank.

On reflection, these objections could actually open up a constructive debate regarding learning historical lessons, strategy and intentions of worker co-ops. Union activists attempting to service members and organise campaigns in the private or voluntary care sector are fully aware that this is often a thankless task of dealing with aggressive employers in a context of poor employment relations or outright lack of recognition. Organising campaigns are tough in these circumstances, especially in striking a balance between the pitch of an organising union, which demands degrees of autonomous action and self-protection, and a servicing offer which precarious and beleaguered workers may crave. There is, therefore, ample motivation to try something different and devise an approach which challenges conventional trade union thinking. Matthew Brown, PCC leader, has urged unions to consider co-operative options within debates around ownership structures, as not to do so risks failing to adequately challenge the status quo, leaving intact extractive businesses and thus surrendering the initiative on long term issues concerning low pay and job security.

Key figures within North West Unison, including importantly Kevan Nelson, the Regional Secretary, have, while maintaining some caution, supported the possibility of working towards a concrete example. This has involved direct meetings with Matthew Brown, key council officers and other elected representatives. Grassroots activists and organising personnel have also met to advance the potential for such developments to connect with a defined organising project in Preston care sector. One of the important supportive factors pertaining to the locality is that the North West Region of Unison, under the leadership of the Regional Secretary and other notable activists, has been in the vanguard of efforts within the union to transform itself into an organising union. The North West region has sponsored various imaginative and effective organising programmes and is not absent from organising in the care sector, including constructive utilisation of the union's Ethical Care Charter[6] and pursuance of living wage demands within a Care Workers for Change campaign.[7] Consequently, the region leads the union in membership recruitment.

Conclusion

One of the main casualties of the neoliberal hegemony has been a crisis of legitimacy for democracy itself. Diminished public trust in political and democratic institutions has been matched by unashamed corruption and manipulation of electoral and information systems poorly protected from the influence of dark money amid a dirty politics practised by neoliberal insiders (Geoghegan, 2020). As faith in democracy wanes, trade unions are caught up in increasingly important struggles to re-establish their own legitimacy and renew themselves as potent agents within the state, workplaces and communities, and perhaps, reverse the losses surrendered to decades of neoliberal power. The answer is not to give up on democracy but to seek to establish more and better democracy. There is a need to both reinvigorate attachment to enfranchisement and offer more deeply democratic, participatory opportunities for people to express their wants and will in a range of contexts. The world of work represents one such opportunity and focusing union organising campaigns on worker co-operatives offers one set of democratic solutions.

Union organising programmes are themselves implicitly democratic, enhancing employee voice within the workplace and bolstering the ties of solidarity between workers. But such extensions of democracy only go so far. Worker and union cooperatives place democracy at the heart of union organising and, within opportune environments such as provided by the Preston Model, have the potential to extend democratic participation beyond the workplace into communities. Sectors of the economy under stress or typified by market failure, such as the care sector, offer real opportunities to explore union sponsored worker ownership. Despite the large UK unions operating in the care sector being committed to insourcing and public ownership, the development of co-operatives remains a viable alternative where this is not possible.

Castells's claim (Castells, 1996: 354) that workers' movements are 'unable to remake society' was arguably premature, but unless union renewal programmes succeed, and deepen solidarity with wider community interests, the legitimacy crisis for unions will persist. Forms of worker or union cooperatives offer the labour movement one way to shift from the defensive, rear-guard fight against neoliberalism to the vanguard of reshaping the very organisation of work along co-operative and democratic lines. Such a shift is arguably best supported in the context of broader union renewal programmes, ideally those which balance workplace and community organising to connect with other progressive social movements and, in alliance with these, locate the realisation of workers' rights with other social rights and societal transformations. Achievement of such goals would represent something of a resurgence of older syndicalist ideals and emphasis upon class identity as a crucial axis for movement politics and action (Burgmann, 2005).

The Preston Model, and other new municipal approaches to create fairer economies, provide an advantageous context for enacting such change, eventually linking workplace democracy to progressive civic engagement and a more active, participatory democratic involvement of all citizens in the local polity. Furthermore, in line with the objectives of the Preston Model, worker co-operatives can form an integral part of such local and regional regeneration initiatives, helping to fight inequalities, protect the environment, support sustainable local economic growth, and ensure the locally-created wealth never leaves the area. The development of new worker co-ops in Preston is at an early stage, but the efforts of local activists, in solidarity with significant national and international allies, has laid a substantial foundation and exciting times lay ahead. Solidarity lies at the heart of the labour movement, so should therefore also represent its future.

Notes

1 For a more detailed understanding of co-operative approaches see the ICA definition at www.ica.coop/en/cooperatives/cooperative-identity
2 See www.ilo.org/empent/Publications/WCMS_311447/lang–en/index.htm
3 Other evidence of UK collaborations between union and cooperative movements includes www.uk.coop/sites/default/files/uploads/attachments/tuc_co-operatives_uk_-_guidance.pdf and www.thenews.coop/39882/sector/retail/co-operatives-uk-and-tuc-team-protect-public-service-mutuals
4 See https://wcownit.org.uk
5 See www.apse.org.uk/apse/index.cfm/research/current-research-programme/insourcing-a-guide-to-bringing-local-authority-services-back-in-house
6 See Unison's Ethical Care Charter at www.unison.org.uk/content/uploads/2013/11/On-line-Catalogue220142.pdf
7 See www.unisonnw.org/care_workers_for_change

References

Anderson, J., Hamilton, P. and Wills, J. (2010), The Multi-scalarity of Trade Union Practice, in McGrath-Champ, S., Herod, A. and Rainnie, A. (eds), *Handbook of Employment and Society: Working space*, Edward Elgar, Cheltenham, 383–397.

Barandiaran, X. and Lezaun, J. (2017), The Mondragón Experience, in J. Michie, J.R. Blasi, and C. Borzaga (eds), *The Oxford Handbook of Mutual, Co-Operative, and Co-Owned Business*, Oxford University Press, Oxford, 279–294.

Bird, A. (2015), Why We Need to Update the Co-operative Principles. Retrieved from www.alex-bird.com/why-we-need-to-update-the-co-operative-principles/. Accessed 5 November 2020.

Bird, A., Conaty, P., McKeown, M., Mangan, A. and Ross, C. (2020a), Democracy and work, In M. Parker (ed.), *Life After Covid: The Other Side of Crisis*, Bristol University Press, Bristol, 63–72.

Bird, A., Conaty, P., McKeown, M., Mangan, A. and Ross, C. (2020b), *Union Co-ops UK: A Manifesto for Decent Work*, Union Coops UK, Manchester. Retrieved from www.co-op.ac.uk/Handlers/Download.ashx?IDMF=92f4e857-b317-4581-8f40-26961b1ee810. Accessed 5 November 2020.

Brecher, J. and Costello, T. (1990), Concluding Essay: Labor-Community Coalitions and the Restructuring of Power, In J. Brecher and T. Costello (eds), *Building Bridges: The Emerging Grassroots Coalition of Labor and Community*, Monthly Review Press, New York, 325–345.

Burgmann, V. (2005), From Syndicalism to Seattle: Class and the Politics of Identity, *International Labor and Working-Class History*, 67 (1): 1–21.

Button, D and Bedford, S. (2020), *Ownership in Social Care: Why it Matters and What Can Be Done*, New Economics Foundation, London. Retrieved from https://new economics.org/2020/01/ownership-in-social-care. Accessed 5 November 2020.

Castells, M. (1996), *The Rise of the Network Society Vol 1: The Information Age: Economy, Society and Culture*, Wiley-Blackwell, Oxford.

Clarke, A., Coleman, A., Hayden, E., Jennings, S., Munby, S., Small, N., Davies, J. and Lucas, K. (2020), *Who Cares? Reinventing Adult Social Care: Insourcing and Restoring the Public Good*, report prepared by a Scrutiny Panel established by the Social Care and Health Select Committee of Liverpool City Council, Liverpool. Retrieved from https://d3n8a8pro7vhmx.cloudfront.net/unisonnw/pages/2539/atta chments/original/1596036758/Insourcing_Adult_Social_Care__-_FINAL_Amended__29_July_2020_v2.pdf?1596036758. Accessed 5 November 2020.

Conaty, P., Bird, A. and Ross, C. (2018), *Working Together: Trade Union and Co-operative Innovations for Precarious Workers*, Co-operatives UK, Manchester. Retrieved from www.uk.coop/sites/default/files/uploads/attachments/working-together_final_web-version.pdf. Accessed 5 November 2020.

Crosby, J. (2005), Democracy, Density, And Transformation: We Need Them All. *Journal of Labor and Society*, 8 (6): 733–753.

Crouch, C. (2011), *The Strange Non-Death of Neo-Liberalism*, Polity Press, Cambridge.

Fiorito, J. and Jarley, P. (2010), Understanding Organising Activity Among US National Unions, *Industrial Relations Journal*, 41 (1): 74–92.

Gall, G. (2009), *Union Revitalisation in Advanced Economies: Assessing the Contribution of Union Organising*, Palgrave, London.

Geoghegan, P. (2020), *Democracy for Sale: Dark Money and Dirty Politics*, Head of Zeus, London.

GM Commission (2020), *A Cooperative Greater Manchester: People and Communities Working Together to Improve the Environment, Create Good Jobs and Sustainable Growth*. Retrieved from https://gmcommission.coop/report-published

Goodwin, T., Burch, D. and McInroy, N. (2020), A Progressive Approach to Adult Social Care: How Markets Can Be Made or Shaped by Policymakers and Commissioners. Retrieved from https://cles.org.uk/publications/a-progressive-approach-to-adult-social-care. Accessed 5 November 2020.

Gumbrell-McCormick, R. and Hyman, R., 2019. Democracy in Trade Unions, Democracy through Trade Unions?, *Economic and Industrial Democracy*, 40 (1): 91–110.

Heery, E. (2015), Unions and the Organising Turn: Reflections after 20 Years of Organising Works, *The Economic and Labour Relations Review*, 26 (4): 545–560.

Hoerr, J. (1997), *We Can't Eat Prestige: The Women Who Organized Harvard*, Temple University Press, Philadelphia, PA.

Holgate, J. (2004), *Black and Minority Ethnic Workers and Trade Unions: Strategies for Organisation, Recruitment and Inclusion*, Trades Union Congress, London.

Holgate, J. (2015), Community Organising in the UK: A 'New' Approach for Trade Unions?, *Economic and Industrial Democracy*, 36 (3): 431–455.

Howard, N. (2020), A World of Care, in M. Parker (ed.), *Life After Covid: The Other Side of Crisis*, Bristol University Press, Bristol, 21–30.

Hyman, R. (2007), How Can Trade Unions Act Strategically?, *Transfer: European Review of Labour and Research*, 13 (2): 193–210.

International Co-operative Alliance (2018), Cooperative identity, Values and Principles. Retrieved from www.ica.coop/en/cooperatives/cooperative-identity. Accessed 5 November 2020.

Jackson, M. and McInroy, N. (2015), *Creating a Good Local Economy: The Role of Anchor Institutions*, Centre for Local Economic Strategies (CLES), Manchester.

Laliberté, P. (2013), Trade Unions and Worker Cooperatives: Where Are We at?, *International Journal of Labour Research*, 5 (2): 173–177.

Lerner, S. (2003), An Immodest Proposal: Remodeling the House of Labor, *New Labor Forum*, 12 (2): 9–30.

Manley, J. (2018), *Preston City Council Strategy: The Preston Co-operative Development Network*, Preston Co-operative Councils Innovation Network (PCCIN), Preston. Retrieved from www.councils.coop/wp-content/uploads/2018/04/Strategy-Co-operative-Development-Network-Preston-City-Council.pdf. Accessed 5 November 2020.

Manley, J. and Froggett, L. (2016), Co-operative Activity in Preston: A Report for PCC. Retrieved from http://clok.uclan.ac.uk/14526. Accessed 5 November 2020.

McInroy, N. and Calafati, L. (2017), Local Government and The Commons: The Time Has Come. Retrieved from https://cles.org.uk/blog/local-government-the-commons-the-time-has-come. Accessed 5 November 2020.

Meardi, G., Simms, M. and Adam, D. (2019), Trade Unions and Precariat in Europe: Representative Claims, *European Journal of Industrial Relations*. Online ahead of print. doi:10.1177/0959680119863585.

Monaco, M. and Pastorelli, L. (2013), Trade Unions and Worker Cooperatives in Europe: A Win-Win Relationship: Maximizing Social and Economic Potential in Worker Cooperatives, *International Journal of Labour Research*, 5 (2): 227–249.

Morris, D. (1992), *The Mondragon System: Cooperation at Work*, Institute for Local Self-Reliance and Infinity, Washington, DC. Retrieved from www.ilsr.org/wp-content/uploads/files/images/mondragon.pdf. Accessed 5 November 2020.

Murray, G. (2017), Union Renewal: What Can We Learn from Three Decades of Research?, *Transfer: European Review of Labour and Research*, 23 (1): 9–29.

Nissen, B. and Jarley, P. (2005), Unions as Social Capital: Renewal through a Return to the Logic of Mutual Aid?, *Labor Studies Journal*, 29 (4): 1–26.

O'Halloran, L. (2006), *Relational Organising: A Practical Guide for Unionists*, Association of University Staff, New Zealand.

Quick, A. and Martin, A. (2020), Financialised Care is Crumbling. How Can Workers Shape What Comes Next? Retrieved from www.opendemocracy.net/en/oureconomy/financialised-care-crumbling-how-can-workers-shape-what-comes-next. Accessed 5 November 2020.

Quiggin, J. (2012), *Zombie Economics: How Dead Ideas Still Walk Among Us*, Princeton University Press, Princeton.

Reich, A.D. (2012), *With God on Our Side: The Struggle for Workers' Rights in a Catholic Hospital*, ILR/Cornell University Press, Ithaca, NY.

Roper, C. (2020), Union Membership Rises for Third Year Running to 6.4 Million. Retrieved from www.tuc.org.uk/blogs/union-membership-rises-third-year-running-64-million. Accessed 5 November 2020.

Saundry, R. and McKeown, M. (2013), Relational Union Organising in a Healthcare Setting: A Qualitative Study, *Industrial Relations Journal*, 44 (5–6): 533–547.

Simms, M., Holgate, J. and Heery, E. (2013), *Union Voices: Tactics and Tensions in UK Organizing*, Cornell University Press, Ithaca, NY.

Simms, M., Holgate, J. and Roper, C. (2019), The Trades Union Congress 150 Years on: A Review of the Organising Challenges and Responses to the Changing Nature of Work, *Employee Relations*, 41 (2): 331–343.

Taylor, S. (2017), Union Co-operatives: What They Are and Why We Need Them, *New Internationalist*. Retrieved from https://newint.org/blog/2017/01/13/union-co-operatives-what-they-are-and-why-we-need-them. Accessed 5 November 2020.

Taylor, S. (2014), An Opportunity Missed? Trade Union Responses and Attitudes to Coalition Policies on Mutuals, Social Enterprises and Co-operatives. Dissertation, Ruskin College, Oxford.

Thomas, A. (2004), The Rise of Social Cooperatives in Italy, *Voluntas: International Journal of Voluntary and Nonprofit Organizations*, 15 (3): 243–263.

TUC (2010), Civic Society and Public Services: Collaboration not Competition. Retrieved from www.tuc.org.uk/research-analysis/reports/civil-society-and-public-services-collaboration-not-competition. Accessed 5 November 2020.

Unison (2020), 'We Need our Union to be Stronger than Ever' Dave Prentis Tells NEC'. Retrieved from www.unison.org.uk/news/article/2020/07/necjuly2020/. Accessed 5 November 2020.

Vandaele, K. (2020), Newcomers as Potential Drivers of Union Revitalization: Survey Evidence from Belgium, *Relations Industrielles/Industrial Relations*, 75 (2): 351–375.

Weaver, B. and Nicholson, D. (2012), Co-producing Change: Resettlement as a Mutual Enterprise, *The Prison Service Journal*, 204: 9–17.

Weaver, B. (2016), Co-producing Desistance from Crime: The Role of Social Cooperative Structures of Employment. Retrieved from https://strathprints.strath.ac.uk/65053/1/Weaver_ECANB_2016_Co_producing_desistance_from_crime_the_role_of_social.pdf. Accessed 5 November 2020.

Whyte, W.F. and Whyte, K.K. (2014), *Making Mondragon: The Growth and Dynamics of the Worker Cooperative Complex*, Cornell University Press, Ithaca, NY.

Wills, J. and Simms, M. (2004). Building Reciprocal Community Unionism in the UK, *Capital and Class*, 28 (1): 59–84.

7 Stevenage

A distinct community wealth building journey

Michael Brookes, Christopher Nicholas, Tracy Walsh, Anita Sharma and Sarah Wolfe

Context

Stevenage is a town in north Hertfordshire approximately 30 miles north of London. Although a settlement recognisable as Stevenage is identifiable as far back as the Doomsday Book its current size and formulation is a relatively recent development. This was driven by Stevenage being identified as the first 'New Town' in the 1946 New Towns Act and significant housing developments throughout the 1950s and subsequent decades led to an exponential increase in the population. The current population of Stevenage is around 88,000, which is more than 5 times the size of its pre-war level.

In relation to community wealth building (CWB), although there has been strong growth in interest in CWB across the country in the last 6 or 7 years, Stevenage is somewhat unusual in that it is one of the few initiatives based in the more affluent areas of the country. While Stevenage is nominally classified as in the Eastern region, it is very much within the hinterland of London and the South East. Central London is roughly 30 minutes away by direct train and Stevenage's position right next to the A1(M) makes many parts of North London relatively easily accessible and, as a result, London based employment is an important source of income for many Stevenage households. However, despite its proximity and ease of access to the UK's most lucrative labour market, there is still significant evidence of Stevenage as a community that could benefit to a large extent from a successful CWB programme.

It is estimated that there are 56,000 people of working age (i.e. between 16 and 64 living in Stevenage); this is broken down as 48,200 economically active, 1500 unemployed, and 6300 inactive. The reported unemployment rate is 3.1% but, given the claimant count of 3340 (i.e. 6%) and the inactivity rate of 11%, there are a significant number of people whose current earnings do not meet their needs or could make a greater contribution to the Stevenage economy if the opportunities existed. Furthermore, for Stevenage as a whole, the median earnings by residence is £557.5 per week, which compares to a median of £587 per week for Great Britain. Therefore, once again despite the proximity and ease of access to the London labour market, the majority of Stevenage residents are significantly lower paid in comparison to the rest of the country. Although, obviously all the above is likely to change significantly as the economic impact of the current COVID-19 crisis unfolds, it does translate into real challenges with respect to levels of deprivation within Stevenage.

The UK government uses the English Index of Multiple Deprivation (IMD or EIMD) to capture the level of deprivation across England, and thereafter, to inform policy decisions (Petrovic et al., 2019). It has been broadly applied to many government departments including health, education, and transportation among others. An example for education is that the IMD is being used as part of a formula to distribute school funding by the UK government (Education and Skills Funding Agency, 2020). In health, an illustrative application is that the IMD is utilised to measure associated risks between deprivation and childhood obesity (Davies 2019), and more recently, COVID-19 (Public Health England, 2020). There is, however, no unified IMD measure across the UK. Instead, there are country-specific IMDs with slight differences in the data collection methods. Thus, England has the EIMD (Ministry of Housing, Communities and Local Government, 2019), Scotland (Scottish Government, 2020) and Wales (Welsh Government 2019) their own measures, while Northern Ireland has the MDM equivalent (Northern Ireland Statistics and Research Agency, 2017). In England, Noble et al. (2019: 5) promote the use of EIMD as an 'important tool for identifying the most deprived areas of England'. Local policy makers and communities can also use this tool to ensure that their activities prioritise the areas with greatest need for services. An example of a country specific application, for transport in England, is that under the London-based 'Mayor's Transport Strategy 2018', London boroughs can apply for grants to promote Healthy Streets and Healthy People. Camden, one of these boroughs, has used the EIMD as one of many measures in the application of this (Camden Creative Services, 2019). The use of IMD in government reports is ubiquitous, thus has important policy considerations (Petrovic et al., 2019).

The EIMD has been in existence since the turn of the century and fulfils the function of enabling comparisons to be made, across both time and location, in terms of relative levels of multiple and combined deprivation. It has given rise to a large number of academic publications in the intervening years highlighting the extent and impact of deprivation across England. For those seeking a deeper understanding of the index, Noble et al. (2006) outlines the background to the development of the various component indices of deprivation in England, including the key principles underpinning the construction and the statistical techniques utilised to operationalise them. The large body of empirical work that has emanated from the EIMD is disproportionally focused within the realms of health inequalities. Examples of this include; Hiscock et al. (2013) highlighting the impact of socioeconomic status on the likelihood of quitting smoking, as well as Kontopantelis (2018) who, somewhat topically in advance of the current COVID-19 crisis, undertook a study of epidemiology and found that socioeconomic deprivation is a key determinant for health and its effects are very stubborn over time.

Although to date there has been relatively little attempt to utilise the EIMD to establish empirically the effectiveness of policies and interventions targeting the development of social value, it does offer a potentially rich source of evidence for CWB. The low level of collection unit, i.e. the lower-layer super output areas, plus the fact that it is secondary data collected on an annual basis by the Office for National Statistics, means that the evolution of social value development on the back of the application of CWB can be clearly and effectively mapped over time. For Stevenage, the evidence presented below, clearly highlights Bedwell and Shephall as the two wards with the highest levels of deprivation within the borough. Therefore, detailed analysis of the EIMD in these two wards, plus the factors having the greatest influence, are a readymade and easily accessible means of accurately establishing the impact of Stevenage's developing CWB project.

In order to understand what we can establish as a benchmark for Stevenage at the outset of its CWB project, the following describes precisely what the EIMD measures and what it indicates for the wards within the borough. In 2019 England is divided into 32,844 areas which contain roughly 1,500 residents (or 650 households) called lower-layer super output areas (LSOA). The deprivation of each LSOA is measured through use of 37 indicators across 7 weighted domains: income deprivation (22.5%), employment deprivation (22.5%), education, skills and training deprivation (13.5%), health deprivation and disability (13.5%), crime deprivation (9.3%), barriers to housing and services deprivation (9.3%), and living environment deprivation (9.3%) (Noble et al., 2019). Income deprivation measures the proportion of the population with a low income. Employment deprivation measures the proportion of the working age population who involuntarily do not participate in the labour market. Health and Disability deprivation measures the risk of premature death and poor physical and mental health. Education, Skills and Training deprivation measures the lack of necessary skills and development. Crime deprivation measures the risk of being a victim of crime. Barriers to Housing and Services deprivation measures the financial and geographical barriers to housing and services. Living Environment deprivation measures the quality of the indoor and outdoor environment. The deprivation measure is ranked compared to all the LSOAs to measure relative deprivation.

For the context of this project, the boundaries of the 2010, 2015, and 2019 EIMD data were converted from LSOAs to the boundaries for the relevant local authority wards to better reflect the elected officials' responsibilities for each area. Figure 7.1 portrays the level of deprivation for Stevenage Wards when ranked against all other Wards in England for each year. There was a notable improvement in the relative deprivation of Stevenage from 2010 to 2015 with three of the 13 Wards within the second quintile (i.e. 40% most deprived Wards in England) by 2015. This trend reverses by 2019 with six out of the 13 Wards within the second quintile making Stevenage relatively more deprived than in 2010. Throughout the years, the three Wards of Bedwell, Pin Green and Shephall remained within the most deprived 40%.

Figure 7.1 English index of multiple deprivation quintiles for Stevenage Wards in 2010 (left), 2015 (centre), and 2019 (right)
Source: maps created in ArcMap10 by the authors using data from Ministry of Housing, Communities and Local Government (2010, 2015, 2019)

In breaking down the EIMD, Table 7.1 shows the domains for each of the 13 Wards in Stevenage for 2010, 2015, and 2019. The table generally follows the overall IMD trend with relative improvement in rank across multiple domains between 2010 and 2015 before reversing from 2015 and 2019 and becoming relatively more deprived compared to 2010. Health and Disability Deprivation followed this trend but maintained some of the improvements in deprivation in 2019. Notable expectations to this trend were the Education, Skills and Training Deprivation which deteriorated from 2010 to 2015 before stabilising and Crime Deprivation which showed a continued deterioration from 2010 to 2019. Four Stevenage Wards; Bedwell, Old Town, Pin Green and Shephall had at least one domain within the first quintile (i.e. 20% most deprived Ward in England) in 2019. Of concern is Bedwell which consistently had at least one domain and often multiple domains within the first quintile across all the years. Despite Hertfordshire being noted as a relatively affluent county, there are significant societal causes for concern for Stevenage (given its geographical location and proximity to its more affluent neighbouring areas). Therefore, potential exists for meaningful benefits from an effective and successful CWB programme in Stevenage. The focus of any social impact arising from a CWB programme should target the Bedwell and Shephall wards specifically.

Local government

The local administration is Stevenage Borough Council (SBC) and, in partnership with the University of Hertfordshire, have been exploring the potential and applicability of a CWB initiative within the borough. Most notably this has led to the undertaking of a scoping pilot project led by Professor Michael Brookes from the Global Work and Employment Research Group at the University of Hertfordshire, and including all of the co-authors for this chapter, as well as the adoption of a CWB Charter for the Borough Council as a whole. The full wording of the Charter is as follows:

> That this Council understands the benefits of community wealth building, drawing from learning both nationally and internationally, and believes that further opportunities can be unlocked for the local economy and our residents through work with partners in the town around;

- procurement and social value
- training and skills
- growing the social economy
- effectively tackling climate change

> This Council commits to developing an inclusive Economy charter based on these foundations to build community wealth, to ensure that future regeneration and growth in Stevenage works for everyone.
>
> (Stevenage Borough Council, 2020)

Table 7.1 Domains of the English index of multiple deprivation for 2010, 2015 and 2019 Stevenage Wards (shaded quintiles: 1 = within 20% most deprived and 2 = within 40% most deprived)

Stevenage Wards	Income Deprivation			Employment Deprivation			Education, Skills and Training Deprivation			Health and Disability Deprivation		
	2010	2015	2019	2010	2015	2019	2010	2015	2019	2010	2015	2019
Bandley Hill	2	2	2	3	2	2	3	2	2	2	3	3
Bedwell	1	1	1	1	2	1	2	1	1	1	2	2
Chells	3	3	3	3	3	3	3	2	2	1	4	3
Longmeadow	3	2	2	3	3	2	3	2	2	2	3	3
Manor	5	4	5	5	4	5	4	3	4	4	5	4
Martins Wood	2	2	2	2	2	2	3	2	2	2	3	3
Old Town	2	2	2	3	3	3	3	2	3	3	4	3
Pin Green	2	2	2	2	2	2	3	2	2	2	3	2
Roebuck	2	2	2	2	2	2	3	2	2	2	3	3
Shephall	2	2	2	2	2	2	2	1	1	1	3	2
St Nicholas	2	2	2	3	2	2	3	2	2	2	3	3
Symonds Green	2	2	2	3	3	3	3	2	2	2	3	3
Woodfield	3	3	3	4	3	3	4	3	3	4	3	3

	Crime Deprivation			Barriers to Housing and Services			Living Environment Deprivation		
	2010	2015	2019	2010	2015	2019	2010	2015	2019
Bandley Hill	2	3	3	3	2	2	5	5	4
Bedwell	4	2	1	1	3	2	4	5	4
Chells	3	2	3	2	3	2	4	5	4
Longmeadow	3	3	3	3	3	2	5	5	5
Manor	4	4	4	4	4	2	5	5	5
Martins Wood	4	4	2	3	4	3	5	5	4
Old Town	5	1	1	2	4	3	3	4	3
Pin Green	4	2	1	1	3	2	4	5	4
Roebuck	3	2	2	2	3	3	5	5	3
Shephall	5	2	1	1	5	4	4	5	4
St Nicholas	5	3	2	2	4	3	4	5	5
Symonds Green	3	4	4	4	3	2	5	5	4
Woodfield	2	2	2	3	2	1	4	5	5

Source: data taken from Ministry of Housing, Communities and Local Government (2010, 2015, 2019)

The Charter was presented to a full council meeting in January 2020 and was adopted as a strategic policy objective for the borough. Of the 38 seats on the council, Labour currently holds 26, hence any motion presented by the council leadership is likely to garner sufficient support to be passed. However, on this occasion, the leaders of both the Conservative and Liberal Democrat groups spoke in favour of the motion and it received unanimous support across the chamber.

The initiative began following an approach from Professor Brookes to all 11 of the local authorities, including the county council, within Hertfordshire and there was immediate traction and interest from within SBC. This approach was driven by an understanding of the many challenges present within communities in Stevenage, outlined by the deprivation data earlier in the chapter, as well as in other Hertfordshire communities and a desire to inform policies to address these. On the back of a series of visits by Professor Brookes to Preston and meetings with Matthew Brown, Leader of the Preston City Council, and Dr Julian Manley from the University of Central Lancashire, a deeper understanding of the Preston Model was developed. This deeper understanding encompassed both the transformative potential of the Preston Model as well as the practicalities of implementing and maintaining a CWB strategy. On the back of this, Professor Brookes became convinced that CWB offered the most effective and achievable means of addressing the many deprivation challenges within Hertfordshire, hence the initial approach to local authorities was made.

There was already an existing initiative within Stevenage focused upon the Cooperative Network seeking to promote and support employee-owned enterprises within the local communities. Therefore, initiatives such as the Mondragon Corporation in Spain, the Evergreen co-operatives in Cleveland, Ohio as well as the Preston Model were already well known within SBC and its network of community focused organisations. Consequently, the university was largely pushing at an open door in developing a CWB based narrative and seeking a partnership with SBC. The Stevenage approach to community wealth building, which has evolved over the last 18 months, is a pragmatic amalgamation of academic input from the University of Hertfordshire allied to long-standing and deep-seated links with communities provided by the local council.

In line with Steve Dubb (2016), Professor Brookes presented a CWB narrative to SBC revolving around leveraging the local authority, as well as other local anchor institutions, to provide development support for more inclusive growth. Throughout the period of austerity SBC had experienced rising frustrations with the current provision and its inability to support the local economy in an acceptable and sustainable fashion and most of the limitations of the status quo, again highlighted by Dubb (2016), could be witnessed. These included collaborating with footloose multinationals, incubation activities focused on conventional SMEs, locational tax incentives leading to the creation of marginal and precarious jobs, outsourcing as well as Public-Private Partnerships. Therefore, Professor Brookes had a relatively easy task in terms of looking for a collaborative commitment from SBC and an agreement to partake in an initial pilot project.

Although there was an existing strong commitment towards co-operatives within SBC and Stevenage in general, there was also recognition of the difficulties in developing and sustaining a local economy, as well as a CWB project, predominantly around co-operative enterprises. In previous times Cornforth and Thomas (1990), as well as Spear (2004), have highlighted many of the challenges facing a co-operative-based local economy, most notably maintaining continued engagement with the collective objectives of the enterprise over extended periods. With this in mind, along with the recognition that although co-operatives can make a significant contribution towards positive outcomes within a CWB framework, they are not a necessary condition for its success and important gains can still be captured for the local economy without their presence. As a result, it was decided, at least for the initial pilot phase, that the focus would simply be on the procurement and employment practices of SBC and other anchor institutions. The thinking being that significant benefits can still be captured for the communities of Stevenage through getting anchor institutions and their suppliers to behave differently, without, at least in the initial phase, seeking to develop local co-operatives to fill gaps in the anchor institutions' procurement chains. With this in mind a large data collection and scoping exercise was undertaken, within SBC's existing procurement contract holders, by a research team from the University of Hertfordshire under the leadership of Professor Brookes.

Data analysis

Alongside the *inclusive economy charter*, the pilot project has been progressing under the stewardship of the University of Hertfordshire and to date detailed analysis has been undertaken of SBC's contract register, as well as two data collection exercises with current procurement contract holders. From these various pieces of analyses the following has been established.

The initial analysis utilising the SBC contract register shows 41 contracts with a combined value of £19,455,409 and breaking down by service area reveals the following;

Corporate services and transformation	£11,054,402
Finance and estates	£373,997
Housing and investment	£2,132,026
Communities and neighbourhood	£2,976,586
Regeneration	£117,800
Property and estates	£1,500,000
Stevenage direct services	£869,589
Planning, regeneration, and transport	£35,275
Planning and regulatory	£123,501
Corporate policy and partnerships	£91,110
Human resources	£31,123
Housing development	£150,000

Within the overall spend over £14 million is allocated to four specific areas. £7 million goes towards various contracts in relation to 'supply services of personnel including temporary staff', therefore investigating the basis under which people within these contracts is an obvious starting point for CWB. Then £3 million is paid to a large national construction company for materials and maintenance services so digging into the supply chain below this could be a rich source of CWB benefits. Thirdly, almost £3 million is spent on CCTV monitoring operatives, so a detailed analysis of the basis that these people are employed could also be a useful source for CWB capture. Finally, £1.5 million is paid for electricity supply, this may be a longer-term initiative but many local authorities as part of the CWB programmes have set up their own energy companies, so this may well be of interest for future extensions of the project.

From a Qualtrics survey administered by Stevenage Borough Council and circulated to all their existing procurement contract holders 47 responses were received.

Using extrapolation from the responses received we can deduce that these companies hold around £3.5 million worth of contracts with Stevenage Borough Council with the average being approximately £81,000 per company. From these contracts 22.5% is on average paid to suppliers and/or sub-contractors to deliver on the contracts, this equates to £789,250 and £18,265 on average per contract. Clearly this represents a sizeable sum, since if this is consistent across all SBC's procurement contracts, this would represent around £10 million per year being paid to suppliers/sub-contractors out of their procurement spend. Hence, a detailed study of the underpinning supply chains is needed to identify how much of this £10 million per annum has the potential to be captured for greater social impact.

The respondents to the survey are predominantly private limited companies, with these being 36 out of the 45 who replied to this question. For the remainder there are four PLCs, two charities, one partnership and one sole trader, there is also one public sector organisation which is Hertfordshire Country Council. Although there is wide variation, 1% being the lowest and 38% being the highest, the SBC procurement contracts make up 9.85% on average of the overall total annual revenue of their contract holders. Therefore, there is not insignificant leverage for SBC to try to influence the behaviour of their contract holders in the future.

Although there is widespread coverage of staff training, with only one of the 47 respondents not providing any, there is relatively little formal training. Only 12 currently offer apprenticeships, eight training towards professional or industry qualifications, three graduate training and six offering regular CPD, with those firms that do offer formal training tending to offer a range of the four options above. Therefore, there is considerable scope for skills development within the contract holders.

There is a wide range in terms of size among the contract holders, the smallest having only two employees and the largest 8500, and this gives an average of 653 per firm. In response to where their employees live they record; 23% in

Stevenage, 21% Hertfordshire and 50% outside of the Eastern region. There-fore, once again, significant potential for capturing more of the procurement spend for the local economy.

In an interview conducted with one of the survey respondents (a national, not for profit organisation), it was clear that the contracts held by the organisation had benefits for the local community: they not only provided a 'in' to the services offered for residents in Stevenage, but also training for volunteers, who would often stay with the organisation for a 'significant period of time'. In 2019, the organisation supported 12 volunteers back into paid work, through their highly valued training programme, many of whom had been long term unemployed, or away from the workplace bringing up a family.

The organisation is also contracted by SBC to provide a representation ser-vice for tenants, supporting them with alternatives to eviction, offering debt advice and keeping them in homes in the local area.

The long-standing contracts with SBC make up nearly a third of the organi-sation's annual revenue, so they are able to use that funding to do other work in the local area: 'helping Stevenage residents is a key partnership area' (Inter-view 1).

The contract is for services, not for goods, and the services in the con-tracts held are provided directly by the organisation, nothing is outsourced by them, keeping the wealth in the local area. The organisation contracts in some services which overlap with the SBC contracts, such as IT and accountancy, which are local to Stevenage and Hertfordshire, hence there is evidence that some of the principles of CWB are already embedded infor-mally within the relationships between SBC and its existing providers. As a result, there is likely to be relatively limited resistance to a more formal expansion of these principles.

Social value

As part of this pilot project, we have sought to develop a Social Value Measure that can be utilised effectively within both the award of procure-ment contracts, as well as the subsequent management of those contracts. This will ensure that the bids with the greatest potential for creating social value will have an increased probability of being awarded the contracts in the first place and it will then enable them to evidence their subsequent social impact more clearly.

The construction of a social value measure follows a similar initiative by the central government (Cabinet Office, 2019); this involves the introduction of additional questions asked to potential suppliers during the bidding process. The additional questions are based on general 'themes' and associated policy outcomes that can be tailored by the relevant government authority. The gen-eral themes and policy outcomes are:

Table 7.2 Social value themes

Themes	Policy outcome
Diverse supply chains	Supply chain available to SMEs (Small/Medium Enterprises) and VSCEs (Volunteer, Social, Community Enterprises)
	Supply chain available to business owned/led by under-represented groups
Skills and employment	Improved employability and skills
Environmental sustainability in support of the 25-year environmental plan	Environmental impacts are reduced
Inclusion, staff mental health and wellbeing	Ensuring businesses in the supply chain encourage improved gender pay balance
	Ensuring businesses in the supply chain encourage increased representation of people with disabilities and under-represented groups in the workforce
	Ensuring businesses in the supply chain encourage inclusion and improved staff mental health and wellbeing
	Ensuring businesses in the supply chain encourage more cohesive communities
Safe and secure supply chains	Cyber security risks are reduced
	Modern slavery risks are reduced

Source: Cabinet Office (2019)

To operationalise the policy outcomes, a potential supplier is asked questions to prove they are contributing to each of the policy outcomes. The responses are given values that together would provide a social value measure of the potential supplier. This metric will be added to the standard evaluation of bidders and all factors would be weighted according to the preference of the local authority. Furthermore, evidencing the creation of social value will become an integral part of the requirements for suppliers in delivering upon the councils' contracts.

However, having established the principles and key criteria that should underpin SBC's approach to progressive procurement, it does not address the pragmatic issues that are present. Put simply, how can SBC manage the processes of initially awarding procurement contracts based on CWB and progressive procurement principles and then subsequently how they manage those contracts, ensuring that the promised impacts upon social value are delivered.

An initial suggestion from the Procurement Team at SBC was to make use of the Social Value Portal. This commercially available service gathers evidence in relation to the social value emanating from specific contracts. It is based upon themes, outcomes and measures that emerged from a National Social Value conference in 2017, with the key themes being as follows;

1   Jobs: promote local skills and employment.
2   Growth: supporting growth of responsible regional business.
3   Social: healthier, safer and more resilient communities.
4   Environment: decarbonising and safeguarding our world.
5   Innovation: promoting social innovation.

As an approach, the Social Value Portal has significant appeal for the implementation of CWB in Stevenage since it already exists, is immediately available and promises effective evidencing of social impacts that are of critical importance to the communities within the area. However, it was decided that, although the portal should be utilised in the short term, it does not offer the most effective means of awarding and managing procurement contracts to the benefit of the local community in the long term. There were 3 reasons why the Social Value Portal was not viewed as a long-term solution. Firstly, there was still a separation between the award of the contract and the subsequent management, SBC were hoping to integrate both of these processes into the same online platform. Secondly, there was a cost implication, since there was a charge in the region of £600–800 per contract for the collection of the social impact evidence. SBC were concerned that this cost would simply be passed on to the council, with any charge for evidence gathering being added to tenders being submitted for procurement contracts. Therefore, they were keen to explore the possibility of cheaper alternatives. Finally, there were also concerns about the effects upon local SMEs. It was thought likely that the upfront cost of the evidence gathering charge, disproportionately large for smaller enterprises, may act as a barrier and dissuade small local SMEs from bidding for contracts. Since these are clearly important agents and drivers within a successful CWB initiative, an approach that did not disadvantage local SMEs would obviously be preferable.

As a result of the 3 limitations outlined above SBC opted to utilise the Social Value Portal in the short term. This would enable their CWB to get off the ground and start to embed the principles of social value within their wider procurement stakeholders. While, at the same time, exploring the possibility of developing their own online platform for awarding and managing contracts that offer more effective long-term outcomes. The next section outlines the progress that has been made on this front.

Innovative delivery

As part of the partnership project between SBC and the University of Hertfordshire innovative approaches have been explored for more effective and efficient awarding and management of procurement contracts. This has led SBC and the UH team to pursue the possibility of a blockchain technology-based solution to these challenges.

From all of the above it is clear that there is potential within Stevenage Borough Council's existing procurement spend to significantly improve the quality of lives for people across the borough, but most specifically for those within the more disadvantaged wards. The challenge being to set up and implement a system that enables effective awarding and monitoring of contracts, while ensuring that the key areas of social value are delivered and evidenced within that system. One possibility that has emerged as a potential solution to this challenge is as a result of an existing collaboration between Hertfordshire Business School and Criterium Solutions; the latter is a consultancy firm specialising in digital solutions, which utilises blockchain technologies to develop effective business solutions. Below is an outline of what is planned to be put in place for SBC.

Driving innovation in procurement in Stevenage

The University of Hertfordshire is working in partnership with Criterium Solutions - an international specialist in Business Transformation - who last year, successfully completed a major project in the US focused on harnessing new technology to transform global procurement systems. Leveraging the University and Criterium's combined experiences creates an opportunity for SBC to be at the forefront of innovation in local authority procurement by conducting a small-scale pilot study to trial a transformative new technology approach in collaboration with two or three of its major suppliers. It has already been established from the Contracts Register that the bulk of SBC's procurement spend is destined for a small number of very large contracts, so this small pilot will still cover the bulk of the council's total procurement spend. It is envisaged that significant cost savings and process improvements will ensue as well as giving full transparency to sourcing product and prioritising local suppliers in the Stevenage first policy arena.

New technology approach

The technology set to transform supply chains globally is called Blockchain. Due to the powerful encryption the technology uses it provides a fully secure method for tracking a product from source to acquisition and payment that is free from tampering, counterfeiting or fraud. As we emerge from COVID-19, it will be critical for all businesses and local authorities to have 100% traceability of product and the ability to track its progress throughout all stages of the supply chain.

The critical start point for this journey is to authenticate the product at source and then - supporting the Council's transition from paper-based records - capture the 'truth' about the product in a digitised form, i.e. create a 'digital asset' which is fully visible, trackable and traceable within Stevenage's supply chain ecosystem. Blockchain is the mechanism by which this is implemented.

Benefits of this transformative approach

Deployment of so-called smart contracts, enabling tamper proof agreements between parties which can execute themselves automatically according to preset terms. These contracts verify each transaction and can include automated payments that drastically reduce or eliminate back office invoice management and procure to pay processes. These contracts are fully auditable and transparent to agreed stakeholders. The technology (Blockchain) maintains the privacy and confidentiality of individual contract terms.

Full transparency and authenticity of goods can be achieved, and relevant authorisations, credentials and certifications cannot be compromised. Transparency embeds trust between the actors in the procurement cycle, reducing manual due diligence and paper processes. The quality of goods and services supplied can be visibly rated together with the performance of the supplier.

Purchase order management can be vastly improved with transactions visible to both the Council and Suppliers rather than using paperwork files. Placing, validating, and approving orders (as well as invoicing and payment) is often a manual process or uses older tech while here, Blockchain allows you to streamline the entire request to receipt process.

Additionally, since supplier onboarding and transparency can be enhanced, Stevenage can over time look to encourage local suppliers and local policy initiatives (e.g. fairer trading or minimum wage agreements) and capturing more of the procurement spend for the local economy. The overall upshot being that SBC will end up with an online platform for awarding and managing procurement contracts that is effective both in terms of awarding contracts to those suppliers most likely to have a significant impact upon social value and in terms of then subsequently being able to evidence the social value that is created. It will also ensure that the entire procurement process can be undertake in a more secure and transparent fashion while delivering cost savings for the management of contracts both for suppliers and for SBC themselves.

Concluding remarks

This chapter outlines and evidences the need for a CWB initiative within Stevenage, it also indicates the scope and potential within the current procurement spend to capture more of this for the greater benefit of the local economy. In addition it also suggests a social value measure that can be integrated as a key decision making and monitoring tool within the procurement process, finally, it also suggests one possible route through which all of this can be delivered, monitored and evidenced.

The last suggestion, developing a Blockchain technology solution, also offers the possibility of contract holders fully or partially funding the initial investment, since there are clear benefits and cost savings to both the Council as well as the contract holders. The solution can also underpin a compliance regime for the CWB initiative.

References

Cabinet Office (2019), Social Value in Government Procurement: A Consultation on How Government Should Take Account of Social Value in the Award of Central

Government Contracts. Retrieved from www.gov.uk/government/consultations/social-value-in-government-procurement. Accessed 5 November 2020.

Camden Creative Services (2019), *Healthy Streets, Healthy Travel, Healthy Lives: Camden Transport Strategy 2019–2041*, Camden Borough Council, London. Retrieved from www.camden.gov.uk/documents/20142/18708392/1925.7+Camden+Transport+Strategy_Main+Document_FV.pdf/d7b19f62-b88e-31d4-0606-5a78ea47ff30. Accessed 5 November 2020.

Cornforth, C. and Thomas, A. (1990), Cooperative Development Barriers, Support Structures and Cultural Factors, *Economic and Industrial Democracy*, 11 (4): 451–461.

Davies, S. (2019), Time to Solve Childhood Obesity: An Independent Report by the Chief Medical Officer. Retrieved from https://assets.publishing.service.gov.uk/government/uploads/system/uploads/attachment_data/file/837907/cmo-special-report-childhood-obesity-october-2019.pdf. Accessed 5 November 2020.

Dubb, S. (2016), Community Wealth Building Forms: What Are They and How to Use Them at the Local Level, *Academy of Management Perspectives*, 30 (2): 141–152.

Education and Skills Funding Agency (2020), Schools Block Funding Formulae 2020 to 2021: Analysis of Local Authorities' Schools Block Funding Formulae. Retrieved from https://assets.publishing.service.gov.uk/government/uploads/system/uploads/attachment_data/file/901324/Proforma_publication_commentary_2020_to_2021.pdf. Accessed 5 November 2020.

Guinan, J. and O'Neill, M. (2019), From Community-Wealth Building to System Change, *IPPR Progressive Review*, 25 (4): 383–393.

Hiscock, R., Murray, S., Brose, L., McEwen, A., Leonard, J., Dobbie, F., and Bauld, L. (2013), Behavioural Therapy for Smoking Cessation: The Effectiveness of Different Intervention Types for Disadvantaged and Affluent Smokers, *Addictive Behaviours*, 38 (11): 2787–2796.

Kontopantelis. E., Mamas, M.A., and van Marwijk H. (2018), Geographical Epidemiology of Health and Overall Deprivation in England, its Changes and Persistence from 2004 to 2015: A Longitudinal Spatial Population Study, *Journal of Epidemiol Community Health*; 72(2): 140–147.

Ministry of Housing, Communities and Local Government (2010), English Indices of Deprivation 2010. Retrieved from www.gov.uk/government/statistics/english-indices-of-deprivation-2010

Ministry of Housing, Communities and Local Government (2015), English Indices of Deprivation 2010. Retrieved from www.gov.uk/government/statistics/english-indices-of-deprivation-2015

Ministry of Housing, Communities and Local Government (2019), English Indices of Deprivation 2019. Retrieved from www.gov.uk/government/statistics/english-indices-of-deprivation-2019. Accessed 5 November 2020.

Noble, M., Wright, G., and Smith, G. (2006), Measuring Multiple Deprivation at the Small-Area Level, *Environment and Planning*, 38 (1): 169–185.

Noble, S., McLennan, D., Noble, M., Plunkett, E., Gutacker, N., Silk, M., and Wright, G. (2019), *The English Indices of Deprivation 2019: Research Report*, Ministry of Housing, Communities and Local Government, London. Retrieved from https://assets.publishing.service.gov.uk/government/uploads/system/uploads/attachment_data/file/833947/IoD2019_Research_Report.pdf. Accessed 5 November 2020.

Northern Ireland Statistics and Research Agency (2017), Northern Ireland Multiple Deprivation Measure 2017. Retrieved from www.nisra.gov.uk/statistics/deprivation/

northern-ireland-multiple-deprivation-measure-2017-nimdm2017. Accessed 5 November 2020.

Petrovic, A., Manley, D., and van Ham, H. (2019), Freedom from the Tyranny of Neighbourhood: Rethinking Socio-spatial Context Effects, *Progress in Human Geography*, 44 (6): 1103–1123.

Public Health England (2020), Disparities in the Risk and Outcomes of COVID-19. Public Health England. Retrieved from https://assets.publishing.service.gov.uk/government/uploads/system/uploads/attachment_data/file/908434/Disparities_in_the_risk_and_outcomes_of_COVID_August_2020_update.pdf. Accessed 5 November 2020.

Scottish Government (2020), The Scottish Index of Multiple Deprivation 2020. Retrieved from www.gov.scot/publications/scottish-index-multiple-deprivation-2020. Accessed 5 November 2020.

Spear, R. (2004), Governance in Democratic Member-Based Organisations, *Annals of Public and Cooperative Economics*, 75 (1): 33–60.

Stevenage Borough Council (2019), *Equality & Diversity Information for Stevenage 2018–19*. Retrieved from www.stevenage.gov.uk/documents/equality-and-diversity/equality-and-diversity-report-2018-19-acc.pdf. Accessed 16 November 2020.

Stevenage Borough Council (2020), Community Wealth Building. Retrieved from https://democracy.stevenage.gov.uk/ieDecisionDetails.aspx?Id=1444. Accessed 16 November 2020.

Welsh Government (2019), Welsh Index of Multiple Deprivation. Retrieved from https://gov.wales/welsh-index-multiple-deprivation. Accessed 5 November 2020.

8   The economics of the Preston Model

Philip B. Whyman

From humble beginnings ...

The Preston Model emerged out of the collapse of a £700 million Tithebarn retail regeneration scheme[1], as a direct consequence of the credit crunch and economic stagnation following the 2008 global financial crisis. The resulting coalition government austerity policies, and the most severe reductions in public spending since the Second World War, resulted in a 49.1% real terms reduction in central government funding to local authorities between 2010–11 and 2017–18, with less affluent areas experiencing disproportionate cuts (Pugalis and Bentley, 2014: 669; NAO, 2018: 15). Perhaps, not surprisingly, this has been described as a period of 'super-austerity', with effects being compounded upon local communities through multiplier effects and economic growth paths degraded (Townsend and Champion, 2014: 49; Lowndes and Gardner, 2016: 358–359).

This combination was, and indeed, still remains particularly problematic for an area like central Lancashire. Yet, unlike many other local authorities who have adopted 'austerian realism' with varying degrees of enthusiasm or attempted mitigation (Davies and Blanco, 2017), the response in Preston, by policy makers and key local stakeholders, has been innovative (Lyall and Lua, 2015). The stress that austerity placed upon the local delivery of services would appear to have created the 'push' incentives for certain local policy makers to experiment with alternative forms of economic development (McInroy, 2016: 25), where weakened or 'hollowed out' local authorities seek to *steer* rather than *direct* activity (Rhodes, 2007: 1254–1257). In that, to quote Plato (*Republic*, Book II), 'the true creator is necessity, who is the mother of our invention'.

The economic foundations of the Preston Model

As stated elsewhere in this book, the Preston Model is a particular type of community wealth building (CWB). The intent is to mobilise under-utilised local assets and capacity, in the form of human (i.e. skills and knowledge), social (i.e. personal networks, culture and community solidarity), environmental (i.e. the built environment and natural assets), institutional (i.e. local authorities and educational institutions) and physical capital (i.e. local firms and local savings), to drive economic development (Tomaney, 2010: 6; Pugalis and Bentley, 2014). Rather than subsidising the activities of trans-national firms attracted into the area, the CWB approach seeks to develop existing local assets to expand economic activity while ensuring that much of the resulting gains are retained and anchored in place, to the benefit of the local community. In this sense, Preston is not unique, as many aspects of the approach are shared by other localities, both in the UK (i.e. Oldham, the Wirral, Glasgow, North Ayrshire, North of Tyne, Birmingham, Manchester, Bristol and the London boroughs of Newham, Islington and Hackney), Canada (i.e. Ontario) and the USA (i.e. Cleveland Ohio, New York City, Albuquerque New Mexico and Richmond Virginia). However, few have embraced as many of the facets of the approach as thoroughly as Preston.[2] That is why the Preston Model has been considered to be the 'exemplar of this approach' (Heslop et al., 2019: 8).

The Preston Model is an *indirect* policy initiative, with the primary initiator of the strategy, Preston City Council (PCC), acting as the mobilising agent to encourage other organisations to reconfigure their own activities to generate local economic benefit. Thus, while PCC can act as role model, encourage, facilitate and structure debate, it has little direct control and depends upon anchor-partners to initiate most activity. This has caused criticism that such initiatives are 'piecemeal' (Bailey, 2003: 443), although others argue that the value of coordinating the actions of stakeholders to regenerate their local communities has considerable value (Thake, 2001). The Preston Model is therefore an interesting example of policy strategy, in that it is coordinated by a central actor weaker in resource terms than most anchor participants, yet it has nevertheless successfully framed the CWB approach and mobilised local capacity to address three primary motivations, namely:

i   a reaction to an unfavourable economic environment;
ii the need to develop an alternative model of economic development reliant more upon the 'economics of place' rather than seeking to attract footloose external capital; and
iii regaining (or 'taking back') greater control over the local economy for the benefits of its citizens.

The specific approach adopted, and the pathways to achieving social and economic objectives, are illustrated in Figure 8.1.

Anchor institutions

The importance of major local employers to local economies has long been recognised, by those charged with steering regional economic development. However, the combination of globalisation, deindustrialisation, capital relocating away from urban areas and the neglect of active regional policy measures due to neo-liberal hegemony deindustrialisation, resulted in greater emphasis being placed upon those large-scale employers which became increasingly important for local economies (Maurrasse, 2001; Smallbone et al., 2015: 2).

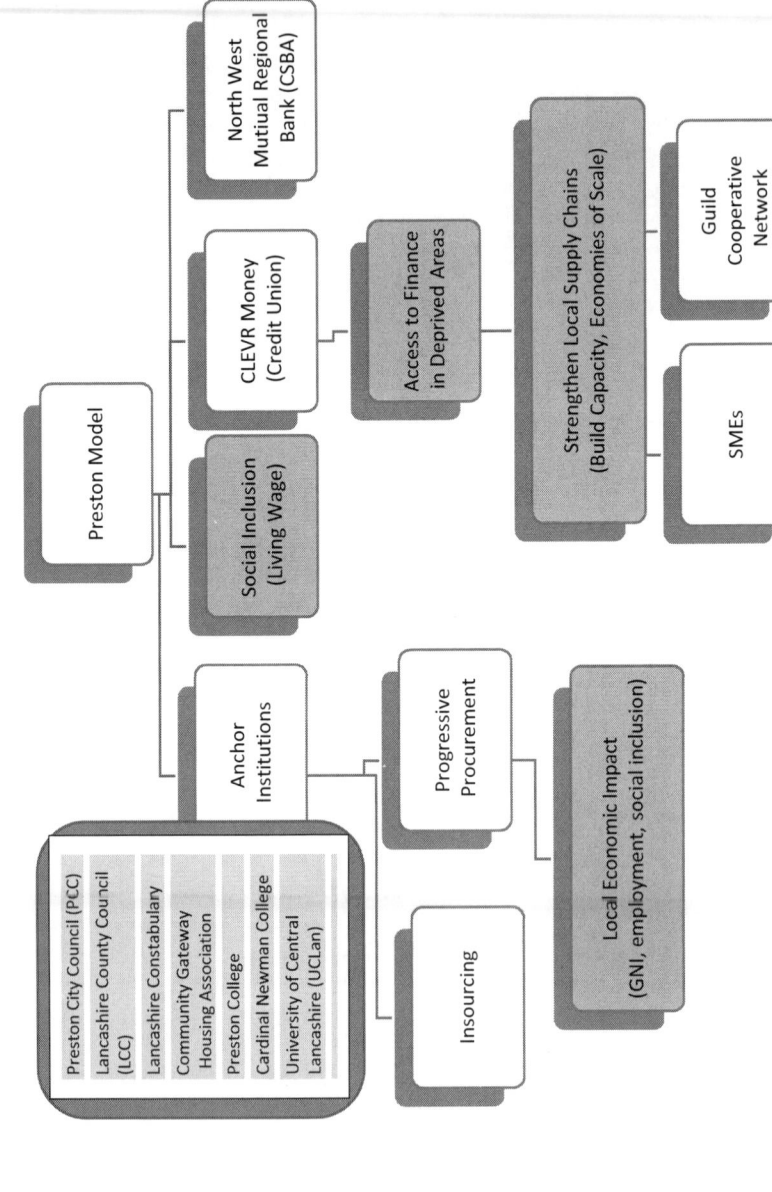

Figure 8.1 The Inter-Related Aspects of the Preston Model

The concept of 'anchor institutions' emerged from the USA in response to the perceived need to harness the potential of existing institutions to address the needs of urban communities. Anchor institutions share certain characteristics which ties them to the local area. This can be through the investment of significant sunk capital, or their relationship with stakeholders (i.e. customers, employees, supportive institutions and local policymakers), their institutional mission (Webber and Karlstrom, 2009; Smallbone et al., 2015). As such, anchors tend to be 'sticky' or spatially immobile, and unlikely to relocate. They are also likely to have a significant presence in the local community, whether through their direct employment, procurement expenditure, their provision of human capital formation or their importance in innovation spillovers. The two most prominent examples of anchor institutions are universities and hospitals – the so-called 'eds and meds' (Harkavy and Zuckerman, 1999; Bartik and Erickcek, 2008). Nevertheless, there are a range of potential anchor organisations, including other higher and further education institutions, cultural institutions including theatres, museums and libraries, religious and faith-based establishments, military bases and sports clubs (Smallbone et al., 2015:vii).

Local economic development is not a primary objective for anchor organisations. However, they do have an enlightened self-interest in the creation of an attractive local environment, as this assists their attraction and retention of staff and customers (Dubb and Howard, 2012; Smallbone et al., 2015: 2). They have the potential to generate local economic impact in a number of ways, whether directly, through their employment or remuneration decisions, investment in infrastructure, human capital development or the services they offer to the community, or indirectly, through the use of procurement policy to strengthen local supply chains, their influence over wages more generally within the local labour market and spillovers ranging from productivity effects to mitigating crime and enhancing civic engagement. The multifaceted contributions that anchor institutions can make to the local community, drawn from the literature, are summarised in Table 8.1, with those areas where the Preston Model anchor institutions have made distinctive contributions illustrated in darker shading, and unshaded cells representing those in the process of development.

There is a sizeable literature which has considered the social and economic impact that anchors can make in their local area. Increased expenditure by anchors has been found to raise wages for the local population (Moretti, 2004), and enhance innovation (Bartik and Erickcek, 2008: 19). Universities and other higher education providers can generate 'export' or 'import substitution' effects, through attracting students and high skilled staff into the locality; an effect particularly significant in smaller metropolitan areas (Bartik and Erickcek, 2008: 7–8). Local firms (particularly SMEs) benefit from many of the management and leadership development programmes run by local universities, while start-ups can benefit from business incubation facilities (Smallbone et al., 2015: 15). Other spillover benefits are more difficult to quantify, such as lower crime rates and improvements to community health and civic responsibility, yet even here there is tentative evidence to suggest that impact can be identified. Finally, it is

Table 8.1 Anchor institutional framework

	Potential anchor impact		
	Economic development	Physical	Community building
Provision of products and services tailored to local community	DC		
Insourcing of services	PCC/CLES		
Channelling financial capital to the local economy	DC, WF, PCC/CLES		
Plurality of ownership of the economy (co-operatives, municipal ownership)	PCC/CLES		
Access to finance in deprived areas			
Procurement (GNI multiplier, build local supply chains)	ICIC, DC, WF, WK, PCC/CLES		
Employer (local)	ICIC, DC, WF, BE, WK		
Social inclusion and fair employment (minority employment, living wage)	DC, PCC/CLES		
Developing local labour force skills	ICIC, WF, BE		
Attract inflow of high skilled workers	WF, WK		
Raises wages in local labour market	BE		
Increases productivity	BE		
Stimulate innovation and research capacity (R&D spillovers)	WF, BE, WK		
Business start-ups and Incubation	DC, BE, WK		
Cultural development, heritage preservation	DC, WF		WF
Reputational capital (identity)	WF, WK		
Real estate development		ICIC, WF, WK	
Affordable housing		DC	
Infrastructure and neighbourhood (i.e. streetscape)		DC, WF, PCC/CLES	
Community infrastructure (capacity building resources)			ICIC, DC, WF, PCC/CLES
Education and outreach			ICIC, DC, WF, WK
Enhance public discourse and public life			WF, WK
Healthy community			DC, WK
Healthy local environment			DC
Safe environment			DC, WK

Source: adapted from Bartik and Erickcek (2008) [BE]; Webber and Karlström (2009) [WK]; ICIC (2011) [ICIC]; Dubb et al. (2013) [DC]; Ehlenz (2018); Jones and Leibowitz (2019) [PCC/CLES]; Morris et al. (2020) [WF]

suggested that anchor institutions can assist in contextualising the community and its networks, and thereby enhance the resilience of the community in difficult times (Clopton and Finch, 2011: 70–73).

Not all effects are necessarily beneficial, of course. An influx of highly skilled workers may place upward pressure upon house prices, which may benefit those with property assets but increase affordability concerns for younger, less affluent members of the local community. The University of Pennsylvania, for instance, has long faced critiques of 'Penntrifying' its immediate locality, with the consequence of squeezing out existing residents over the medium term (Ehlenz, 2018: 88). Similarly, while the evidence suggests that the inward attraction of skilled labour and the development of high skilled job opportunities does tend to benefit the local economy as a whole, this is unlikely to be evenly distributed across the local community and many of these newly created posts may require skill or education levels in excess of those held by particularly disadvantaged groups (Dubb and Howard, 2012: 14–15).

One additional observation from the literature, which is worthy of note, concerns the possibility that social and economic impacts may remain suboptimal, as anchor institutions tend to over-estimate the financial cost and reputational risk associated with engaging in initiatives to benefit the local community (Webber and Karlström, 2009: 17–18). To the extent that a coordinated approach (such as the Preston Model) can demonstrate the potential of anchor institutional local economic impact then, *ceteris paribus*, net social and economic benefits should be enhanced.

Procurement

Procurement, if used strategically, can build supply chains and has been used in countries such as the USA to further innovation, develop high technology industries and reduce economic imbalances pertaining across the UK, thereby facilitating sustainable economic development (HMG, 2017: 18, 21). It can facilitate environmental goals, by encouraging small scale farmers to link more directly with sections of the public sector (i.e. schools, hospitals, elderly care facilities and/or prisons), where the sourcing of local foods could enhance the quality of meals while delivering environmental benefits through shortening supply chains and reducing food miles (Jones and Leibowitz, 2019: 9). Moreover, local procurement can be used to reduce leakages from a local economy, while strengthening supply chains, attracting skilled workers to an area and boosting growth potential (HMG, 2017: 120).

Rules imposed by the European Union, to protect the integrity of the single internal market, prevent preference being awarded to a particular firm, industry or locality in the awarding of a contract (HMG, 2017: 71).[3] However, the introduction of new procurement rules, and their transposition into UK law via the Public Services (Social Value) Act 2012,[4] enabled the splitting of large procurement contracts into smaller segments and use of a 'balanced scorecard' approach to allow 'social value' criteria to be included alongside cost considerations in the awarding of contracts (HMG, 2017: 18, 71–72). Value could, thereafter, be considered to reflect social, environmental, and wider economic aspects, rather than simply least cost solutions. Contract criteria could, therefore, include workforce diversity, collaboration with the voluntary and community sector, establishing minimum labour standards, skills development, promoting access to digital technology, encouraging health and wellbeing, the creation of employment opportunities within a local community or disadvantaged groups, enhanced opportunities for SMEs, enhancing the UK economic growth, heritage protection, carbon reductions and environmental protection (DCMS, 2018: 2–3). It is this enhanced procurement flexibility which has enabled the Preston Model to use procurement to enhance social, environmental and economic aspects of the local economy. Withdrawal from the EU would further simplify procurement rules, if these were subject to WTO rules.

Insourcing of services

The outsourcing of organisational internal activities, undertaken to reduce costs and diversify risk; subcontracting tasks to firms capable of carrying them out more efficiently, and enabling the organisation to focus upon core competencies (Feenstra, 1998). However, outsourcing incurs costs associated with a lack of control of activity, weakness in transparency and loss of employee morale (Lankford and Parsa, 1999). Consequently, there has been a recent trend to revise supply chains by bringing some previously outsourced activities back in house, thereby reinstituting greater control and aspects of vertical integration into the production process (Ellram et al., 2013; Drauz, 2014). In Preston, both the Lancashire Constabulary and Community Gateway anchor institutions have both made decisions to bring previously outsourced services back in-house over recent years, with the intention to strengthen employment terms and conditions, while generating greater local economic benefit and strengthening democratic oversight of the service (Jones and Leibowitz, 2019: 27).

Steering finance

Successful economic development strategies rest upon access to inexpensive and patient finance to increase flows of productive investment. The Mondragon co-operative group in the Basque Country of Spain, for example, was facilitated by the establishment of the Caja Laboral bank, while Sweden has the Jord Arbete Kapital Medlemsbank (Land Labour Capital Members Bank) and Germany the state-owned regional Landesbanken, all promoting a mixture of co-operative, public purpose and regional development objectives. An important element, in the Mondragon scheme, is the combination of training, business support and access to finance to facilitate the establishment of a network of co-operatives; the Evergreen co-operative network, in Cleveland Ohio, has sought to achieve similar objectives through its Fund for Employee Ownership (Jones and Leibowitz, 2019: 27).

In the UK, proposals have been made to harness existing wealth within a locality to increase flows of capital for local investment opportunities through a combination of the establishment of mutually owned regional banks and the redirection of public sector pension fund focus from global to local investment opportunities. One example of the former, in the UK, is the Community Savings Bank Association (CSBA) which aims to establish 18 regional co-operative banks across the UK.[5] If achieved correctly, the steering of investment could combine a good rate of return for investors with increased investment to local communities.

The Preston Model incorporates three main initiatives related to local finance. The first involved the incorporation of a financial co-operative, CLEVR Money[6] credit union, operating across Blackpool, Preston and the Fylde coast, where its 4700 anchor employees and community members have deposited £5 million payroll savings which in turn, has resulted in £13 million 'affordable' loans. The intention is to support access to finance in deprived areas of the city. The second initiative concerns steering a proportion of the investment portfolio of the Lancashire Government Pension Fund (LGPF), towards local rather than global projects. Out of total assets of £5.5 billion, the LGPF has thus far allocated approximately £100 million for investment in Preston and South Ribble, and an equivalent amount across the remainder of Lancashire (Jones and Leibowitz, 2019: 15). Projects include the construction of new student accommodation, the redevelopment of the Park Hotel and renewable energy (Lockley and Glover, 2019: 13, 23). Finally, the PCC is investigating the possibility of establishing a regional bank, supported by the patronage of the anchor institutions, and with the intention of providing an alternative source of inexpensive finance for local SMEs.

Plurality of ownership

The plurality of ownership often forms an element of CWB strategies, because it is perceived as reducing the influence of powerful, vested interests, and thereby enhancing participative democracy across civil society (Jackson and McInroy, 2015: 6). This could be achieved through the establishment of municipal enterprises or through the establishment of worker co-operatives. PCC and the University of Central Lancashire (UCLan) have introduced initiatives intended to diversify ownership. One approach has been to work with a network of technology co-operatives (Co-Tech) to bid to supply services for local schools and universities. Similar initiatives have involved working with the Community Gateway Housing Association, a tenant-led housing cooperative, and an employee-owned transport consultancy (TAS) (Brown and O'Neill, 2016: 71). A 'Guild Co-operative Network' was established, now replaced by the Preston Cooperative Development Network, to provide the training, business support and access to start-up finance to generate growth of co-operatives in the city.

Critique

Given the prominence that the Preston Model has assumed in the political debate over the previous few years, and the potentially transformational nature of the initiative if adopted more widely across the UK, it is not surprising that it has received considerable criticism, particularly from orthodox economists.

The most prominent critique of the Preston Model concerns the inefficiency of protectionism. If local producers are preferred to more efficient external suppliers, then *in the short run at least*, this will be expected to increase costs and reduce efficient allocation of activity; in economic terminology, it will be Pareto inefficient. Moreover, a range of studies forecast potential welfare gains from the liberalisation of public procurement (Dixon et al., 2017). A prominent 2018 article in *The Economist* magazine founded their opposition to widespread adoption of the Preston Model on this basis.

There are a number of weaknesses with this conclusion, not the least of which concerns the assumptions inherent in the economics textbook view of the world upon which this criticism is based, such as the assumption of continuous market clearing, the operation of Say's Law, rational expectations and an industrial structure characterised by perfect competition. None is this reflects reality. Economies rarely (if ever) operate in conditions of steady-state equilibrium, with the full employment of all resources. Even a cursory glance at the UK's own history over the past two decades will attest to the inadequacy of the neo-classical model on this crucial point. Thus crowding out is far less of a problem than many orthodox economists assert. Pareto efficiency, where resources are efficiently allocated and rewards distributed according to individual effort or abilities, is hard to justify where Gini coefficients indicate substantial inequalities in income and the work of Piketty (2013) and others highlights the widening inequalities in wealth. As a result, predictions of the beneficial impacts arising from economic liberalisation often over-estimate realisable gains, while few seek to quantify the distribution of predicted benefits. It is quite likely that some countries will gain little, or indeed suffer losses in terms of output and employment, even as consumers in aggregate may benefit from price reductions. Moreover, these studies do not seek to include externalities into their modelling, even though social and environmental impacts are often key motivations for social value procurement practices.

Moving away from the restrictive assumptions underpinning neoclassical theory, it may be necessary, when designing economic policy interventions to deal with real world problems, not to sacrifice a realisable second-best outcome by chasing after an unrealisable textbook optimum solution. Rodrik (2000: 180–183) highlighted the policy trade-offs that face public policy makers seeking to achieve simultaneously deep economic integration, national sovereignty and maintain democratic and/or policy autonomy. The logic of this 'inescapable trilemma' is that nations, which prioritise sovereignty and democratic policy autonomy may need to disengage from certain aspects of globalisation. The alternative is for economic integration to place a 'golden straightjacket' upon policy options.

Perhaps not surprisingly, therefore, a consensus does not exist within the economics literature that protectionism is always inefficient and produces negative outcomes. There are, for example, arguments relating to its necessity in the development of infant industries and others which possess competitive advantages but high scale thresholds, while active industrial policies that facilitate the development of domestic industries and encourage R&D expenditure can produce macroeconomic benefits, particularly for those nations suffering significant trade deficits or structural unemployment (Orchard and Stretton, 1997: 416; Mazzucato, 2013). Furthermore, the evidence is quite strong that those economies which utilised active industrial policy outperformed other large OECD economies between 1950 and 1987 (Chang, 2009: 7–8). Thus, a final judgement upon the relative merits of protectionism and interventionism would appear to depend upon the type proposed, the prevailing circumstances and acceptance of policy trade-offs to be achieved.

The economic literature considering the type of local protectionism, ascribed to the Preston Model, is less developed. Nevertheless, it would seem plausible that local communities might engage with the policy trade-offs that Rodrik's trilemma describes, and as a result, to prioritise local democratic empowerment over the dictates of economic integration. Particularly for more marginalised or 'left behind' communities, where market forces have not worked to the advantage of the local population, there may be strong arguments for regaining greater control over their economic lives and thereby helping to preserve aspects of social identity and cohesion (Goff, 2007: 5–6, 14–15).

In addition, advocates of CWB claim that it may create a more efficient spatial distribution of goods and services, due to a relocation of activity towards areas of higher unemployment and spare capacity (Dubb and Howard, 2012: 2; Jones and Leibowitz, 2019: 9). If, for example, the Preston Model results in a relocation of activity from the over-heated southeast to less affluent localities in the north of England, this would deliver the kind of macroeconomic rebalancing that successive Chancellors of the Exchequer have advocated, and which forms the rationale for the creation of the Northern Powerhouse policy programme. Thus, to this extent, even if the Preston Model is considered to be an example of economic protectionism, which is certainly not a straightforward conclusion to reach, there may be perfectly valid justifications for the adoption of certain elements of protectionism to empower economically marginalised areas.

A second, and related criticism, is that protectionism will result in a reduction in competition, as external firms are excluded or local firms given precedence, while the inclusion of *any* additional factors into procurement determination, rather than simply awarding contracts on the basis of lowest cost, will inevitably increase costs (Lockley and Glover, 2019: 30–31).

The impact of the Preston Model upon competition has not yet been established. However, it is certainly quite plausible for the splitting of tenders into smaller segments to encourage a greater proliferation of SMEs to bid for contracts, thereby enhancing competition, while one stated aim of CWB is to facilitate service innovation and the development of new areas of activity which, if realised, would increase consumer choice (Dubb and Howard, 2012: 2).[7] It is also important to recognise that there is no single *modus operandi* which ensures superior outcomes. The use of the Compulsory Competitive Tendering (CCT) process, to liberalise local authority service provision during the 1980s, had mixed results, trading off initial cost savings (which tended to decline over time) while introducing additional transaction costs, rent-seeking behaviour on the part of private contractors, alongside issues relating to service quality, trust and transparency (Boyne, 1998: 703–704, 710; Bovaird, 2016: 67–68). The CCT process additionally tended to create oligopolistic rather than competitive markets (Reimer, 1999: 123). Moreover, the reliance upon least cost contract awards omitted consideration of externalities, leading to awards which were not socially optimum. The recognition of this fact led to the introduction of the Public Services (Social Value) Act 2012. Hence, a criticism that the local procurement may have a broader focus than the sole goal of minimising cost of service delivery, is the explicit intention of EU and UK government policy. Rather than focus upon issues of cost in isolation, the critique should instead seek to ascertain whether the local procurement approach takes into account externalities effectively, so that social benefits are optimised.

A third criticism focuses upon the scalability of the Preston Model.[8] To the extent that procurement preference schemes succeed, firm beneficiaries may wish to realise economies of scale through expanding sales beyond regional boundaries, thereby reducing local purchasing elsewhere. If so, the Preston Model becomes a self-defeating example of a zero-sum game – displacing rather than enhancing activity.[9] Moreover, this becomes an economic loss if efficient activity is displaced by less efficient local producers, or other areas engage in retaliation against what they regard as unfair trade advantages.

This argument presumes that scalability cannot occur within a local or regional market. Yet, the regional equivalent of the infant industry argument suggests that this can certainly occur, at least in the short or medium term, as fast growth (scale-up) SMEs have their development facilitated, thereby enhancing the efficiency of the local economy. This, in turn, may facilitate macroeconomic regional rebalancing and allow faster growth to occur without stoking up inflationary pressures. It may be accurate to surmise that, in the long term, these firms may wish to expand beyond regional boundaries, but as Keynes was apt to note, in the long run we are all dead! In the meantime, emergent SMEs will have enhanced their efficiency and among these fast growth firms may be international champions of the future.

The critique additionally downplays potential social and economic benefits which may arise from the assisted development of different types of organisation. Elsewhere in this book, the potential economic advantages of co-operatives and democratic firms have been evaluated. There is, for example, a solid evidence base for longer term decision making, greater use of teamwork and other forms of functional flexibility, higher organisational commitment leading on to enhanced performance and more resilient (DeCotiis and Summers, 1987; Kurtulus and Kruse, 2017: 12).

A fourth line of criticism focuses upon the central feature of CWB, namely the emphasis upon the local economy and community. This can be challenged on the grounds that centring upon a fixed geographical place underpinning long term individual commitment, is too inflexible and idealised. For many highly skilled individuals in particular, occupational mobility necessitates transience, resulting in lower identification with social relations derived from a single geographical location.[10] Mobility can lessen multiplier effects deriving from the activities of a firm operating in a given locality (Whyman, 2018), and can weaken the ability for transient groups to retain or share community wealth following relocation. In addition, it is difficult to define the optimum size of a local community or, indeed, when a firm may or may not be accepted as 'local'.[11] Should the Preston Model be considered to be the 'Lancashire Model', since the impact across the county was always a central feature of the initiative, alongside the benefit to the city of Preston more narrowly? Should Nissan be considered an integral part of the Sunderland economy, despite their foreign ownership, perhaps on the basis of their duration of operations (since 1984) or size of employment? Are subsidiaries of Trans-National Corporations operating within the local economy counted as truly local, even if they have negligible local presence and are little more than letterbox companies? In terms of size and importance of local employment and skills spillovers, British Aerospace is considered to be a central pillar of the Preston/Lancashire economy. Yet, to what extent is the company truly local, since it operates in 40 countries worldwide and with employment at Samlesbury representing only around 3.5% of its global workforce?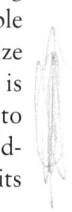

These questions highlight the difficulties inherent in the design of any set of rules underpinning a central CWB approach. Interestingly, certain supporters of the approach concur with this critique, arguing that CWB initiatives should be considered to be more of an 'inspiration' for activity designed to be 'unique to place', rather than an 'off-the-peg' generic model (Jones and Leibowitz, 2019: 22, 25). What this line of criticism does not do, however, is repudiate or reject the Preston Model approach. Rather, it highlights the difficulties inherent in designing a successful policy intervention.

A fifth concern derives from public choice theory, namely that any lack of transparency or ambiguity in contract allocation can potentially give rise to corruption, rent seeking or capture. As a result, favoured producers might charge prices above those that would otherwise be necessary, and this 'economic rent' reduces economic welfare. Firm beneficiaries have an incentive to 'capture' local decision makers, to prevent the weakening of protection advantages, whether through extolling the virtues of retaining protections for the local economy, or through corrupt practices.

The UK is fortunate in that its public servants are overwhelmingly beyond reproach. Nevertheless, the potential for corrupt practices to occur in any walk of life is always a possibility, whether this being in the public or private sectors. Transparency in decision making is a key element in mitigating this risk. Advocates for CWB would argue that its central feature is the engagement and empowerment of the local community, through greater democratic control over the economic sphere, and consequently this might result in greater (not less) scrutiny over key decision making. The Preston Model additionally involves regular meetings of anchor procurement officers, where priorities are discussed and achievements monitored, rather than these decisions being made in isolation by smaller groups of individuals. The possibility of 'capture' by interested parties, who benefit from the introduction of the Preston Model, should act as a cautionary note to policymakers and anchor institutions. However, popular participation within the local community should lessen this possibility, as decisions would ultimately be democratically determined and monitored by community stakeholders.

A sixth criticism claims that the Preston Model will lead to greater vulnerability for the local area, as future budget cuts for public sector anchors, the reorganisation of service delivery or changes in demand may all impact negatively upon the ability of anchor institutions to drive the economic development of the area (Morris et al., 2010; Lockley and Glover, 2019: 29–30). This would be a valid concern but for three things. The first is that, as outlined in the next section of this chapter, fiscal austerity has indeed reduced the total procurement expenditure of the anchor institutions, yet the economic impact on the Preston and Lancashire economies actually improved directly because of the operation of the Preston Model. Moreover, this criticism would have greater validity if focused upon a single anchor institution, underpinning the local economy. However, the Preston Model involves multiple anchors, which naturally diversifies this risk. Furthermore, the critique overlooks the original motivation for introducing the Preston Model, namely that the economy was underperforming because of a lack of investment, while leakages from the local economy were further weakening economic development opportunities. Preston was already vulnerable, and the CWB initiative was introduced as an attempt to rectify this weakness.

Concerns have also been raised over the potential conflict between the fiduciary duty, placed upon local government pension schemes to ameliorate risk and deliver maximum value to policyholders, and the desire to utilise this capital to fund local investment opportunities (Lockley and Glover, 2019: 45–46). This is a valid concern, and monitoring should occur to ensure the viability of local investments. Yet, it is important to recollect what local government pension funds represent, namely the deferred earnings of workers within the local community. Consequently, it would seem justifiable if investment determination was at least partly influenced by the expressed democratic will of the community as a whole, as long as the interests of workers and pensioners were protected in the process.

An eighth criticism notes that there is no *a priori* reason why the CWB approach is necessarily progressive or democratic. This is true. Local economies could be strengthened by encouraging the development of new privately owned firms and need not strengthen local democratic institutions. Yet the anchoring of future wealth is more effective if local communities are empowered and co-operatives or other forms of democratic enterprises are established, since they are more likely to remain rooted within the local economy. Moreover, any lack of grounding in patterns of democratic participation would result in CWB initiatives forfeiting perceptions of legitimacy and the potential inherent in the enthusiastic participation of large sections of the local community (Quinn, 2017: 294). This is not to downplay the difficulties inherent in reconciling 'complexities of empowerment' and mitigating against conflict and the exclusion of marginalised groups (Skerratt and Steiner, 2013: 335). Nevertheless, while a privatised and elite-led variant of CWB might be possible, it would be likely to suffer the lack of transparency and responsiveness to local needs that has so bedevilled previous attempts to embed the private sector into key aspects of public service delivery (Whyman, 2019).

The final critique identifies the possible exceptionalism of the Preston Model. If accurate, rather than the experience of CWB in Preston demonstrating a valid development strategies for other areas of the UK and beyond, it is possible that Preston may be the 'Goldilocks' city for the development of the CWB approach – sufficiently large to possess the infrastructure and range of businesses necessary to take advantage of the opportunities created, but small enough for coordination of a handful of anchor institutions to have a sizeable impact upon the local economy.[12] While Preston may be viewed, by commentators located in London, as relatively peripheral on a national or global comparison, it is the central hub of the Lancashire economy. Consequently, it is important to ascertain whether any successes ascribed to the Preston Model have been distributed widely across the city and/or more peripheral and deprived areas within Lancashire, or gains are disproportionately accrued by already successful firms, sectors and localities.[13]

Evidence

The main body of evidence relating to the performance of the Preston Model, derives from the work of the Centre for Local Economic Strategies (CLES), which were commissioned by PCC to operationalise the procurement element of the Preston Model after they had performed a similar service for the Greater Manchester local authorities. In Manchester, CLES analysis indicated that, between 2008/9 and 2015/16, of the share of procurement expenditure received by the 300 largest suppliers, the proportion retained within the Manchester economy increased from 51.5% to 73.6%, with commensurate increases of supply chain re-spend within the local area from 0.25 to 0.43 over the same time period (Jackson, 2017: 21–22). Given that the total procurement expenditure in question is approximately £1 billion, this equated to around £221 million additional demand circulating in the Manchester economy, which was equivalent to 1.1% of Manchester's annual GVA.

The Preston procurement measures were even more significant for the local economy, with the share of local procurement expenditure (received by the 300 largest suppliers), rising from 5% to 18.2% within Preston, between 2012/13 and 2016/17, and from 39% to 79.2% in Lancashire as a whole. Thus, at a time when austerity measures had reduced the total procurement spend for the five initial Preston Model anchor institutions, from £750 million to £620 million per annum, the realised economic boost from procurement to the Preston economy increased by £74 million and for Lancashire the equivalent gain was £200 million (Jones and Leibowitz, 2019: 11–13, 32). Since the mid-Lancashire (NUTS-3, including Preston) 2017 GVA was £12.1 billion and Lancashire (NUTS-2) as a whole £32.7 billion,[14] Preston Model procurement annual expenditure represented 5.12% of annual Preston GVA and 1.9% for Lancashire. Additional anecdotal evidence emerges from internal analysis of the procurement strategy, from within PCC, which is reported as claiming that more SMEs have bid for procurement contracts, thereby increasing competition and choice, while the large majority of repatriated expenditure has substituted for prior multinational or other large suppliers based in the southeast, thereby leading to greater economic rebalancing.[15]

Given the significant direct economic impacts that CLES figures suggest, this should be corroborated by indirect evidence concerning macroeconomic factors such as growth rates, employment opportunities and human capital investment. Interestingly, ONS figures indicate that both GDP and GDP per head in Mid Lancashire, of which Preston is part, have both been growing faster than the UK average from 2013, when Preston Model initiatives were first introduced.[16] Similarly, in terms of labour productivity (GVA per hour worked), mid Lancashire growth rates exceeded national averages.[17] In terms of unemployment, Preston moved from above to below average, following the introduction of the Preston Model programme, albeit that the impact of the COVID-19 pandemic has negatively impacted upon this area of performance.[18] Not surprisingly, given these trends, Preston's ranking in terms of the Index of Multiple Deprivation has maintained the improvement noted by Lockley and Glover (2019: 34–39).[19] This improvement has been further highlighted by the PriceWaterhouse Coopers Good Growth for Cities annual index. From an initial weak ranking, PwC estimated that Preston was the best performing city in the northwest, and ahead of London on most criteria (Hawkworth et al., 2018: 2, 8, 12, 15–16). Once again, this turning point corresponded to the time period when the Preston Model was introduced.

One point for concern, however, is that the most recent index suggests that Preston's trajectory of improvement has flattened, limited by persistent non-graduate skills deficit, low wages and inequality (PwC, 2019). This raises the question concerning whether the Preston Model has the ability to result in long term, sustainable improvement, or whether it represents an initial short term boost to GVA and employment, but it might not be as effective as achieving efficiency gains necessary to sustain this improvement longer term.

These conclusions appear rather promising. It is, therefore, not surprising that advocates of the Preston Model have taken this as proof of the vitality of the approach. Unfortunately, this evidence is not sufficient to draw this conclusion. The CLES study is not independent, as they were paid by PCC to undertake the work and, moreover, it was largely their efforts that they were analysing. Not surprisingly, therefore, it is difficult to reply upon an organisation paid to undertake a project if it self-reports that it has done a good job. There has been no independent verification of the data and nor the workings used by CLES to reach these conclusions. This is unfortunate, because the research method, as outlined in CLES documentation, seems to be broadly appropriate – based upon a three stage multiplier (LM3) approach,[20] combining internal anchor procurement data with surveys of the 300 largest firms in the supply chain – albeit, that the use of certain local input estimates, drawn from previous studies, and the omission of distinguishing anchor employee local expenditure, may have potentially weakened the accuracy of the conclusions somewhat.

The indirect evidence relating to the improvement in the performance of the Preston economy is suggestive, but no causal link has been established. It may be true that the Preston Model led to these beneficial outcomes and, indeed, the timing of these developments does appear to be suggestive in this direction, but these consequences might equally have been due to other causes. It may, for example, derive from a longer-term variation in the business cycle, which impacts differently upon Preston than many other local economies, due to the persistence of manufacturing industry in the northwest. In the absence of rigorous analysis capable of excluding (econometrically) these other potential explanations, it is not proven whether or not these improvements to the Preston economy have resulted from the Preston Model or another factor(s). The evidence thus presented to date, concerning the impact of the Preston Model, is intriguing and suggestive, but does not constitute rigorous, independent evidence.

The 'What Works' network – a collaboration between the LSE and Centre for Cities, funded through the research councils and four government departments[21] – goes a little further in claiming that there is *no rigorous evaluation evidence* that considers whether local procurement strategies generate local economic growth. This is a little excessive, since there are a number of studies which have examined US experiments in local procurement and, moreover, there are a broader range of studies, many outlined earlier in this chapter, which have examined the local economic impact that anchor institutions (particularly the 'eds and meds') can deliver. However, it is fair to note that this broader literature has two main limitations. The first is that most studies of the economic impact of anchor institutions focus upon a single organisation rather than a network of multiple anchor institutions, such as characterises the Preston Model (Webber and Karlström, 2009: 17–18). Given that a network of anchor institutions, acting in concert, would account for a larger proportion of the local economy, with the potential for the interaction of activity mutually reinforcing and magnifying initial impact, it might be assumed that the existing evidence might underrepresent. Hence, the impact multiplier would be anticipated to be larger. However, this remains a hypothesis until tested.

Secondly, there are a number of methodological weaknesses that have been identified concerning a surprising proportion of these studies. For example, many seem overtly prone to double-counting, the adoption of inconsistent counterfactuals and undependable delineation of geographic boundaries. The estimation of spillovers, while an important element in any comprehensive analysis, is difficult to isolate from other factors which may have caused the ascribed effects. Moreover, the utilisation of 'off the peg' regional input-output models, where these are available for US studies, inevitably builds in a degree of inaccuracy, given that the use of historical coefficients implies the assumption that new expenditures will have the same effect as the average of historical expenditures (Siegfried et al., 2007). Where these regional input-output models are available, their use certainly simplifies the analysis, reducing research time and cost, but at the expense of accuracy. In the UK, no equivalent regional input-output tables are available from the ONS, and even national tables are only calculated every five years, due to the cost involved. Hence, there is a significant time lag between publication of the tables and the activity upon which the tables are based. Since economies can evolve quite significantly over a period of half a decade, even the national tables will only return approximate coefficient relationships. The result for UK researchers is to choose between drawing coefficients from national data, which weakens the efficacy of the analytical method, develop their own custom-built models or to use a combination of internal data on anchor expenditure to capture direct and indirect effects, combined with surveys to estimate induced effects.

The deficiency in evidence in relation to the efficacy of the Preston Model will be rectified in time. Indeed, full disclosure requires the author of this chapter to acknowledge that he is currently engaged in one such project which might shed a little more light upon the performance of the Preston Model within one particular segment of the Lancashire economy. Nevertheless, if a fair and balanced conclusion is to be reached regarding the potential of Preston Model type public policy interventions, further research is required.

Conclusion

The Preston Model is a fascinating example of innovative policy innovation, undertaken by a local community seeking to utilise their existing local assets (people, capital, skills and ideas) to avoid the damaging implications of fiscal austerity and regenerate an economy often overlooked by policy makers operating within larger economic conurbations of London, Manchester or Liverpool. The coordinating of a network of anchor institutions has taken the approach beyond the limitations inherent in over-reliance upon a single dominant employer, while the identification of a multiplicity of ways in which economic impact can be achieved – ranging from procurement to steering productive finance, from SMEs to co-operatives – introduces the potential for individual initiatives to mutually reinforce one another (or alternatively create trade-offs) which could magnify aggregate effects. If introduced intelligently, the approach offers an alternative mode for developing more marginalised areas of the UK, where orthodox economic development strategies have, by definition, been less effective. Moreover, by placing the empowerment of local communities at the heart of the strategy, it offers the intriguing prospect of creating a development strategy that leaves fewer marginalised groups behind. Moreover, in a post-Brexit world, there are many aspects of the approach that might prove to be of particular interest to national, as well as local, policy makers.

It is therefore frustrating that the evidence base for this set of initiatives remains so underdeveloped. Moreover, the lack of rigorous conclusions leaves opinions entrenched; supporters of the approach pointing to Preston's recent improvements as evidence of the success of the programme, and opponents pointing to the follies of beggar-thy-neighbour protectionism and zero-sum consequences if the approach were to be replicated more widely. This is too important an issue to neglect.

Notes

1 See www.bbc.co.uk/news/uk-england-lancashire-15571764
2 See https://oxfamblogs.org/fp2p/is-community-wealth-building-a-solution-to-local-depriva tion-in-poor-countries-as-well-as-the-uk/; https://cles.org.uk/blog/community-wealth-buil ding-from-the-uk-to-australia/; www.stirtoaction.com/blog-posts/beyond-municipal-protectionism
3 For further discussion, see https://europa.eu/youreurope/business/selling-in-eu/public-contracts/public-tendering-rules/index_en.htm and https://ec.europa.eu/growth/sin gle-market/public-procurement/rules-implementation/thresholds_en
4 See www.legislation.gov.uk/ukpga/2012/3/enacted; https://assets.publishing.service. gov.uk/government/uploads/system/uploads/attachment_data/file/690780/Comm issioner_Guidance_V3.8.pdf; www.gov.uk/government/publications/social-value-act-information-and-resources/social-value-act-information-and-resources
5 See www.csba.co.uk
6 See https://clevr.money
7 See https://moneyweek.com/487565/how-the-left-behind-took-back-control-in-preston
8 See https://whatworksgrowth.org/resources/local-procurement-1/
9 See https://moneyweek.com/487565/how-the-left-behind-took-back-control-in-preston
10 See https://failedarchitecture.com/community-wealth-building-an-idea-afraid-of-its-own-radical-potential
11 See https://whatworksgrowth.org/resources/local-procurement-1
12 See www.youngfabians.org.uk/the_preston_model_municipal_socialism_or_protec tionist_conjuring_trick
13 See www.youngfabians.org.uk/the_preston_model_municipal_socialism_or_protec tionist_conjuring_trick
14 See www.lancashire.gov.uk/lancashire-insight/economy/businesses-and-economic-wea lth/gross-value-added-for-lancashire/
15 See https://scopeni.nicva.org/article/social-value-could-regenerate-local-economies-for-the-benefit-of-their-people
16 See www.ons.gov.uk/economy/grossdomesticproductgdp/bulletins/regionaleconomica ctivitybygrossdomesticproductuk/1998to2018; www.ons.gov.uk/economy/grossdom esticproductgdp/datasets/regionalgrossdomesticproductallnutslevelregions
17 See www.ons.gov.uk/employmentandlabourmarket/peopleinwork/labourproductivity/ articles/regionalandsubregionalproductivityintheuk/february2020
18 See www.ons.gov.uk/employmentandlabourmarket/peoplenotinwork/unemployment/ datasets/claimantcountbyunitaryandlocalauthorityexperimental
19 See www.gov.uk/government/statistics/english-indices-of-deprivation-2019

20 See www.nefconsulting.com/our-services/evaluation-impact-assessment/prove-and-improve-toolkits/local-multiplier-3
21 See https://whatworksgrowth.org/about-us

References

Bailey, N. (2003), Local Strategic Partnerships in England: The Continuing Search for Collaborative Advantage, Leadership and Strategy in Urban Governance, *Planning Theory and Practice*, 4 (4): 443–457.

Bartik, T.J. and Erickcek, G. (2008), *The Local Economic Impact of 'Eds and Meds': How Policies to Expand Universities and Hospitals Affect Metropolitan Economies*, Metropolitan Policy Programme, Brookings Institution, Washington DC. Retrieved from www.brookings.edu/wp-content/uploads/2016/06/metropolitan_economies_report.pdf. Accessed 1 September 2020.

Bovaird, T. (2016), The Ins and Outs of Outsourcing and Insourcing: What Have We Learnt from the Past 30 Years?, *Public Money and Management*, 36 (1): 67–74.

Boyne, G.A. (1998), Competitive Tendering in Local Government: A Review of Theory and evidence, *Public Administration*, 76 (4): 695–712.

Brown, M. and O'Neill, M. (2016), The Road to Socialism is the A59: The Preston Model, *Renewal*, 24 (2): 69–78.

Chang, H-J. (2009), Industrial Policy: Can We Go Beyond an Unproductive Confrontation?, *Plenary Paper for Annual World Bank Conference on Development Economics*, Seoul, South Korea, 22–24 June. Retrieved from http://siteresources.worldbank.org/INTABCDESK2009/Resources/Ha-Joon-Chang.pdf.

Clopton, A.W. and Finch, B.L. (2011), Re-conceptualizing Social Anchors in Community Development: Utilizing Social Anchor Theory to Create Social Capital's Third Dimension, *Community Development*, 42 (1): 70–83.

Davies, J.S. and Blanco, I. (2017), Austerity Urbanism: Patterns of Neo-liberalisation and Resistance in Six Cities of Pain and the UK, *Environment and Planning A*, 49 (7): 1517–1536.

DCMS (2018), *The Public Services (Social Value) Act 2012: An Introductory Guide for Commissioners and Policymakers*, Department for Digital, Culture, Media and Sport, London. Retrieved from https://assets.publishing.service.gov.uk/government/uploads/system/uploads/attachment_data/file/690780/Commissioner_Guidance_V3.8.pdf. Accessed 11 September 2020.

DeCotiis, T.A. and Summers, T.P. (1987), A Path Analysis of a Model of the Antecedents and Consequences of Organizational Commitment, *Human Relations*, 40 (7): 445–470.

Dixon, P. B., Rimmer, M.T., and Waschik, P.G. (2017), Macro, Industry and Regional Effects of Buy America(n) Program: USAGE Simulation's, Center of Policy Studies (CoPS), Working Paper No. G-271 (April), Victoria University. Retrieved from www.copsmodels.com/ftp/workpapr/g-271.pdf. Accessed 3 September 2020.

Drauz, R. (2014), Re-Insourcing as a Manufacturing-Strategic Option During a Crisis: Cases from the Automobile Industry, *Journal of Business Research*, 67 (3): 346–353.

Dubb, S. and Howard, T. (2012), Leveraging Anchor Institutions for Local Job Creation and Wealth Building, retrieved from https://community-wealth.org/content/leveraging-anchor-institutions-local-job-creation-and-wealth-building. Accessed 2 July 2020.

Dubb, S., McKinley, S., and Howard, T. (2013), *The Anchor Dashboard: Aligning Institutional Practice to Meet Low-Income Community Needs*, Democracy Collective,

University of Maryland, Takoma Park, MD. Retrieved from http://community-wealth. org/sites/clone.community-wealth.org/files/downloads/AnchorDashboardComposite Final.pdf. Accessed 1 September 2020.

Ehlenz, M.M. (2018), Defining University Anchor Institution Strategies: Comparing Theory to Practice, *Planning Theory and Practice*, 19 (1): 74–92.

Ellram, L.M., Tate, W.L. and Petersen, K.J. (2013), Offshoring and Reshoring: An Update on Manufacturing Location Decision, *Journal of Supply Chain Management*, 49 (2): 14–22.

Feenstra, R. (1998), Integration of Trade and Disintegration of Production in the Global Economy, *Journal of Economic Perspectives*, 12 (4): 31–50.

Goff, P.M. (2007), *Limits to Liberalisation: Local Culture in a Global Marketplace*, Cornell University Press, Ithaca, NY.

Harkavy, I., and Zuckerman, H. (1999), *Eds and Meds: Cities' Hidden Assets*, Center on Urban and Metropolitan Policy, The Brookings Institution, Washington, DC.

Hawkworth, J., Mason, G., Goode, V., and Tren, D. (2018), *Good Growth for Cities 2018*, PriceWaterhouse Coopers, London.

Heslop, J., Morgan, K. and Tomaney, J. (2019), Debating the Foundational Economy, *Renewal*, 27 (2): 5–12.

HMG (2017), *Building Our Industrial Strategy – Green Paper*, The Stationery Office, London. Retrieved from www.gov.uk/government/uploads/system/uploads/attachm ent_data/file/585273/building-our-industrial-strategy-green-paper.pdf. Accessed 3 September 2020.

ICIC (2011), Inner City Insights: Anchor Institutions and Urban Economic Development, from Community Benefit to Shared Value, retrieved from http://icic.org/wp-content/up loads/2016/04/ICIC_Anchors-and-Urban-Econ-Dev.pdf?af674c. Accessed 1 September 2020.

Jackson, M. (2017), The Power of Procurement II: The Policy and Practice of Manche-ster City Council – 10 Years on, retrieved from https://cles.org.uk/wp-content/uploa ds/2017/02/The-Power-of-Procurement-II-the-policy-and-practice-of-Manchester-City-Council-10-years-on_web-version.pdf. Accessed on 7 September 2020.

Jackson, M. and McInroy, N. (2015), Creating a Good Local Economy: The Role of Anchor Institutions, retrieved from www.preston.gov.uk/media/819/The-role-of-Anchor-In stitutions/pdf/Anchor-institutions.pdf?m=636934398910770000. Accessed 2 July 2020.

Jones, F. and Leibowitz, J. (2019), How We Built Community Wealth in Preston: Achievements and Lessons, retrieved from https://cles.org.uk/wp-content/uploads/ 2019/07/CLES_Preston-Document_WEB-AW.pdf. Accessed 19 August 2020.

Kurtulus, F.A. and Kruse, D.L. (2017), *How Did Employee Ownership Firms Weather the Last Two Recessions?: Employee Ownership, Employment Stability, and Firm Survival in the United States: 1999–2011*, Upjohn Institute for Employment Research, Kalamazoo, MI. Retrieved from https://research.upjohn.org/cgi/viewcontent.cgi?arti cle=1259&context=up_press. Accessed 7 September 2020.

Lankford, W.M. and Parsa, F. (1999), Outsourcing: A Primer, *Management Decision*, 37 (4): 310–316.

Lockley, A. and Glover, B. (2019), *The 'Preston Model' and the New Municipalism*, Demos, London. Retrieved from https://demos.co.uk/wp-content/uploads/2019/06/ June-Final-Web.pdf. Accessed 19 August 2020.

Lowndes, V. and Gardner, A. (2016), Local Governance under the Conservatives: Super-Aus-terity, Devolution and the 'Smarter State', *Local Government Studies*, 42 (3): 357–375.

Lyall, S. and Lua, A. (2015), *Responses to Austerity: How Groups Across the UK Are Adapting, Challenging and Imagining Alternatives*, New Economics Foundation, London. Retrieved from www.barrowcadbury.org.uk/wp-content/uploads/2015/02/responses_to_austerity_NEF.pdf..

Maurrasse, D. J. (2001). *Beyond the Campus: How Colleges and Universities Form Partnerships with their Communities*. Routledge, New York.

Mazzucato, M. (2013), *The Entrepreneurial State: Debunking Public v's Private Sector Myths*, Anthem Press, London.

McInroy, N. (2016), *Forging a Good Local Society: Tackling Poverty through a Local Economic Reset*, Centre for Local Economic Strategies, Manchester. Retrieved from https://cles.org.uk/wp-content/uploads/2016/10/Forging-a-good-local-society3.pdf.

Moretti, E. (2004), 'Estimating the Social Return to Higher Education: Evidence from Longitudinal and Repeated Cross-sectional Data', *Journal of Econometrics*, 121 (1–2): 175–212.

Morris, K., Jones, A., and Wright, J. (2020), *The Role of Anchor Institutions in the Regeneration of UK Cities*, The Work Foundation Research Paper 2, The Work Foundation, London. Retrieved from www.researchgate.net/publication/303751278_Anchoring_Growth_The_role_of_%27Anchor_Institutions%27_in_the_regeneration_of_UK_cities. Accessed 2 July 2020.

NAO (2018), *Financial Sustainability of Local Authorities 2018*, HC 834, National Audit Office, London. Retrieved from www.nao.org.uk/wp-content/uploads/2018/03/Financial-sustainabilty-of-local-authorites-2018.pdf. Accessed 12 September 2020..

Orchard, L. and Stretton, L. (1997), Public Choice, *Cambridge Journal of Economics*, 21 (3): 409–430.

Piketty, T. (2013), *Capital in the Twenty-First Century*, Harvard University Press, Cambridge, MA.

Pugalis, L. and Bentley, G. (2014), (Re)appraising Place-Based Economic Development Strategies, *Local Economy*, 29 (4–5): 273–282.

PwC (2019), *Good Growth for Cities 2019*, PwC, London. Retrieved from www.pwc.co.uk/government-public-sector/good-growth/assets/pdf/good-growth-for-cities-2019.pdf. Accessed 12 September 2020.

Quinn, M. (2017), Place Leadership and the Social Contract: Re-examining Local Leadership in the East Midlands, *Local Economy*, 32 (4): 281–296.

Reimer, S. (1999), Contract Service Firms in Local Authorities: Evolving Geographies of Activity, *Regional Studies*, 33 (2): 121–130.

Rhodes, R.A.W. (2007), Understanding Governance: Ten Years On, *Organization Studies*, 28 (8): 1243–1264.

Rodrik, D. (2000), How Far Will International Economic Integration Go?, *Journal of Economic Perspectives*, 14 (1): 177–186.

Siegfried, J.J., Sanderson, A.R., and McHenry, P. (2007), The Economics Impact of Colleges and Universities, *Economics of Education Review*, 26 (5): 546–558.

Skerratt, S. and Steiner, A. (2013), Working with Communities-of-Place: Complexities of Empowerment, *Local Economy*, 28 (3): 320–338.

Smallbone, D., Kitching, J., and Blackburn, R. (2015), *Anchor Institutions and Small Firms in the UK: A Review of the Literature on Anchor Institutions and their Role in Developing Management and Leadership Skills in Small Firms*, UK Commission for Employment and Skills, Wath-upon-Dearne. Retrieved from https://assets.publishing.service.gov.uk/government/uploads/system/uploads/attachment_data/file/414390/Anchor_institutions_and_small_firms.pdf. Accessed 2 July 2020.

Thake, S. (2001), *Building Communities, Changing Lives: The Contribution of Large, Independent Neighbourhood Regeneration Organisations*. Joseph Rowntree Foundation, York.

Tomaney, J. (2010), *Place-Based Approaches to Regional Development: Global trends and Australian implications*, Australian Business Foundation, Sydney.

Townsend, A. and Champion, T. (2014), The Impact of Recession in City Regions: The British experience, 2008–2013, *Local Economy*, 29 (1–2): 38–51.

Webber, H.S. and Karlström, M. (2009), *Why Community Investment is Good for Non-profit Anchor Institutions: Understanding Costs, Benefits and the Range of Strategic Options*, University of Chicago, Chicago, IL. Retrieved from https://community-wea lth.org/sites/clone.community-wealth.org/files/downloads/report-webber-karlstrom. pdf. Accessed 1 September 2020.

Whyman, P.B. (2018), The Local Economic Impact of Shale Gas Extraction, *Regional Studies*, 52 (2): 184–196.

Whyman, P.B. (2019), Street Trees, the Private Finance Initiative and Participatory Regeneration: Policy Innovation of Incompatible Perspectives, *Political Quarterly*, 91 (1): 156–164.

Part II

Beyond municipalism, beyond Preston

The new socio-economic democracy

9 Economic democracy and local economic development

Philip B. Whyman

What is economic democracy?

At its most basic level, economic democratisation refers to the extension of democratic control over the economic sphere. Whereas within capitalism, it is the private owners of capital who largely determine the objectives for, and working patterns of, productive organisations, economic democracy initiatives seek to increase the participation and influence of workers, consumers and/or members of the wider community within economic decision-making. This can be at the level of the firm, where one natural expression of economic democratisation would be the development of co-operatives or labour-managed firms. Here, organisations (firms and enterprises) are owned and run according to democratic principles (Archer, 1990: 38). Alternatively, economic democracy can be reflected at national or international level, by securing increased control for labour and/or the community over the productive sector of the economy. This can be achieved through socialisation of investment, either channelled through a state or municipal agency, or alternatively through examples of collective employee investment fund initiatives.

Economic democracy can be considered to be an extension of industrial democracy which seeks to extend employee influence over their immediate work process (see Figure 9.1). Industrial democracy introduces *microeconomic* restrictions upon management's right to manage arbitrarily, and thereby expands the degree of participation of workers and, in particular, their influence over decision making within organisations. This enhanced participation may cumulate in co-determination, whereby managers and employees make joint decisions over a range of matters pertaining to the operation of the organisation. Participation can be promoted through the introduction of legislation, for example including the role of trade union safety representatives within workplace health and safety legislation, through to laws requiring firms to create worker representatives on company boards.

Nevertheless, industrial democracy remains subject to restrictions placed upon these initiatives by owners of these enterprises. Using Hirschman's terminology, while industrial democracy extends employee influence through 'voice' within an organisation, the owners of capital possess both 'voice' and can use the threat of 'exit' as an ultimate means of control (Hirschman, 1970). Workers can use exit or the temporary withdrawal of their labour as a means of exerting

INDUSTRIAL DEMOCRACY

Participation in decision-making

collective bargaining

works councils

minority employee board representation

Co-Determination - joint decisions

ECONOMIC DEMOCRACY

Financial Participation - ownership of capital

Individual employee share ownership (ESOPs)

collective employee ownership (EIFs)

social or community share ownership (social funds, municipal funds)

Cooperatives

Community Wealth Building

Figure 9.1 Differentiating between industrial and economic democracy

influence over their employer, but the relative mobility of capital means that it can make more effective use of exit control (Archer, 1990: 42). Moreover, it is the relative scarcity of capital that gives its private owners the ability to dominate the productive sphere within capitalism, as capital purchases labour power (or more specifically, labour potential) for a specified period of time rather than the other way around. It also enables capital to exercise authority over labour, as the former seeks to impose restrictions upon behaviour at work and the monitoring of performance, to increase work intensity and ensure the quality of the work produced (Williamson, 1985: 229). It is this exercise of authority, together with criticisms that excessive control over people's working lives reduces the opportunity for self-expression and creativity that has formed the basis of a critique of capitalism and a desire for its transcendence through economic democratisation.

Economic democracy involves the extension of democratic control over all aspects of production through worker financial participation and ownership of capital. It seeks to transcend the limitations experienced by industrial democracy initiatives through employee and/or social ownership. In a fully fledged economic democracy, labour would hire capital, rather than the other way around, and labour would receive whatever profit or surplus the organisation would generate as a result of its activities.

Transition: alternative models

Short of a severe economic crisis or revolution, complete with the wholesale replacement of capitalist forms of production by a perfectly formed model of economic democracy, economic theorists have debated the merits of taking steps towards greater economic democratisation within an economy where capital remains the focal determinant of economic activity – capitalism. There are a multiplicity of options available to those who wish to pursue a transition towards a more democratic model of economic activity.

The simplest approach is to establish autonomous communities of producers, such as those advocated by Owen, Saint-Simon, and Fourier. The isolation of these communities, however, together with difficulties surrounding methods of pricing work according to the Labour Theory of Value, weakened this approach as a means of transforming society (Engels, 1975: 50–62). Nevertheless, co-operatives have proven rather resilient (Mayo, 2017). Defined by the International Co-operative Alliance (ICA, 2015) as 'an autonomous association of persons united voluntarily to meet their common economic, social, and cultural needs and aspirations through a jointly-owned and democratically-controlled enterprise', co-operatives can be quite diverse, depending upon their objectives. Membership may comprise either individuals or other organisations who use the co-operatives services (i.e. marketing, distribution, housing, finance and insurance) or participate in its activities as workers, consumers or independent business owners such as agricultural and fisheries or marketing and distribution co-operatives (ICA, 2015: 8). Co-operatives can vary greatly in terms of the degree of financial participation expected from their members, ranging from a nominal sum for large consumer co-operatives, where the bulk of capital derives from retained earnings and is held in common, to worker co-operatives where contributions may occur in the form of sweat capital or individual investment, with ownership either held in common or via individual holdings. These differences can have a significant effect upon the development of the organisation in the long run.

Labour-managed (LM) firms can be viewed as a distinctive sub-set of co-operatives in that they are not typically self-financed but rather funded through loan capital. This removes the dualism that critics assign to other types of co-operatives; with consumers and workers arguably becoming their own capitalists, since their income is comprised of both labour and capital contributions (Jossa, 2005: 14). Asset owners receive compensation for the utilisation of their assets, allocated through market forces or democratic mechanism, and may require insurance to guarantee against asset loss or damage (Vanek, 1970: 5). For this model to work effectively, however, it requires either an accessible financial sector, willing to lend to democratic firms at similar rates to conventional firms, or for a combination of LM firm group cross-funding and/or provision of capital via state or other public bodies. However, reliance upon external sources of funding has the potential to impair the autonomy of the organisation.

Friendly Societies and other forms of mutual organisation (such as insurance companies, credit unions and building societies) have a long history, emerging out of the self-help aspect of the medieval guild system. They are similar to consumer co-operatives, in that they are owned by, and run for the benefit of, their members, albeit that no direct contribution of capital is required, other than through payment for services provided (i.e. mortgage, insurance policies) or through temporary deposits of savings.

The John Lewis Partnership is yet another variant of the co-operative model, in that employee-partners have the ability to appoint directors, participate in decision-making through democratic councils and share in organisational prof-its. One strength of this approach is that the shares are held for the benefit of employee-partners through a legal trust, thereby securing the long term viability of the organisation from any short termism displayed by a majority of the partners. However, this also implies that the trust is only subject to their indirect control, thereby creating the possibility of decision-making dominance by a combination of managers and trustees.[1]

Individual employee ownership can be facilitated through an Employee Share Ownership Plan (ESOPs), which provide tax incentives to participant compa-nies and their employees to encourage employee financial participation in the enterprise. Employees have the option of purchasing shares in the company, with the cost partly offset through individual tax incentives. ESOPs are typically quite limited in scope, being used more as a tax-efficient way of combining profit-sharing incentives with an attempt to influence the perception of employees that their interests are aligned with those of their employing organi-sation. There is no reason, however, why employee shareholding should neces-sarily be restricted through use of the ESOP scheme. Indeed, they are frequently used to facilitate succession planning in private companies where passing con-trol to other family members is not an option.

Community wealth building (CWB) has the potential to encourage a broad-ening of democratic ownership and control of production, through its primary focus upon utilising under-utilised local talent, capacities, assets, and institu-tions, to strengthen local economies and ensure that a greater proportion of resultant wealth is anchored in place, to the benefit of the local community. There is no *a priori* reason why CWB is necessarily equated with economic democracy. It can be used, for example, to strengthen local communities by encouraging the development of new privately owned firms. Yet, the objective to anchor future wealth and in the process to empower local communities, means that CWB initiatives often involve the establishment of co-operatives and other forms of democratic enterprises. The Evergreen project, in Cleveland (USA), and the Preston Model, in Lancashire (UK), are two such examples.

The generation of capital that can facilitate the spread of economic democracy can be achieved via an expansion of communal saving, carried out through budget surpluses or a combination of social and/or collective employee investment funds (Esping-Andersen, 1985; Olsen, 1992: 12). Examples of social funds embraces pen-sion fund investments (Deaton, 1989) and labour-sponsored venture capital funds promoting regional economic development in Canada (Quarter, 1995). Collective wage-earner funds were established for a period in Sweden (Pontusson and Kuruvilla, 1992; Whyman, 2006, 2008). To the extent that collective capital expanded sufficiently that capital scarcity was reduced (or eliminated), then there would be no reason why capital should hire labour and not the other way around (Keynes, 1973 [1936]: 376). Communal saving could, therefore, provide the foundations for the establishment of economic democracy across the economy as a whole.

Balancing the interests of workers and wider society

One key aspect of proposals for economic democracy concerns the balancing of interests between different groups within society. Resource scarcity and opportunity costs reflect conflicts of interest (Nove, 1983: 85). There is always the potential for a conflict between sectional interests and the general public interest (Bahro, 1977: 537; Södersten, 1982: 144). By definition, each individual enterprise represents only a fragment of the community. Hence, individual democratic organisations, whether consumer co-operative or worker self-managed enterprise, may act in their own vested interests by seeking to utilise their market position against the interests of other workers (with whom they may be in competition) and/or society as a whole.

Consumer co-operatives have the potential to pursue the sectional interests of their members, at the expense of wider societal or employee interests. However, it is perhaps more probable that a divergence of interests may occur between those of members, whose living is derived from outside the co-operative movement, and those employed by the organisation. If the consumer co-operative sought to maximise value to its membership through reducing costs, the temptation exists to squeeze wages and working conditions to deliver lower prices charged to consumers (Webb and Webb, 1975 [1920]: 22). The presence of independent trade unions might act as a necessary counterweight, to prevent consumer co-operatives becoming 'an instrument of positive oppression' (Webb, 1891: 194–196).

For self-managed firms, the tension is more likely to occur between societal interests and the organisation pursuing its narrow interests and abusing its market position (particularly in imperfectly competitive markets); in the process degenerating into 'sectional egoism' (Cole, 1928 [1913]: 368, 408–409; Poole and Jenkins, 1990: 11). Indeed, the Fabian critique claims that the 'self-governing workshop' could potentially negate, rather than advance, democracy (Webb and Webb, 1975 [1920]: 3, 18–19, 27–28, 103, 160). As a result, various propositions have been made to restrict the ability for self-managed firms to and/or to operate for the benefit of society as a whole rather than the narrower interests of their worker-members.

One solution could be through the centralised control over the means of production and with individual firms being subservient to the requirements of central planning (Marx, 1871: 152, 155). This would, of course, violate the autonomy of the self-managed firm, and consequently would undermine one of the key principles of democratic firms. Another option could be to reconcile potentially divergent interests of producers and the wider community, through the adoption of a system of multiple sovereignty, with the state owning the means of production but guilds controlling production (Cole, 1917: 129). Or again, through a combination of public management in large enterprises, to realise large economies of scale, and self-management in smaller companies.

Much the same solution was proposed sixty years later by the advocates of LM firms, who advocated separating the bundle of rights associated with capital ownership into *use* and *basic* components, with employees exercising users' rights to control the enterprise, but basic capital ownership would rest with the state, municipalities, trade unions, employee investment funds, private individuals or be held in trust for the wider community as a form of Wigforssian 'enterprise with no owners' (Vanek, 1970: 315). The important point being that ownership of capital does not entitle owners to interfere in the management of the firm but only to receive rent (interest) according to the relative scarcity of capital in the economy (Thomas and Logan, 1982: 7). This would ensure efficient economic performance and avoid a misallocation of resources, while capital would be protected from deterioration or consumption, and increasing when revenue exceeds costs. This may require the constraint of short-term objectives, even if democratically determined, in favour of long term expert analysis. The operation of democratic firms would, additionally, take place within national democratic governance which might seek to balance civic and labour interests, providing a 'guarantee that local strivings for advantages will be held within reasonable limits', thereby ensuring social solidarity and long term productive efficiency (Abrahamsson and Broström, 1980: 233).

Another option could be to introduce a form of intermediary to balance sectional, collective labour and civic interests. The Austrian Chambers of Labour (*Arbeiterkammern*) might provide one such approach, since employees elect representatives to enact socio-political functions separate from traditional trade union roles (Meidner, 1980: 366). A final option might be to consider exploring the community wealth building examples provided in this book. This offers a flexible approach to reconciling divergent interests, through a greater involvement of the local community.

Economic democracy – anticipated impact

The introduction of economic democratisation is likely to have significant impacts upon the economy, the work environment and working lives of those individuals employed within engaged organisations, and have a broader influence upon the wider community.

Microeconomic effects

Personal development

One of the long-standing aspirations of worker co-operatives and labour managed firms is the creation of conditions more conducive to both individual and collective self-expression through work, leading to enhanced dignity (Mill, 2008a [1848]: 153) and a corresponding reduction in the sense of powerlessness, alienation and anomie (Seeman, 1991). This was often discussed in moral or ethical terms, as being a benefit in its own right (Mill, 2008a [1848]: 155–156; Marshall, 1997 [1890]: 236–237). The expansion of democracy cultivating economic as well as political citizenship (Wigforss, 1922). In the process, it was anticipated that democratisation of the workplace would enable latent productive energies to be released and thereby increase productivity (Mill, 2008a [1848]: 153).

Technical efficiency

One area where efficiencies may be achieved is through diminishing diseconomies arising from what is known in economics as the principal-agent problem. This is when an agent, designated to act on the behalf of the principal, may have different interests and thereby act in ways contrary to their best interest. The principal, in this description, could be the owner of an organisation and the agent the manager or workers within that organisation. Democratising the organisation would at least partially address this inefficiency as worker and/or community participation in the setting of organisational objectives is likely to increase identification with organisational goals and (at least partly) legitimise business strategy (Mill, 2008a [1848]: 149, 153; Bonin et al., 1993: 1303).

To the extent that greater organisational consensus and identification was achieved, there would be less need for monitoring, thereby reducing numbers of supervisory staff with resultant cost savings (Simon, 1991). Industrial relations would be expected to be improved with the removal of divergent interests between owners and workers in the organisation, resulting in fewer restrictive practices and shirking, thereby increasing labour productivity (Marshall, 1997 [1890]: 253; Jones, 1976: 11). In addition, absenteeism and labour turnover may decline, which in turn reduces costs and facilitates higher human capital investment and resulting productivity improvements (Thomas and Logan, 1982: 9; Olsen, 1992: 22).

The evidence relating to technical efficiency would indicate that firms governed by their workers perform at least as efficiently as conventional firms (Abell, 1983: 89). However, direct comparisons are difficult due to the multiplicity of objectives that democratic firms often seek to pursue, such as job security, improvement in working conditions, education and training to promote self-fulfilment, pursuing ethical trading or empowering individuals through self-governance (Vanek, 1970; Archer, 1990: 166).

Financial participation

Financial participation in the organisation, either through direct ownership of the firm or through profit sharing, has the potential to incentivise employees

(Mill, 2008a [1848]: 140–144; Robson, 1968: 266). There is a natural tension here, between the solidarity between workers within a democratically controlled organisation, and the design of remuneration schemes intended to incentivise and reward differential performance. Nevertheless, if it is possible to reconcile this tension, the greater trust engendered by an organisation where employees either hold a financial stake or participate in decision making, has the potential to create workplace incentives that are more widely accepted across the whole workforce, with potentially commensurate productivity effects (Mill, 2008a [1848]: 149–150). The economics literature would appear to suggest, despite the limitations of data on the issue, that economic democratisation has the potential to stimulate employee motivation, providing greater incentives to raise productivity, without raising labour intensity through weakening safety standards or threatening unemployment (Vanek, 1970: 402; Olsen, 1992: 21).

Allocative efficiency

Aside from considerations of labour productivity and other technical efficiencies, the economics literature raises the possibility that democratic firms have the potential for promoting allocative efficiency. This is where the price that consumers pay reflects the marginal cost of production. At this point, assuming that all resources are fully employed, scarce resources are best allocated to the production of those goods and services that society values.

One way that this might occur is that consumer co-operatives, by contrast, could use their position as 'democracies of consumers' (Webb and Webb, 1975 [1920]: 3, 18–19) to gain competitive advantage through refraining from short term opportunistic behaviour and corrupt practices (Gide, 1898: 495–499; Jones and Kalmi, 2009). Trust in the quality of goods and services provided, together with the distribution of the surplus generated through business activities through dividends, could thereby enhance consumer sovereignty and further encourage customer loyalty (Marshall, 1997 [1890]: 233–236; Mill, 2008b [1879]: 421). Research indicates that loyalty can influence the profitability of organisations and is a substitute to monitoring (Simon, 1991). It also means that there would be less necessity for advertising and more confidence in the quality of goods and services provided, since there was 'no inducement to adulterate their own goods' (Marshall, 1997 [1890]: 232, 254).

Consumer co-operatives may additionally seek to promote ethical trading and at least partially negate market failure which reduces the efficiency of a market economy by failing to fully reflect social costs and benefits (externalities), such as the 'reckless exploitation of natural resources' (Gide, 1898: 495–499; Robertson, 1923: 101–112). Co-operatives have long claimed their pursuit of multiple objectives, whereas other firms have only belatedly adopted corporate social responsibility initiatives which cover some of the same ground, and accordingly, it would not be particularly surprising that co-operative performance would appear to be more advantageous when social as well as private costs and benefits are included in any comparison (Galbraith, 1974).

A further potential allocative efficiency gain could result from an extension of consumer co-operatives and a reduction in the number of distributors – what Robertson termed 'superfluous middlemen' – to that minimum level required for the efficient realisation of their role of bringing goods and services to consumers, rather than waste scarce resources in a costly multiplicity of distributors, when these could be put to more productive uses (Mill, 2008a [1848]: 153; Robertson, 1923: 101–112). One allocative disadvantage, suffered by smaller co-operatives when compared to large transnational competitors, is the difficulty in integrating logistics and supply chains to deliver economies of scale, and thereby reduce costs which may (or may not) be passed on to consumers in the form of lower prices. Indeed, it is perfectly plausible for large organisations, who do not comply with marginal cost pricing and therefore make excess profits, may still deliver lower costs for consumers when compared to smaller competitors, who do comply with marginal cost pricing, but whose scale is insufficient to realise similarly low average costs. One solution could be for the formation of co-operative networks which, through combination, could deliver economies of scale and thereby enhance allocative efficiency (Marshall, 1997 [1890]: 234–236). The establishment of networks would be particularly important to worker or LM co-operatives, for example, because economic theory would suggest that these are likely to be relatively small in size and thereby otherwise lack the degree of scale economies available to larger, trans-national competitors (Vanek, 1970: 119–120).

Governance and management

The ability to realise potential advantages for democratic firms is dependant, at least in part, upon the combination of efficient but relatively selfless behaviour would be more likely to realise greater returns (Robson, 1968: 265). The reduction in informational asymmetry and principal-agent problem inefficiency, in self-managed firms, could provide the basis for more effective governance (Jones, 1976: 12, 21). Moreover, any reduction in mistrust across the organisation would improve industrial relations and create conditions more conducive to more flexible decision-making (Vanek 1970: 258).

There are two main criticisms levelled at democratic firms. The first relates to inefficiencies in collective decision-making, related to the paucity of knowledge and experience among those 'amateur committee-men' upon which the governance of the organisation relied (Robertson, 1923: 105–112, 134–147). Moreover, relatively egalitarian remuneration systems make it more difficult to attract experienced managerial and/or entrepreneurial talent (Robertson, 1923: 133; Ben-Ner, 1987). The more detailed the scrutiny of managerial decisions, the greater the perceived potential for friction (Marshall, 1997 [1890]: 243–244). Yet, the less scrutiny, or the imperfect operation of democratic oversight, might result in managers and skilled workers asserting dominance over co-workers, with resulting de-legitimisation of decision making for the workforce as a whole (Burkitt, 1983: 111).

A second criticism focuses upon the difficulties inherent within self-managed organisations, where employee-owners are required to submit to the authority of managers that they have collectively elected or employed to perform this role, to ensure the smooth running of production. Yet, they additionally participate in the collective scrutiny of the performance of these same managers, and establish their strategic priorities (Webb, 1891: 127–128, 152–153). Arguably, this might reduce managerial authority and cause risk-averse decision-making, such as the deferral of difficult decisions which may result in rationalisation or imposing changes within working arrangements.

It is possible to reconcile these inherent tensions within the democratic model of enterprise governance by noting that management within a democratic enterprise requires a new ethos and acceptance of limitations placed upon managerial autonomy, but in return, decisions are likely to be perceived as more legitimate, thereby potentially increasing both management authority and satisfaction (Carnoy and Shearer, 1980: 123; Archer, 1990: 170).

A second potential solution to managerial and governance weaknesses lies in the objective, shared by many democratic enterprises, to provide an education service for worker-members. This has the potential to address any initial shortage of managerial skills and ability (Cole, 1917: 75; Carnoy and Shearer, 1980: 123). However, it could simultaneously explain and promote the advantages of the economic democracy approach, and indicate the opportunities for participation for each member. In addition to providing a means to deliver personal development, this could facilitate the development of a more co-operative organisational culture. Moreover, it could also help to enhance the capacity of citizens to the wider benefit of the community.

Innovation and dynamic change

One area where expectations of democratic firms is more mixed, concerns their ability to innovate and invest in new technology. Financial participation might create an incentive to innovate, if resultant improvements led to members sharing increased rewards (Mill, 2008a [1848]: 140). However, profit sharing, as a means of incentivising a workforce, is hardly restricted to democratic firms. Another suggestion is that democratic organisations are more likely to network and thereby create agglomeration (or clustering) effects, such as skills and knowledge spillovers (Marshall, 1997 [1890]: 232–236). Networks of democratic firms could mutually reinforce their own activities, offering 'infant industry' protection to organisations in the early stages of their development, while clustering offers the opportunity for the development of economies of scale (Marshall, 1997 [1890]: 234–236; Mill, 2008a [1848]: 153). In addition, it has been suggested that democratic firms may have a 'slight advantage' over other types of enterprise due to greater trust embedded in the organisation and hence lower levels of resistance to changes in work organisation (Vanek, 1970: 295).

In contrast, other theorists point towards a tendency, among workers in self-managed firms, to avoid the disruption caused by innovation (Webb, 1891: 150).

Moreover, it has been noted that employees may have higher levels of risk associated with the success or failure of their organisation, given that this may impact upon the future prospects of their working lives and threaten the investment in status and security built up over time through seniority within the organisation. Financial participation may further increase risk, to the extent that profit-sharing may replace a share of fixed wages, as incomes may fluctuate with the business cycle and the relative success of the firm (Hart and Hübler, 1989: 4).

Demographic distribution of benefits and the risk of degeneration

The particular sub-set of democratic firms, which require a significant (rather than nominal) injection of employee-member savings, raises the greatest concerns in this context (Clayre, 1980: 79). For example, even if it is possible for employees to be able to withdraw their savings capital, this may require replacement with new employee-members to prevent the degeneration of the firm, and is only likely to occur during favourable economic conditions. Hence, there is a danger of an employee's savings being 'locked in' to the employing organisation, and hence, in these circumstances, transaction costs of moving savings are higher than in an equity market, since employee-shareholders must change jobs (Clayre, 1980,: 9–80). The owners of smaller, private firms, may shoulder equivalent risks, but private owners of capital may risk the loss of only part of their portfolio, if their holdings are diversified via the medium of shareholding in publicly limited firms. To the extent that this characterisation is accurate, this may lead to more risk adverse behaviour in democratic firms, which may reduce innovation.

The discussion of risk leads on to a second potential disadvantage of democratic firms, namely the presence of tensions relating to the generational distribution of gains and investments (in capital or in sweat labour) to individual workers and the related possibility for their long term decomposition (Burkitt, 1983: 111). Democratic organisations involving the assignment of individual shares in the value of the enterprise can result in the fracturing of solidarity between workers, as those who have been with the organisation for the longest will have amassed significant value through 'sweat equity' and the return on their initial membership contribution, which may make it expensive for newer workers to match in new (cash) investment upon joining the organisation. One solution would be to create different categories of workers within the same organisation, denoting different ownership value, but this would undermine the democratic nature of the organisation and create insider 'small masters' employing outsiders much as occurs with capitalist firms (Webb, 1891: 45, 150).

For firms where ownership remains collective, then more recent recruits may benefit from a degree of expropriation of the value of the time and/or financial investment provided to the organisation by their colleagues with longer service records (Archer, 1990: 169). Younger workers may, additionally, favour self-financing to produce future income streams and accept current consumption restriction, whereas older workers may prefer financing the organisation through borrowing, as this will generate a higher present income stream, while having less concern about long term debt problems the firm may face after they have retired. The creation of 'internal capital accounts', representing individual employee assets and liabilities created during their employment and redeemable at retirement, may resolve this particular issue, but at the cost of weakening the capital base of the organisation should a disproportionate number of employees retire in any specific period.

Macroeconomics effects

Aside from the microeconomic effects debated in the economics literature, there are a number of macroeconomic impacts that may arise from a shift towards greater economic democratisation.

Income distribution

Concerns have been raised over concentration of ownership and power inherent within capitalist economies (Dahl, 1985). Yet, the achievement of significant redistribution is limited by the private control over investment (Whyman, 2008). If redistribution occurs, increasing the labour share of national income at the expense of capital, then the incentive to invest is adversely affected, which in turn undermines capital accumulation and growth. Governments find themselves in a trilemma, unable to simultaneously pursue policies of capital accumulation and growth without regressive distributional consequences (Esping-Andersen, 1985: 232).

One solution is to socialise investment, which could facilitate full employment and reduce economic instability (Keynes, 1973 [1936]: 375–378; Whyman, 2008: 228). Another is through the LM form of employee self-management. In this model, labour hires capital, the owners of capital – whether this resides in state, municipal, employee, community or private hands – are divorced from control over the firm. Capital receives rent (interest) in accordance with its scarcity within the economy, whereas the surplus (profit) accrues to worker-members. As a result, differentials within democratic organisations will be significantly reduced (Nove, 1983: 216). While the introduction of LM would likely reduce fundamental inequality within society, there would remain a need for government intervention to redistribute income between different sections of society, and between employees working in LM firms, due to the heterogeneous market conditions facing individual firms. Irrespective of the quality or quantity of work performed, or the knowledge and skill sets of worker-members, some sectors in the economy benefit from higher demand relative to costs, thereby facilitating higher levels of reward (Nove, 1983: 134–135; Weisskopf, 1992: 8–9). Nevertheless, the fact that self-management forms of economic democracy do not solve all distributional issues should not detract from their overall benefits in this and other areas.

Reducing instability

There are three reasons to suspect that economic democratisation may reduce the instability inherent within a capitalist economy. The first relates to a reduction in the inequality and cyclicality of income distribution (Hamilton, 1964: 10). It has been proposed that a combination of broader social considerations and acceptance of a lower return to capital could help to minimise certain under-investment tendencies associated with the private ownership and control of the investment function (Whyman, 2006). Secondly, economic theory hypothesises that LM firms may seek to maximise average earnings per employee rather than profits, subject to investment requirements (Estrin, 1983: 2–3, 12, 16; Vanek, 1970). This might result in a less volatile economy, with greater stability of employment (Vanek, 1970: 204). However, in the absence of sufficient levels of market entry and exist, or an alternative incentive to pursue dynamic adjustment, a greater insensitivity to market forces may cause resource mis-allocation (Estrin, 1983: 2–3, 14; Vanek, 1970: 385). Finally, the persistence of financial speculation and investment short-termism within capitalist economies drains funding away from productive capital to financial assets, thereby sapping the vitality from the real economy. Keynes (1973 [1936]: 159) argued 'when the capital development of a country becomes a by-product of the activities of a casino, the job is likely to be ill done'. To the extent that economic democratisation is less likely to suffer from these deficiencies, it could help to stabilise the economy.

Enhancing growth potential

Economic democracy has the potential to enhance growth potential through its encouragement of greater tolerance of profits, particularly among organised labour, and thereby creating more favourable conditions for an economic policy approach focused upon the pursuit of full employment (Gustafsson, 1981). A second argument suggests that greater openness and common interest between democratic firms could extend co-operation to sharing information and productive technologies, accelerating economic growth (Hedborg cited in Abrahamsson and Broström, 1980: 204).

Full employment

One of the major weaknesses, within capitalist economies, concerns the tendency for the economy to operate at less than full employment for considerable periods of time. The resulting loss of production through less than full employment of capital and labour is a major inefficiency. Keynes (1973 [1936]: 375–378) recognised this issue and advocated comprehensive socialisation of investment to 'augment', or if necessary to replace, a majority of private investment to maintain full employment in the long run. His argument was that a level of investment sufficient to maintain full employment would be unlikely in the absence of state intervention, due to instability caused by uncertainty, speculative entrepreneurial 'animal spirits' (Keynes, 2004b [1980]: 322) and because the maintenance of high rates of capital accumulation and full employment may reduce returns to capital over time (Keynes, 1973 [1936]: 136, 376–378; Hyman, 1975: 360).

It could also eliminate what is termed the 'dynamic inefficiency of capitalism', namely where imperfect information and mistrust between trade unions and employers creates a sub-optimal bargaining solution, and frustrates options for wage moderation to facilitate increased investment and employment opportunities (Lancaster, 1973). Options for resolution are to either accept a regressive income distribution as the price of securing sufficient investment to secure sustainable full employment, or to negotiate a capital-labour partnership, where the rewards of growth are shared in agreed proportions, or alternatively to socialise investment (Hyman, 1975: 38, 368; Whyman, 2006: 51–52). Robinson (1973: 130) summarised the position thus: 'Keynes was arguing that, if a private enterprise system cannot deal with potential abundance, we must turn it into a system that can.' If Keynes's writings from the 1920s were a guide, that alternative system would include substantial levels of public investment (up to 8% of GDP) to secure full employment, alongside industry characterised by a combination of 'industrial self-government', 'co-operation in the individual factory or workshop', profit-sharing and works councils to develop a form of capital-labour partnership (Liberal Party, 1928: 205–228; Keynes, 2004a [1926]: 101).

Access to capital

Access to capital is a critical factor for the development of any business. Democratic organisations have particular difficulty in raising external capital from the existing financial markets, due to unfamiliarity (or suspicion) relating to un-orthodox business models and perceived estimates of risk. As a result, many such firms seek to reply upon internal equity, generated primarily through membership investment and retained earnings. This preserves independence but seriously limits available investment, thereby restricting potential future growth potential (Clayre, 1980: 3). As a result, many co-operatives operate in sectors where capital intensity is low – i.e. textiles, printing and construction (Ben-Ner, 1988: 10). Differential investment and member equity holdings, could generate more risk capital, but at the cost of undermining the equality of democratic participation and with the ultimate risk of degeneration (Gunn, 1992).

External financing, by contrast, is more efficient, since the price paid for capital reflects its scarcity value, and resolves the inadequacy of funding problem (Vanek, 1970: 305–307; Aoki, 1986). However, it creates an 'agency problem' for external investors, caused by asymmetric information and potential employee opportunism, such as diluting capital to raise short term wages (Clayre, 1980: 2; Engberg, 1993: 282). The result is likely to be higher capital charges, monitoring or management participation, thereby raising capital costs for the firm or violating its autonomy. Debt financing preserves firm autonomy, at known cost, but in difficult economic periods, the debt burden upon a smaller workforce may become problematic.

Reliance upon private external finance may, therefore, result in a higher interest cost than market norms, leading to competitive disadvantage (Clayre, 1980: 3). One solution is for a public body or social-employee investment fund to provide external financing. This agency could establish a relationship between firm and provider of capital, which could limit short-termism and other forms of principle-agent problem (Devine, 1992: 71; Engberg, 1993: 287). They could also simulate a capital market by placing investment funds to maximise marginal returns, thereby ensuring allocative efficiency and facilitating new firm entry (Brus and Laski, 1989: 135–136; Estrin, 1989: 187–189). Another solution could reflect the Mondragon example, combining collective and individual holdings to provide a system of pooled funding to support the co-operative federation (Thomas and Logan, 1982: 7).

Economic democracy and local economic development

One aspect of economic democratisation, which is particularly pertinent to the Preston Model and the range of different perspectives contained within this book, relates the impact on local economic development strategies. A fundamental feature of economic democracy concerns the empowerment of stakeholders in production, whether this be workers, consumers or the citizenry at large, in determining key aspects of production. The decisions taken by firms have a marked impact upon the individuals who work for them and the community in the area immediately surrounding the workplace. Consequently, these stakeholders have a direct interest in how firms impact upon the 'economics of place'. They have an interest in ensuring the retention of well paid, highly skilled jobs in the vicinity for the benefit of the current workforce but also providing future employment opportunities for the wider community.

Economic activity underpins the vitality and gross national income (GNI) of the local economy, and the multiplier effect means that this initial wealth generation causes a positive chain reaction (or knock-on effect) thereby benefitting other local firms, workers and citizenry. Hence, there is an obvious link between economic democratisation encouraging local governance and fostering local economic development. This may be through improving working conditions, environmental protection and regional balance (Meidner, 1980: 364). Or it may be by preventing take-overs which may threaten continued production within the region, or the owners of the existing firms moving operations and capital abroad (Pontusson and Kuruvilla, 1992: 782–783).

Conclusion

This chapter has sought to provide an over-view of the economic literature concerning economic democracy. It has noted the myriad of different forms that economic democratisation can take, and the different methods of transition. It has noted the microeconomic effects that a shift towards greater democratic forms of production may deliver, whether in relation to labour productivity and efficiency, the advantages flowing from trust-based organisations, or the degree of allocative efficiency which may occur. Macroeconomic advantages may include reduction in instability and providing a foundation for economic policies intended to promote growth and full employment. Yet, questions relating to governance, management and access to capital, need to be resolved for economic democracy to realise its potential advantages (Clayre, 1980: 50). Mutual support can help to address some of these issues, through the pooling of finance, access to specialist financial and technical support, together with benefits drawn from R&D and/or legal support (Thomas and Logan, 1982: 7–8: Vanek, 1970: 317–318).

Note

1 See www.hrmagazine.co.uk/article-details/employee-share-ownership-john-lewis-partnership-not-what-it-purports-to-be

References

Abell, P. (1983), The Viability of Industrial Producer Cooperation, in Crouch, C. and Heller, F.A. (eds), *International Yearbook of Organisational Democracy*, Wiley, Chichester.

Abrahamsson, B. and Broström, A. (1980), *The Rights of Labour*, Sage, London.

Aoki, M.C. (1986), Horizontal vs Vertical Information Structures of the Firm, *American Economic Review*, 76 (5): 971–983.

Archer, R. (1990), *Economic Democracy: The Politics of Feasible Socialism*, Oxford University Press, Oxford.

Bahro, R. (1977), *Die Alternative [The Alternative]*, Europäische Verlagsanstalt, Cologne.

Ben-Ner, A. (1987), Producer Co-operatives: Why Do They Exist in Market Economies?, in Powell, W.W. (ed.), *The Nonprofits Sector: A Research Handbook*, Yale University Press, New Haven, CT.

Ben-Ner, A. (1988), Comparative Empirical Observations on Worker-Owned and Capitalist Firms, *International Journal of Industrial Organisation*, 6 (1): 7–31.

Bonin, J.P., Jones, D.C., and Putterman, L. (1993), Theoretical and Empirical Studies of Producer Cooperatives: Will Ever the Twain Meet?, *Journal of Economic Literature*, 31 (3): 1290–1320.

Brus, W. and Laski, K. (1989), *From Marx to the Market*, Clarendon Press, Oxford.

Burkitt, B. (1983), Employee Investment Funds: A Crucial Element in the Transition to Socialism, *Economic and Industrial Democracy*, 4 (1): 103–115.

Burkitt, B. (1984), *Radical Political Economy*, Wheatsheaf, Sussex.

Carnoy, M. and Shearer, D. (1980), *Economic Democracy: The Challenge of the 1980s*, M.E. Sharpe, New York.

Clayre, A. (1980), *The Political Economy of Co-operation and Participation*, Oxford University Press, Oxford.

Cole, G.D.H. (1928 [1913]), *The World of Labour*, Macmillan, London.

Cole, G.D.H. (1917), *Self-Government in Industry*, G. Bell, London.

Dahl, R.A. (1985), *A Preface to Economic Democracy*, University of California Press, Berkeley.

Deaton, R.L. (1989), *The Political Economy of Pensions*, University of British Columbia Press, Vancouver.

Devine, P. (1992), Market Socialism or Participatory Planning?, *Review of Radical Political Economics*, 24 (3-4): 67–89.

Engberg, L. (1993), Financing Employee-Managed Firms: Some Problems of a Wider Extension, *Economic and Industrial Democracy*, 14 (2): 277–300.

Engels, F. (1975), *Socialism: Utopian and Scientific*, Foreign Language Press, Peking.

Esping-Andersen, G. (1985), *Politics Against Markets: The Social Democratic Road to Power*, Princeton University Press, Princeton, NJ.

Estrin, S. (1983), *Self-Management: Economic Theory and Yugoslav Practice*, Cambridge University Press, Cambridge.

Estrin, S. (1989), Workers' Co-operatives: Their Merits and their Limitations, in Le Grand, J. and Estrin, S. (eds), *Market Socialism*, Clarendon Press, Oxford, 165–192.

Galbraith, J.K. (1974), Professor Galbraith's Reply, *Annals of Public and Cooperative Economics*, 45 (3–4): 310–314.

Gide, C. (1898), Has Co-operation Introduced a New Principle into Economics?, *Economic Journal*, 8 (32): 490–511.

Gunn, C.E. (1992), Plywood Co-operatives in the United States: An Endangered Species, *Economic and Industrial Democracy*, 13 (4): 525–534.

Gustafsson, B. (1981), *I övermorgon Socialism* [*Socialism the Day after Tomorrow*], Gidlunds, Stockholm.

Hamilton, D. (1964), Keynesian Economics and the Co-operative System, *Annals of Public and Cooperative Economics*, 35(2–3): 107–114.

Hart, R.A. and Hübler, O. (1989), *Profit Sharing: Individual Participation and Shares and Effects on Wages, Labour Mobility and Working Time*, University of Sterling Discussion Paper in Economics, University of Stirling, Stirling.

Hirschman, A.O. (1970), *Exit, Voice and Loyalty*, Harvard University Press, Cambridge, MA.

Hyman, S. (1975), International Politics and International Economics: A Radical Approach, in Lindberg, L.N., Alford, R., Crouch, C., and Offe, C. (eds), *Stress and Contradiction in Modern Capitalism: Public Policy and the Theory of the State*, Lexington Books, London, 355–372.

ICA (2015), *Guidance Notes to the Co-operative Principles*, International Cooperative Alliance, Brussels. Retrieved from www.ica.coop/sites/default/files/publication-files/ica-guidance-notes-en-310629900.pdf. Accessed 2 June 2020.

Jones, D.C. (1976), British Economic Thought on Association of Labourers, 1848–1974, *Annals of Public and Cooperative Economics*, 47 (1): 5–36.

Jones, D.C. and Kalmi, P. (2009), Trust, Inequality and the Size of the Co-operative Sector: Cross-Country Evidence, *Annals of Public and Cooperative Economics*, 80 (2): 165–195.

Jossa, B. (2005), Marx, Marxism and the Co-operative Movement, *Cambridge Journal of Economics*, 29 (1): 3–18.

Keynes, J.M. (1973 [1936]), *The General Theory of Employment, Interest and Money*, Macmillan, London.

Keynes, J.M. (2004a [1926]), The End of Laissez-Faire, in Keynes, J.M., *The End of Laissez-Faire and The Economic Consequences of the Peace*, Prometheus Books, London.

Keynes, J.M. (2004b [1980]), Activities 1940–1946, in Moggridge, D. (ed.), *Collected Writings of John Maynard Keynes: Volume 27, Shaping the Post-War World: Employment and Commodities*, Macmillan, London.

Lancaster, K. (1973), The Dynamic Inefficiency of Capitalism, *Journal of Political Economy*, 81 (5): 1092–1109.

Liberal Party (1928), *Britain's Industrial Future*, Ernest Benn, London.

Marshall, A. (1997 [1890]), *Principles of Economics*, 8th edition, reprinted by Prometheus Books, Amherst, NY.

Marx, K. (1871), The Civil War in France, reprinted in Horvat, B., Markovic, M.,, and Supek, R. (eds), *Self-Governing Socialism: A Reader*, vol. 1, Progress Publishers, Moscow, 148–159.

Mayo, E. (2017), *A Short History of Co-operation and Mutuality*, Co-operatives UK, Manchester. Retrieved from www.uk.coop/sites/default/files/uploads/attachments/a-short-history-of-cooperation-and-mutuality_ed-mayo-web_english.pdf. Accessed 1 June 2020.

Meidner, R. (1980), Our Concept of the Third Way, *Economic and Industrial Democracy*, 1 (3): 343–369.

Mill, J.S. (2008a [1848]), *Principles of Political Economy*, 7th edition, Oxford University Press, Oxford.

Mill, J.S. (2008b [1879]), Chapters on Socialism, reprinted in *Principles of Political Economy*, Oxford University Press, Oxford, 371–436.

Nove, A. (1983), *The Economics of Feasible Socialism*, Unwin Hyman, London.

Olsen, G.M. (1992), *The Struggle for Economic Democracy in Sweden*, Avebury, Aldershot.

Pagano, U. and Rowthorn, B. (1996), *Democracy and Efficiency in the Economic Enterprise*, Routledge, London.

Pontusson, H.J. and Kuruvilla, S. (1992), Swedish Wage-Earner Funds: An experiment in economic democracy, *Industrial and Labor Relations Review*, 45 (4): 779–791.

Poole, M. and Jenkins, G. (1990), *The Impact of Economic Democracy: Profit-sharing and Employee-Shareholding Schemes*, Routledge, London.

Quarter, J. (1995), *Crossing the Line: Unionised Employee Ownership and Investment Funds*, James Lorimer and Co, Toronto.

Robertson, D.H. (1923), *The Control of Industry*, Cambridge University Press, Cambridge.

Robinson, J. (1973), What Has Become of the Keynesian Revolution?, in Robinson, J. (ed.), *Collected Economic Papers* V, Blackwell, Oxford, 168–177.

Robson, J.M. (1968), *The Improvement of Mankind*, University of Toronto Press, Toronto.

Seeman, M. (1991), Alienation and Anomie, in Robinson, J.P., Shaver, P.R. and Wrightsman, L.S. (eds), *Measures of Personality and Social Psychological Attitudes*, Academic Press, London, 291–371.

Simon, H.A. (1991), Organisations and Markets, *Journal of Economic Perspectives*, 5 (2): 25–44.

Smith, H. (1962), *The Economics of Socialism Reconsiderd*, Oxford University Press, London.

Södersten, B. (1982), Towards a Labour-Managed Sweden?, in Ryden, B. and Bergström, V. (eds), *Sweden: Choices for Economic and Social Policy in the 1980s*, George Allen Unwin, London, 142–163.

Sterner, T. (1990), Ownership, Technology and Efficiency: An empirical study of co-operatives, multinationals and domestic enterprises, *Journal of Comparative Economics*, 14 (2): 286–300.

Thomas, A. (1990), Financing Worker Co-operatives in EC Countries, *Annals of Public and Cooperative Economics*, 61 (2–3):175–211.

Thomas, H. and Logan, C. (1982), *Mondragon: An Economic Analysis*, Allen and Unwin, London.

Vanek, J. (1970), *The General Theory of Labor-Managed Market Economies*, Cornell University Press, Ithaca, NY.

Webb, B. (1891), *The Co-operative Movement in Great Britain*, Swan Sonnenschein, London.

Webb, S. and Webb, B. (1975 [1920]), *A Constitution for the Socialist Commonwealth of Great Britain*, Cambridge University Press, Cambridge.

Weisskopf, T.E. (1992), Towards a Socialism for the Future, *Review of Radical Political Economics*, 24 (374): 1–28.

Whyman, P.B. (2006), Post-Keynesianism, Socialisation of Investment and Swedish Wage-Earner Funds, *Cambridge Journal of Economics*, 30 (1): 49–68.

Whyman, P.B. (2008), The Case for the Swedish Wage-Earner Funds: A Post Keynesian Solution to the Dynamic Inefficiency of Capitalism through the Socialisation of Investment, *Journal of Post Keynesian Economics*, 30 (2): 227–258.

Wigforss, E. (1922), *Industrins Demokratisering*, [*Democratising Industry*], Tidens Förlag, Stockholm.

Williamson, O. (1985), *The Economic Institutions of Capitalism*, Free Press, New York.

10 The role of social enterprises in local democratic governance

Co-operation or competition?

Mike Aiken

Introduction

This chapter explores the role of social enterprises in emergent democratic models of local urban regeneration and 'community wealth building' (CLES and Preston City Council, 2019: 12). It draws on emerging experience from what is known as the 'Preston Model' (Singer, 2016) in England as well as similar initiatives elsewhere. This exploration takes place in the context of changing relations between social enterprises and local government in the United Kingdom since the 1990s. This has arisen in part due to steady shifts in the roles and activities of both entities. For example, local authorities across the UK probably still exhibit greater homogeneity as organisations – with clear public recognition and legitimacy due to their statutory roles and local democratic mandate. Nevertheless, they have faced severe and successive budget cuts, have needed to outsource mainstream public services (including waste collection, care services and social housing), or been dependent on large scale private sector re-development to yield *quid pro quo* planning gains for public amenities.

Meanwhile, social enterprises still exhibit greater diversity in terms of their sizes and variety of activities when compared to local authorities. They were usually formed by citizens in a given locality to address a social need. Their legitimacy comes from working closely with a particular client group (e.g. people with disabilities) or an issue (e.g. recycling waste materials or running a community café) and they can be understood as organisations trading for a social purpose. Twenty years ago, as Spear (2001: 254) pointed out, the term, 'social enterprise' was 'only occasionally used in the UK' and covered a broad set of very different organisations. Even today, the list of organisational types covered by this umbrella term may include 'worker co-operatives; social care co-operatives; social firms; mutual organisations; trading voluntary organisations; community businesses; and public sector spin offs in the health, housing and leisure field' (Spear, 2001: 255–257). This provides a broad framework for the types of social enterprise discussed here.

Most social enterprises remain small and close to their particular client group or social issue. They are likely to be involved in supportive networks as in Preston to share local information, to access training and business advice, and to collaborate with others in a community of common interests. On the other hand, over time some social enterprises can become significant and busy economic entities in the local – and even national – economy. Hence, what roles may social enterprises play in local democratic governance in relation to the Preston Model? Further, as organisations with social and enterprise objectives, where might their development trajectories be pulled towards co-operative or competitive impulses?

This chapter explores these issues in the following way. First, there is a brief outline of the Preston Model's key features – including how governance mechanisms may involve both local authorities and social enterprises – and an indication of similar initiatives in other locations. These aspects are then related to broader theory on governance. This is followed by an examination of dilemmas social enterprises may face within competitive markets for social goods. A brief examination of the pressures facing local authorities is provided, after which the analysis in the final section discusses some possible tensions social enterprises and the local authority may face and considers some possible future trajectories.

The Preston Model: local procurement and collaboration

A fuller discussion of the Preston Model is provided elsewhere in this volume. However, a summary here of the context and key elements of the model may aid an understanding of the local democratic governance arrangements and the importance of growing social enterprise organisations.

The city of Preston has a history reaching back to Roman times and, during the industrial revolution, it was a major trading centre for textiles and engineering. Today the city and surrounding conurbation, with a population of just over 141,000, has faced significant industrial decline. Initially, the 'traditional' regeneration remedy was proposed, namely, building a giant shopping centre with a corporate superstore as the retail anchor. However, when these macro arrangements collapsed in 2011, more creative ideas began to surface within council and other local institutions, which are sometimes referred to as the 'New Municipalism' (Ball, 2019). Some encouragement to these initiatives has come from legislative clauses in the Public Services (Social Value) Act (2012), which includes 'collaborating with the voluntary and community sector' as well as Small and Medium Enterprises (SMEs) and social enterprises in relation to local authorities' procurement processes. The emergence of the 'Preston Model' represents a creative set of inter-linked social and economic initiatives aimed at regenerating the city and building wealth in local communities.

Singer's analysis was that:

> Traditional city growth models, based on attracting inward investment for big infrastructure projects, could no longer be relied upon. Nor, under conditions of recession and austerity, could conventional tax-and-spend redistribution.
>
> (Singer, 2016)

In 2013, CLES (Centre for Local Economic Strategies) was asked to identify key anchor institutions in Preston including the city, county council, university, police, and hospital. Their analysis of Preston's anchor institutions had shown that 'from £750m spent, only 5% is spent in Preston' (CLES and Preston City Council, 2019: 7). Subsequent work involved identifying and mobilising the spending power of existing 'anchor' organisations and redirecting their spending to local businesses and co-operatives wherever possible. The aim has been to fuel the local economy by encouraging the growth of networks of small businesses and social enterprises through the circulation of local trade with a focus on local procurement where feasible.

Matthew Brown and colleagues at Preston Council included within this alternative growth model other elements including: the adoption of the 'living wage employer' status; establishing a credit union to combat payday lenders; founding a not-for-profit energy firm; and encouraging worker-owned co-operatives (Eaton, 2018). The university and college in Preston set up training courses and local networking events to bring people together. The council also drew inspiration from models developed in Cleveland, Ohio where the 'Evergreen' co-operatives were established in poorer neighbourhoods. This enabled workers there to gradually earn a stake in these small businesses which focussed on local need. In addition, Preston established a partnership with the Mondragón co-operatives in the Basque region to draw on learning from their nearly 70 years of development (Whyte and Whyte, 1991).

'Community Wealth Building' in Preston is the name given to ways that local people might ensure that the benefits of local growth are invested locally and used to support investment in productive economic activities. It also aims to enable people and their local institutions 'to work together on an agenda of shared benefit' and with 'a more diverse blend of ownership models: returning more economic power to local people and institutions' (CLES and Preston City Council, 2019: 8, 23). Nevertheless, on procurement, there were agreements that any new large scale outsourcing of mainstream public services would be avoided wherever this was feasible to avoid hollowing out the public sector. Meanwhile this would leave plenty of existing small contracting opportunities for local organisations to provide goods and services.

The activities discussed above can be understood as part of formal and informal governance in a number of ways: (1) by bringing together different institutions, organisations and communities for learning, co-operation and possible joint work, (2) identifying local needs and ways for local small businesses, co-operatives, or anchor organisations to address them, and (3) providing training, support and opportunities to network. In particular, these activities are 'an opportunity for local people ... to ensure that the benefits of local growth are invested in their local areas' and also for local organisations to 'work together on an agenda of shared benefit' (Preston City Council, website, 2019). These actions also implied (4) an overarching common purpose shared by local community and social enterprise organisations and the importance of collaborative work (CLES and Preston City Council, 2019). Hence the development work in the Preston Model has included meetings and workshops with key public sector anchor organisations involved in local procurement and there was agreement between them for 'a long term collaborative commitment to community wealth building' (CLES and Preston City Council, 2019:12).

Governance: the approaches and value of broad mechanisms of involvement

The dimensions of the Preston Model sketched in the previous section require moving beyond the official committees of local *government* and other public sector bodies. Initiatives of this dimension also need to reach further than the executive boards of social enterprises, charities and local co-operatives: collaborative local social and economic work inevitably relies on broader notions of *local governance*. This needs to be understood as an inherently messy and contested terrain. Hence governance involves incorporating opinions, views and perspectives from a much broader constituency of local residents, groups and stakeholders. Yet, from Preston to Cleveland and Mondragón 'governance' is never a completed system. Rather it remains an active set of processes involving a variety of stakeholders that requires adaption for new circumstances and new constituencies.

Governance remains critical to the local development process as it represents, metaphorically, the ship's engine room (for harnessing energy) and bridge (for navigating a course). From Gaventa's (2004: 21) perspective this means asking: how far are social enterprises' engagements in governance processes, 'fundamentally embodied' by participants as necessary – and important for themselves and wider local groups?' Alternatively, how far is organisational engagement likely to be, according to Gaventa (2004: 22) 'instrumentalised' and rather shallow or expedient – and oriented solely towards individual organisational gains? Hence, multiple spaces for mutual discussion between stakeholders become crucial elements of the Preston Model rather than expedient locations for discussing sub-contracting of services.

It will be useful to summarise a few illustrative elements related to governance that may apply to the discussion on the Preston Model. These three elements may involve formal, semi-formal or informal spaces where agreements, information, news, practices, opportunities, opinions, or agreements/ disagreements may arise.

First, Mordaunt (2006) suggests examining the following three interacting spheres of a governance system relating to accountability in organisations, namely, their structures, operating environment, and wider environment. These three elements may also usefully aid an understanding of governance in collaborative networks. They are seen as helpful in understanding the ways in which any emerging tensions between stakeholders may be reconceptualised as 'shared dilemmas' for negotiation (Mordaunt, 2006: 124). Second, Evers (2005), points to the importance of being aware that 'the legitimacy of community-based organisations requires connection with a given community and an associated stock of social capital'. Third, governance also relies on general assumptions that the networks' actions are 'desirable, proper, or appropriate within some socially constructed system of norms, values, beliefs and definitions' (Suchman, 1995: 574) rather than being simply understood in narrow commercial or instrumental terms (Dart, 2004).

In summary, the combined framework suggests a governance structure for the network within the Preston model might need to be attentive to (1) structures, operating environment, and wider environment, (2) connection with a given community, and (3) agreement on norms, beliefs and definitions of the work.

These elements may help inform an understanding of emerging governance patterns that are not just organisational and formal in character, but also draw on a wider community of actors and agencies as in Preston. In addition, it is envisaged that some of the network structures and activities may range from formal, semi-formal to informal and an indicative illustration of this is offered by the author in Table 10.1.

Overall, it is suggested that the Preston Model's structure can be understood as a 'relational accountability' that 'involves local stakeholders and will always be open to challenge ... [and] is likely to involve some degree of skill in active engagement' (Cordery, 2013). These ideas also draw on Gaventa's (2004) notion of receptive governance where accountability takes place between many actors rather than being simply steered by a formal repertoire of council committees and elected officials.

Local authorities will always retain their formal organisational functions of local democracy and statutory obligations, but some of the processes may need to be more permeable to wider influence from other local agencies and stakeholders. Meanwhile, the Mondragon co-operatives' organisational model, for example involves a highly detailed set of interlinking committee structures and consultative processes, as Stocki's (2017) work illustrates. This complexity can slow down decision making, yet, arguably better decisions may be made, owned and implemented. This resembles a complex type of 'associative democracy' (Hirst, 1994) between different (but linked) organisations within the Mondragón family of co-operatives. From this analysis, the Preston Model is not

Table 10.1 Illustrative elements of governance locations

Formal structures	Semi-formal	Informal
City Council (and County Council) meetings of elected councillors voted in from the population; anchor institutions' boards of governors; social enterprises' boards of governors or general meeting;	Training events; workplaces, workshops and networking events, international and local learning exchanges, sharing practice.	Networking and social events, informal contact in the street, shops, workplace or home.

ultimately represented by a single entity but, rather, resembles a collaboration of common interests across a range of stakeholders. The structure of meetings, events, and training activities in Table 10:1 aims to provide a sketch to illustrate what participants may focus on within their own organisation as well as where they may contribute to common interests with others in a wider pattern of local governance.

Overall, these structures and processes leave open the possibility of competition, as well as collaboration, between social enterprises participating in the work of the Preston Model. This may arise particularly with larger social enterprise organisations operating at scale (at national or regional level) whose interests could cut across the local governance arrangements that have been developed. Nevertheless, social enterprise leaders – when speaking at national or local conferences – have often appeared comfortable with alternatively collaborating and then, at a later time competing, with a given organisation. Hence, social enterprises involved in the Preston Model may have the potential to play both co-operative and competitive roles in relation to work in the city or further afield depending on the size; organisational expertise; and geographic reach of another social enterprise.

Social enterprises: from local roots to co-option and outsourcing

It is important to understand the nature of social enterprise organisations as they play important roles in the wealth-building, shared ownership and governance arrangements within the Preston Model. However, the 'social enterprise' term can refer to a multitude of organisational trading activities undertaken by, for example, worker co-operatives, charities, community businesses and others. These organisations may also each hold a variety of legal identities for their different activities, including Community Interest Company (CIC), Company Limited by Guarantee (CLG), Industrial and Provident Society (IPS), and charity.

In this section, a brief overview of the emergence of social enterprise in the UK is offered to understand its roots in community action, local campaigns, and aspirational work to improve neglected neighbourhoods and create work opportunities. These values and commitments – which are close to many of the current aspirations in Preston – still apply in many cases. However, there has been systematic work over the last 25 years, from social enterprises, umbrella organisations as well as funders and central government, to 'scale up' these organisations to be deliverers of outsourced public services at scale following competitive tendering. This can, to some degree, weaken their accountability to local communities and strengthen their links with commissioning bodies.

In the 1980s social enterprises were often a loose knit group of organisations that had arisen endogenously, usually in urban areas facing decline and often sparked by community activists. The focus may have been on the closure of a local launderette in Glasgow or in response to derelict land in the midlands; or squatting a treasured building to provide homes and workspace in London.

Pearce (1993: 3) identified 'community enterprise organisations' that had 'roots in the community action tradition of the 1960s and early 1970s'. These included, for example, Westway Trust (then known as North Kensington Amenity Trust) established in 1971. Other community organisations in this era were 'not generally involved in self-financing operations, let alone the commercial development of property' (Duncan, 1992: 44). Meanwhile in 1984, activists set up Coin Street Community Builders on the banks of the Thames with social and economic objectives: including affordable housing, play space, pop up amenities, community festivals alongside encouraging local restaurants and small shopping units for local businesses and artists. Later, analysts noted this dual nature and described them as hybrid organisations (Billis, 2010) that combined business and social logics within a mutual or philanthropic legal structure. Social enterprises' common features were addressing local social needs and engaging in some economic activity to support this end.

The ideas of 'independent organisations' that were 'trading for a social purpose' had roots back in the strong mutual and co-operative movement of the 19th century that yielded Building Societies, the Co-operative stores and contributory sickness and benevolent funds. The term 'social enterprise', was not common in the UK before the 1980s; however, by the mid-1990s, Thake (1995) could point to a range of these new neighbourhood-based regeneration organisations emerging. At the start of the 20th century, researchers noted the emergence of these alternative regeneration models (Thake, 2001) although policy initiatives had lagged behind practitioners' 'social inventions' (Whyte and Whyte, 1991). The Labour government (1997–2010) drew on these initiatives to set up various regeneration programmes involving social enterprises that were aimed at capacity building and urban partnerships.

In order to understand possible tensions and trajectories in the broad third sector (including social enterprises, co-operatives, charities and community organisations) it is important to consider the rapid changes in this arena. By the start of the 21st century, there was growing awareness of the role the sector could play in the growth of public sector commissioning and procurement (Macmillan, 2002) and the UK Government's policy agenda was soon focused on directly expanding the roles third sector organisations would play in the provision of public services (National Audit Office, 2005). Further, terms such as 'earned income', 'grant dependence' and 'sustainable funding' became a common language in the public and third sector. There was an explicit project to build the third sector organisations ability to deliver public services through a range of capacity building and funding programmes from 2002. For example, the Adventure Capital Fund (ACF) gained £2 million from government to 'create sustainable community enterprises through social investment'. ACF had received £17 million from the government by 2006, to offer grants and loans to social enterprises for these endeavours. From 2007, the narrative changed as ACF re-named itself Social Investment Business Ltd (SIB) and ran the Futurebuilders Fund, which 'disbursed £145m in grants and loans'. In 2009 it was also managing the £98 million Social Enterprise Investment Fund for the government's Health Department and a further £70 million for SIB. SIB's aims were to equip third sector organisations 'to win public service contracts', 'secure other forms of investment' and 'run local services'. In the same period 'public service mutuals emerged as spin-offs from public sector services in social work, probation, children and youth services, and libraries' (Spear, 2015: 58).

These shifts raised important tensions concerning the role of these apparently independent organisations and their future trajectories in relation to the public and private sectors. Critical voices, such as Crouch (2011), illustrated that neo-liberal narratives – despite the economic crashes of 2009 – still saw markets, rather than governments, as the primary way of organising national and local economic life. Meanwhile, although hierarchical local authorities may not have always been ideal, notions of network governance and partnership approaches remained as viable alternatives to markets or hierarchies for local co-ordination of services (Lazer et al., 2009). Indeed, partnership approaches still retain importance in Scotland (Cullingworth et al., 2018). Nevertheless, Hirst's (1994: 82) idea of an associative democracy – and a possible governance model of local networks involving citizens in community and co-operative organisations that would be 'better able to deal with crises and natural disasters' – appeared to have receded. Indeed, any envisaged role for mobilised and active communities engaged in a local, democratic, social and economic economy, was replaced by an ever more competitive, contract culture with bids based on a wider geographic scale, involving lower unit costs.

Three key national infrastructure organisations – the National Council of Voluntary Organisations (NCVO), the Association of Chief Executives of Voluntary Organisations (ACEVO) and Social Enterprise UK – have explicitly welcomed the widespread contracting out of public services at scale. NCVO (2015) stated that 'The voluntary sector plays an important role delivering public services across the UK' and it put forward 'a wide range of resources to help voluntary organisations shape and deliver public services' (NCVO, 2015). ACEVO (2019) saw the only difficulty as being that smaller organisations in the voluntary sector might not be able to join the party. It sought to explore 'how voluntary organisations of different sizes can work better together in bidding for and delivering public services' (ACEVO, 2019). Floyd (2013) distinguished the differences of scale for contracting social enterprises:

> One is spin-outs, many of whom are competing for large contracts worth tens or in some cases, hundreds of millions of pounds. Another is those social enterprises whose starting point is similar to traditional voluntary sector organisations and who are looking to win relatively small locally-based contracts.
>
> (Floyd, 2013)

Today social welfare activities have tended to become centralised and homo-genised with large private sector organisations operating alongside national charities and regional social enterprises. Hence, notions of local social enterprises and charities being close to their community, with tacit neighbourhood knowledge and undertaking work flexibility, have been largely replaced by multi-national companies operating highly specified standard routines. In contrast, many local organisations may still gain from small contracts (rather than grants) for fairly specific pre-defined tasks within larger programme funding.

The contestation between the idea of community organisations providing 'authentic voluntary action' that is 'vision-led' and 'independent of government' as opposed to acting 'on sub-contracts from the state' Knight (1993: xviii) appears to have declined as the contract culture has gradually become normalised. Nevertheless, it was Beveridge (1948: 322) who suggested that 'the business motive … is seen as in continual or repeated conflict with the philanthropic motive'.

Rochester (2017: 97) argues that social enterprises 'have identified themselves with the market'. In this discussion, the development paths of organisations seeking to provide housing a generation earlier presents instructive learning. Mullins and Pawson (2010: 197) analysis was that Housing Associations were now considered as either delivering services as 'agents of policy' or actually 'for-profits in disguise' as foreseen by Weisbrod (1988) and Knight (1993). Nevertheless, co-operatives, which represent one important type of social enterprise, maintain the importance of the mixture of social, economic and community concerns with their seven co-operative principles (Co-operative Councils, 2020). Meanwhile, a nuanced view from Locality, an umbrella for local community organisations and social enterprises in the UK argued that outsourcing should be at smaller local scale and involve local authorities:

> It's time to turn the tide on large-scale outsourcing … By unlocking the power of community, local authorities can create more responsive services that reduce long-term costs and invest in the local economy … many local authorities have sought savings through big outsourcing contracts.
>
> (Locality, 2020)

These points, in relation to business motives and contracting for welfare services, need to be held in mind particularly with social enterprises which must, by their nature, hold the tension between philanthropic and market values within one organisation. Small-scale co-operatives and voluntary organisations may still be seen to provide important local work and creative solutions to social issues in Preston. However, the development trajectories of social enterprises in this context may tread a narrow path between staying small and locally connected (but financially vulnerable) or growing large by competing for large public service contracts across a wider region (but with a more remote connection to local governance).

It is also important to distinguish in which type of market a particular social enterprise is operating within and the nature of the business model. Hence, a small co-operative providing occasional catering services for special events at the university will face very different challenges and legislative hurdles when compared to the social care co-operative providing daily support to local care homes and individuals living at home. The first organisation may draw from a network of people on an ad hoc basis to provide individuals with a supplementary income. The second organisation requires a significant number of reliable qualified staff in a highly regulated field to provide an on-going service. Both organisations are vulnerable to competitive pressures. However, the regularity of employment required for care duties – and the danger that a rival regional social enterprise may gain from economies of scale – may make the care co-operative more vulnerable.

Local authorities: new roles and broader governance amid cutbacks

In this section, the focus turns to the context for the Preston Model in relation to the changing shape of local authorities. In brief, they have suffered successive cuts in their budget allocations from central government as well as restrictions on the amount of council tax they can gather from the local population. The level of social provision they directly control has been diminished. Legislation and financial pressures have meant that schools; social housing; waste and recycling activities; some aspects of social services; and public transport; are at various stages of externalisation with local government retaining some supervisory roles. Local authorities contract these areas out to private or third sector *providers*. That final word is emphasised as it points to a relation that is not now based on partnerships or networks – or even hierarchies – but market transactions for social goods (Thompson et al., 1993).

During the mid-1980s, some local authorities were part of a strong municipalism movement in London, Sheffield, Glasgow and elsewhere in the UK. This carried echoes from Fabians such as Sidney Webb, a hundred years earlier, who envisaged a deep local municipalism as he famously took a 'walk along the municipal pavement, lit by municipal gas and cleansed by municipal brooms' (Webb, 1898). In its 1980s form, local government sometimes acted as a change agent in the local economy and took a lead on equalities issues (sometimes dubbed 'municipal socialism'). The aims were both to stimulate local growth and to address social inequalities among disadvantaged groups.

The current context is one of deep budget cuts. If grants targeted at education are excluded, it was estimated in 2016 that local councils in England saw 'an average real-terms cut of almost 26% to their funding' over the previous six years while 'revenue from grants and redistributed business rates has fallen by 38%, and revenue from council tax had fallen by 8%' (Smith et al, 2016). Media reports suggest that, since 2010, some local councils have faced budgets cut up to 50% with only children's services showing an increase (Calver and Wainwright, 2018). According to Haughton (2019) local councils had borne 'a 23% real term reduction in funding since 2010', while only care services had increased in spend.

Local social and economic regeneration is a field that social enterprises were heavily engaged with alongside local authorities. The analysis of Lupton and

Crisp (2018) was that the Brown/Blair New Labour (1997–2010) approach, outlined in their report (Social Exclusion Unity , 1998), focussed on the poorest areas and improving public services through renewal policy at neighbourhood level. The current government trends, however, tends to suggest displacing poorer people by going 'beyond the interests of current residents' by 'stimulating new industries and economic growth; incentivising investment raising land values and creating new residential opportunities for people in professional occupations' (Lupton and Crisp et al., 2018: 212). In that sense the Preston Model stands out as also being concerned with *current* residents.

In some cases, as Newman and Clarke (2007: 26) pointed out public sector were staff transferred, as part of the organisation assets, to private or charitable/social enterprise contracting organisations. This commodification of public services has not necessarily been beneficial to local authorities, social enterprises, or the community. In one of many notable cases, the private sector organisation, Coperforma, was contracted to deliver the transfer of patients to hospitals. A skilled public health service workforce was replaced and a national scandal ensued as the privatisation of patient transport descended into 'total shambles' (Campbell, 2016), while an NHS investigation was launched into the £63.5 million contract. In other cases, charities too may, in effect, 'sell' their staff and services to a private sector contractor. Scope, a disability charity, transferred nearly 1600 staff to Salutem Healthcare a private health care company in 2018 (Plummer 2018). Meanwhile Glasius and Ishkanian (2015: 191–192) highlighted how the formal voluntary sector with its leadership bodies and research base had 'separated itself from wider civil society and activist movement'.

Charitable organisations bidding for contracting work now hold budgets comparable to local authorities. A not unusual example, would be Change, Grow, Live, a charity that has worked with 219,000 people across Britain over the year while 16 of their staff each earned more than £100,000; it had a consolidated income for 2018–19 of £212.6 million (Change, Grow, Live, 2019: 22). By way of comparing size, this single charity/company draws from its contracts nearly one third of the gross revenue expenditure of an entire medium sized city such as Brighton and Hove (£777.6 million in 2020/2021). This illustrates the scale of the charitable and social enterprise organisations engaged in competitive bidding for public sector contracts. Hence, Preston's current commitment to not undertake new large-scale outsourcing of public services remains noteworthy.

In relation to governance, despite the financial challenges facing local government, it has also been increasingly interested in legitimacy and broader consultation bodies. Bulmer's (2015) work points to informal structures that can constitute a sense of local governance – sometimes on a temporary basis. These may include citizen's panels, partnership bodies that may be informal structures that can constitute a sense of local governance – sometimes on a temporary basis. These may include citizen's panels, partnership bodies that may be able to propose or suggest ideas and special purpose authorities. During the Labour government (1997–2010), regeneration bodies such as New Deal for Communities represented relatively formal local partnerships – with boards with wide representation from citizens, community organisations, local councillors or paid officials, and key public, private or voluntary sector participants.

The legitimacy of these bodies, and those persons involved within them, will often be contested as will the powers it is deemed to have (or not have). Cornwall (2004) and Gaventa (2001, 2006) argue that there may be shallow participation at times but there is then scope to develop deeper methods of democratic decentralisation (Spear et al., 2014). Further, as with the Mondragón co-operatives actual decision making entails work at a complex set of levels. Decision making may be slower than in conventional businesses or governments, but decisions subjected to greater scrutiny may be better owned.

Chaskin and Abunimah's (1997: 15) study in the United States found that, in general, the

> neighbourhood-based governance entities created by community-building initiatives are accepted by (and acceptable to) local government even if agreements and consensus on roles was not always easy. Indeed, neighbourhood-based governance entities ... were seen as potentially important mechanisms for fostering the kind of sought-after 'partnership' between local government and its neighbourhoods that many officials described as desirable.

This suggests that in Preston, and elsewhere in England, local governance arrangements to include social enterprises and smaller community organisations and co-operatives may hold promise. These might also include meetings between local anchor organisations (including university, hospital, local authority, housing association and police). Network meetings of small start-up co-operatives, influenced by the 'Evergreen' Co-operatives of the Cleveland Model, also provide spaces where informal as well as formal governance processes can flourish.

Analysis

This chapter has summarised aspects of the recent trajectories of both social enterprises and local government. Social enterprises in England can be understand as hybrid mutual organisations, combining social and business goals. Today they can be significant players at a local, regional, or national level, with legal structures that enable them to trade for social purposes and bid for public sector contacts. Meanwhile, local authorities have suffered severe budget cuts over the last 10 years with little in the way of place-based national government programmes. The Preston Model represents an inventive way of using the procurement power of public sector anchor organisations to re-circulate money in the local economy along with encouraging – or setting up – social enterprises/ co-operatives and encouraging training and networking opportunities. This represents not merely a set of economic measures aimed at community wealth building but also a range of networks that can be understood as part of local democratic governance.

Resource dependent pressures can often play a strong part in determining (or rationalising) the development paths taken by the public sector and social enterprises. Hence, looking ahead, in the context of the Preston model, what role will social enterprises play in developing and strengthening *governance* arrangements, as discussed by Gaventa (2004), and specifically relationships with:

- local government and other public anchor institutions (e.g. hospitals and universities);
- other civil society organisations and networks (e.g. social enterprises including co-operatives, charities and community groups; trade unions and activists; trade associations, local micro-business and individual self-employed people); and
- large private sector contractors (e.g. local and regional companies)?

The nexus of social enterprises within the Preston Model's governance structure provides opportunities for either competitive or collaborative trajectories – or mixtures of both tendencies at different times. We may anticipate that collaborative work will be mutually beneficial for the nexus of groups. However, in a version of the familiar prisoner's dilemma, circumstance may emerge that jolt the anticipated co-operative actions. Hence, one of the long-established dilemmas within collective action, as posited by Olson (1971: 27), is 'when it is in the interest of an individual unit in a group to act in the interest of the group as a whole'. Hence, to what extent may social enterprises, as independent organisations, play co-operative or competitive roles within these intra-organisational arrangements? Hence, to what degree might co-operative or competitive behaviours be, respectively, rewarded, or sanctioned? This may involve an important deliberative democracy where no one course of action is agreed upon. In order to illustrate possible dilemmas, we may consider three (invented) scenarios:

- Scenario 1: Social enterprise A in Preston engages in selling a highly lucrative product in another town that potentially undermines the entire regional business of social enterprise B which is also based in Preston. This could be considered by B (and the wider Preston nexus) in various ways: impolite, inappropriate, untrustworthy or unacceptable?
- Scenario 2: Consider (the mythical) Mai Kaldor who invents the delicious Preston Crumble and Rap Pie (CARP to the devotees) but, when it becomes a national phenomenon, she sells the business to McDonalds and retires to France. There is a sense of local disappointment and betrayal, but is this justified?
- Scenario 3: Organisation C joins a national consortium that wins a newly outsourced NHS service in Burnley which then leads to the closure of one

wing of Preston's hospital. C is also engaged in various other tenders for public sector contracts elsewhere in the UK, as part of a wider growth strategy in the north. There is unease among other local co-operatives at this highly competitive behaviour. Can existing governance arrangements cope with the emerging conflict?

These scenarios illustrate dilemmatic cases where governance arrangements might be jeopardised. Trajectories of competitive behaviour within the Preston model may not break formal rules but upset legitimacy, as Gaventa (2004) argued, and thus undermine trust within a co-operative milieu. However, open discussion of these developments could strengthen the role of governance mechanisms even if disagreement remains on actions that have taken place. Some of the formal structures listed earlier in Table 10.1 may be used to regulate rules but could also stifle relational accountability that will offer a more dynamic part of informal network governance.

Overall, the tension between co-operative or competitive behaviours in local governance arrangements may retain necessary dilemmas. The structures can, as Mordaunt (2006) argued, provide shared dilemmas to enable mutual and collective reflections. Alternatively, proposals for increased constitutional procedures and rules to sanction behaviours might be counterproductive and stifling to local information sharing and innovation. The discussion here points to the importance of the perceived 'legitimacy' (Evers, 2005) or otherwise of given actions within the organisational growth trajectories of organisations in a co-operative milieu. Hence, an important question may be: how far will the decisions or actions of individual organisations within the ambit of the Preston Model be considered as 'desirable' and 'appropriate' (Suchman, 1995) for the collective? Formal and informal governance arrangements may not sanction or oppose individual organisational actions. However, they may play roles in creating intra-organisational debate and establishing norms as part of what Cordery describes as a 'relational accountability' (Crawford et al., 2016; Buckley et al., 2017: 46) within learning exchanges and networking activities This may avoid the shallow, expedient or instrumental agreement discussed by Gaventa (2004: 22) and encourage negotiation and on 'shared dilemmas' as proposed by Mordaunt (2006: 124).

Conclusion

This chapter has explored the roles social enterprises may play in democratic governance arrangements within forums and processes that compose the Preston Model. What are the possible trajectories if, or when, some of the principles appear compromised or new challenges emerge? A simple binary between 'co-operative' and 'competitive' behaviour has been sketched here. One response to this could entail deliberative processes to resolve dilemmas among the nexus of organisations. Other responses might involve a rule-based approach by drafting codes of practice, or creating mediation process. However, the Preston model provides opportunities to engage in the real-time development of a wider deliberative democracy for citizens, projects and partners. This may be in informal or formal ways: in co-operative work spaces, citizen forums, social events, in work spaces or training events. Local governance processes may – at best – provide map, compass, and glue. Hence the development of local governance spaces remains vital in providing locations to debate, discuss and influence decisions and trajectories.

References

ACEVO (2019), Working to Ensure Bidding and Commissioning Practices are Fair and Inclusive. Retrieved from www.acevo.org.uk/advocacy/policy-and-research/commissioning-and-public-services. Accessed 10 April 2020.

Adventure Capital Fund (2020), Our History. Retrieved from www.sibgroup.org.uk/our-history. Accessed 12 June 2020.

Ball, J. (2019), What is 'New Municipalism', and Can it Really Combat Austerity? *New Statesman*, 9 April. Retrieved from www.newstatesman.com/spotlight/2019/04/what-new-municipalism-and-can-it-really-combat-austerity. Accessed 12 June 2020.

Beveridge, W.H. (1948), *Voluntary Action: A Report on Methods of Social Advance*, Routledge, London.

Billis, D. (ed.) (2010), *Hybird Organizations and the Third Sector: Challenges for Practice, Theory and Policy*, Palgrave Macmillan, Basingstoke.

Brighton and Hove (2020), Council Budget, 2020/2021. Retrieved from https://new.brighton-hove.gov.uk/council-and-democracy/council-finance/council-budget/cost-our-services-2020/21. Accessed 17 July 2020.

Buckley, E., Aiken, M., Baker, L., Davis, H., Usher, R. and IVAR (2017) *Power to Change*, Research Institute Report No 10, Power to Change and IVAR, London.

Bulmer, E. (2015), *Local Democracy: International IDEA Constitution-Building Primer 13*, International IDEA, Stockholm.

Calver, T. and Wainwright, D. (2018), How Cuts Changed Council Spending. Retrieved from www.bbc.co.uk/news/uk-england-46443700. Accessed 4 May 2020.

Campbell, D. (2016), Ambulance Privatisation Descends into 'Total Shambles', *The Guardian*, 12 April. Retrieved from www.theguardian.com/society/2016/apr/12/patients-wait-hours-for-ambulances-nhs-transport-service-privatised-sussex. Accessed 17 July 2020.

Change, Grow, Live (2019), *Annual Report and Accounts*, CGL, Brighton.

Chaskin, R.J., and Abunimah, A. (1997), A View from the City: Local Government Perspectives on Neighbourhood-based Governance in Community-Building Initiatives, Discussion Paper, the Chapin Hall Centre for Children, University of Chicago, Chicago, IL. Retrieved from http://citeseerx.ist.psu.edu/viewdoc/download;jsessionid=C357E1C49F6264EDAB19FDB2CF28AD20?doi=10.1.1.700.1496&rep=rep1&type=pdf. Accessed 5 November 2020.

CLES and Preston City Council (2019), How We Built Community Wealth in Preston: Achievements and Lessons, CLES and Preston City Council, Manchester and Preston. Retrieved from www.preston.gov.uk/media/1792/How-we-built-community-wealth-in-Preston/pdf/CLES_Preston_Document_WEB_AW.pdf?m=636994067328930000. Accessed 20 July 2020.

Co-operative Councils (2020), Values and Principles. Retrieved from www.councils.coop/resources/the-coop-values-and-principles/. Accessed 18 July 2020.

Cordery, C.J. (2013), Regulating Small and Medium Charities: Does It Improve Transparency and Accountability?, *Voluntas: International Journal of Voluntary and Nonprofit Organizations*, 24 (3): 831–851.

Cornwall, A. (2004), Introduction: New Democratic Spaces? The Politics and Dynamics of Institutionalised Participation, *IDS Bulletin* 35 (2): 1–10. Retrieved from https://opendocs. ids.ac.uk/opendocs/bitstream/handle/20.500.12413/8560/IDSB_35_2_10.1111-j.1759-5436. 2004.tb00115.x.pdf;jsessionid=51E5C4110A3E2D885B94C25ED02F5907?sequence=1. Accessed 5 November 2020.

Crawford, L., Morgan, G.G., and Cordery, C.J. (2016), Accountability and Non-for-Profit Organisations: Implications of an International Financial Reporting Framework, *Financial accountability and management*, 34 (2): 181–205.

Crouch, C. (2011), *The Strange Non-Death of Neo-Liberalism*, Polity Press, Cambridge.

Cullingworth, J., Bummer, R., and Watson, N. (2018), The Operation Modulus Approach: Further Lessons for Public Service Reform – What Works Scotland Case Study. Retrieved from http://whatworksscotland.ac.uk/wp-content/uploads/2018/06/ WWSOperationModulusApproachFurtherLessonsForPublicServiceReform.pdf. Accessed 5 November 2020.

Dart, R. (2004), The Legitimacy of Social Enterprise, *Nonprofit Management and Leadership*, 14 (4): 411–424.

Department for Digital, Culture, Media and Sport (2012), The Public Services (Social Value) Act: An Introductory Guide for Commissioners and Policymakers. Retrieved from www. gov.uk/government/publications/social-value-act-introductory-guide. Accessed 20 July 2020.

Duncan, A. (1992), *Taking on the Motorway: North Kensington Amenity Trust 21 Years*, Kensington and Chelsea Community History Group, London.

Eaton, G. (2018), Corbynism 2.0: The Radical Ideas Shaping Labour's Future, *New Statesman*, 19 September. Retrieved from www.newstatesman.com/politics/uk/2018/09/ corbynism-20-radical-ideas-shaping-labour-s-future. Accessed 20 July 2020.

Evers, A. (2005), Social Enterprises and Social Capital, In Borzago, C. and Defourny, J. (eds), *The Emergence of Social Enterprise*, Routledge, London.

Floyd, D. (2013), Are Social Enterprises Fit for the Future of Public Services?, The Guardian, 13 August. Retrieved from www.theguardian.com/social-enterprise-net work/2013/aug/13/social-enterprises-public-services-spin-outs. Accessed 20 June 2020.

Gaventa, J. (2001), *Towards Participatory Local Governance: Six Propositions for Discussion*, paper prepared for the LOGO Program Officers Retreat, Buxted, Sussex, June .

Gaventa, J. (2004) Strengthening Participatory Approaches to Local Governance, *National Civic Review*, 93 (4): 16–27.

Gaventa, J. (2006), Finding the Spaces for Change: A Power Analysis, *IDS Bulletin*, 37 (6): 23–33. Retrieved from www.powercube.net/wp-content/uploads/2009/12/finding_ spaces_for_change.pdf. Accessed 14 June 2020.

Glasius, M. and. Ishkanian, A. (2015), Surreptitious Symbiosis: The Relationship between NGO's and Movement Activists . *Open Democracy*. Retrieved from http://eprints.lse. ac.uk/63086/1/Ishakanian_Surreptitious%20symbiosis.pdf. Accessed 7 July 2020.

Haughton, S. (2019), Short Term Funding Does Not Make for Long Term Solutions. www.themj.co.uk/Short-term-funding-does-not-make-for-long-term-solutions/214558. Accessed 30 May 2020.

Hirst, P. (1994), *Associative Democracy: New Forms of Economic and Social Governance*, Policy Press, Cambridge.

HM Treasury (2002), The Third Sector Delivering Public Services: An Evidence Review. Retrieved from www.nao.org.uk/wp-content/uploads/2005/06/050675es.pdf. Accessed 5 November 2020.

HM Treasury and Cabinet Office (2007), The Third Sector Delivering Public Services. Retrieved from www.researchgate.net/publication/265198252_The_third_sector_delivering_ public_services_an_. Accessed 5 November 2020.

Knight, B. (1993) *Voluntary Action*, Centris, London.

Lazer, D, Mergel, I., Ziniel, C., and Neblo, M. (2009), Networks, Hierarchies, and Markets: Aggregating Collective Problem Solving in Social Systems. Retrieved from https://dash.harvard.edu/bitstream/handle/1/4481607/Lazer_NetworksHierarchies.pdf?sequence=1&isAllowed=y. Accessed 5 November 2020.

Locality (2020), Keep it Local. Retrieved from https://locality.org.uk/policy-campaigns/keep-it-local/. Accessed 20 April 2020.

Lupton, R. and Crisp, R. (2018), Regeneration Redux? What (if Anything) Can We Learn from New Labour?, In Needham, C., Heins, E., and Rees, J. (eds), *Social Policy Review 30: Analysis and Debate in Social Policy 2018*, Policy Press, Bristol, 209–228.

Macmillan, R. (2002), The Third Sector Delivering Public Services: An Evidence Review, Third Sector Research Centre, Working Paper 20. Retrieved from www.birmingham. ac.uk/Documents/college-social-sciences/social-policy/tsrc/working-papers/working-paper-20.pdf Accessed 8 January 2021.

Mordaunt, J. (2006), Emperor's New Clothes: Why Boards and Managers Find Accountability Relationships Difficult, *Public Policy and Administration*, 21 (3): 120–134.

Mullins, D. and Pawson, H (2010), Housing Associations: Agents of Policy or Profits in Disguise?, in Billis, D. (eds), *Hybrid Organizations and the Third Sector: Challenges for Practice, Theory and Policy*, Palgrave Macmillan, Basingstoke.

National Audit Office (2002), Working with The Third Sector. Retrieved from www.nao.org.uk/wp-content/uploads/2005/06/050675es.pdf. Accessed 20 July 2020.

NCVO (2015), Public Services. Retrieved from www.ncvo.org.uk/practical-support/information/public-services. Accessed 10 April 2020.

Newman, J. and Clarke, J. (2007), *The Managerial State*, Sage, London.

Olson, M. (1971), *The Logic of Collective Action: Public Goods and the Theory of Groups*, Harvard University Press, Cambridge, MA.

Ostrom, E. (1990), *Governing the Commons: The Evolution of Institutions for Collective Actions*, Cambridge University Press, Cambridge.

Pearce, J. (1993), *At the Heart of the Community Economy*, Calouste Gulbenkian Foundation, London.

Plummer, J., (2018), About 1,600 Scope Staff Transferred to Private Care Company. Retrieved from www.thirdsector.co.uk/1600-scope-staff-transferred-private-care-company/management/article/1463607. Accessed 5 November 2020.

Preston City Council (2019) 'What is the Preston Model' https://www.preston.gov.uk/article/1339/What-is-Preston-Model-, accessed 22/3/2021

Rochester, C. (2017), *Rediscovering Voluntary Action: The Beat of a Different Drum*, Palgrave Macmillan, London.

Singer, C. (2016), The Preston Model. Retrieved from https://thenextsystem.org/the-preston-model. Accessed 26 July 2018.

Smith, N.A., Phillips, D., and Simpson, P. (2016), *A Time of Revolution?: British Local Government Finance in the 2010s*, Institute of Fiscal Studies, London.

Social Exclusion Unity (1998), *Bringing Britain Together: A National Strategy for Neighbourhood Renewal*, HMSO, London.

Spear, R. (2001), United Kingdom: A Wide Variety of Social Enterprises, in Borzaga, C. and Defournt, J. (eds), *The Emergence of Social Enterprise*, Routledge, London.

Spear, R. (2015), Mapping Social Enterprise in the UK: Definitions, typologies and hybrids, in Bouchard, M. and Rousselière, D. (eds), *The Weight, Size and Scope of the Social Economy: an International Perspective*, Peter Lang, Brussels.

Spear, R., Cornforth, C., and Aiken (2014), Major Perspectives on Governance of Social Enterprise', in Defourny, J., Hulgård, L., and Pestoff, V. (eds), *Social Enterprise and the Third Sector: Changing European Landscapes in a Comparative Perspective*, Routledge, London.

Stocki, R. (2017), *Co-operatives Viewed from the Systems Theory Perspective: The Role of Values in Equilibrating Four Levels of Organizational Systems to Decrease the Systems' Entropy*, paper presented at the 10th International Critical Management Studies (CMS) Conference, Liverpool, 3–5 July.

Suchman, M.C. (1995), Managing Legitimacy: Strategic and Institutional Approaches, *Academy of Management Review*, 20 (3): 571–610.

Thake, S. (1995), *Staying the Course: The Role and Structure of Community Regeneration Organisations*, Joseph Rowntree Foundation, York.

Thake, S. (2001), *Building Communities, Changing Lives*, Joseph Rowntree Foundation, York.

Thompson, G.F. (1993), *Between Hierarchies and Markets: The Logic and Limits of Network Forms of Organization*, Oxford University Press, Oxford.

Webb, S. (1898), Quotations: Walk along the Municipal Pavement, Lit by Municipal Gas ... [attributed]. Retrieved from www.goodreads.com/author/show/15312770.Sidney_Webb. Accessed 24 July 2020.

Weisbrod, B.A. (ed.) (1988), *To Profit or Not to Profit*, Cambridge University Press, Cambridge.

Whyte, W.F. and Whyte, K.K. (1991), *Making Mondragon: the Growth and Dynamics of the Worker Co-operative Complex*, ILR Press, Ithaca, NY.

11 The pandemic changes everything

Hybrid stakeholder shared ownership models in the USA starting with the union–co-op movement

Michael Alden Peck

Introduction

Writing this chapter just before the November 2020 US Presidential election, events reveal many hard lessons about the state of America. "Self-evident" truths have become disfigured through a combination of partisan culture, stark socioeconomic inequalities and the uncontrolled pandemic.

A self-infecting nation, first opioids and now coronavirus at the latest rate of over seventy thousand daily, with hundreds of thousands more already departed, disappeared, lost, many dying alone. An unchecked biomedical pandemic brought to crescendo deliberately by a US Senate declining to engage tsunamis of food poverty, over forty million unemployed, homelessness and precariat evictions, pervasive generational and racial despair, frontline community economic class abandonment. An America exceptional for its self-righteousness, embedded racism, hypocritical ugliness, and fatally divisive cultural inferiority failing its own people in pandemic droves.

In this worsening dystopia, it is clear that flattening COVID-19 contagion curves compels flattening inequality pandemic curves concurrently. *No healthy economy without a healthy people* is more than a mantra, it is the pandemic survival *sine qua non*. Beyond outsourcing, arbitraging, commoditising and offshoring Labour, a new investment, governance and performance culture is waiting in the wings.

As noted by Ra Criscitiello, Deputy Director, SEIU-UHW, in the July 2020 UK Manifesto for Decent Work, COVID-19 has exposed the fact that 'essential workers' are often people of colour and, because largely misclassified as independent contractors, are denied the protections and benefits of formal employment that are currently so needed. Now more than ever is a time to focus on creating a different kind of economy that centres worker voice, pooled advocacy, employment benefits, and focuses on better work lives for low-wage 'essential' workers who have historically been undervalued in many ways.

Solving the inequalities exposed by COVID-19 means repurposing the most economically vulnerable from the back to the front of the line as the newly indispensable serving others in the context of a greater common good. Inequality is no longer under debate; it is the debate. And this debate, like the pandemic virus itself, will have to come with a vaccine equally viable and accessible for all. Consent of the Governed must be synonymous with Consent of the Employed, the Contracted Out and the Consuming Public in majority consumption-driven GDP socio-economies.

1worker1vote

The 1worker1vote movement I co-started and help to lead believes that the foundational policy for a fair and aspirational economy that works for all is inclusive, broadened and deepened, local stakeholder worker ownership under-girded by workplace democracy practices. Our movement predicts it will be much harder for those committed to predatory patriarchy and 'trickle-down' wealth and opportunity to ignore, bypass, or disenfranchise any worker-owner empowered by an equity share, a voice in decision-making and a vote.

Metrics show broad-based, worker owned social enterprises and ecosystems, through aligned high road principles and practices, are more stable, inclusive, equitable, democratic, resilient, and competitive with fewer job losses, especially during downturns. Research reveals that combining an equity stake with participatory ownership culture (essentially the definition of a worker co-operative) creates upwardly transformative, shared purpose-driven businesses and societies. (Walsh et al, 2018).

The basic democratic principle valued in nation-states and Stakeholder Economy enterprises is one-human/one-vote. An equity share is the right to vote and provides the basis for power-paradigm-changing culture combining inclusive community and individual civic-solidarity mutualism, stability and self-reliance leading to flatter curves sharing more equally fulfilled lives and dignified retirements.

Increasingly, both social impact and traditional (hedge, pension, and private-equity) funders seek to finance worker-takeovers of companies for these uplifting social reasons and because stakeholder-owned firms' superior resiliency and performance improve returns. For capital providers, the 'S' for Social in ESG's (Environment, Social, Governance) metrics dominates and is based on resiliency algorithms. Resiliency and stakeholder ownership are inseparable, one provides the roots and rationale for the other.

The *Impact Alpha* newsletter reports:

> Asset managers compete on impact as investors move beyond ESG. As passive ESG funds emerge as the hottest trend in financial services, active asset managers are touting their 'impact alpha'. Rather than simply tracking the market, they are looking for outperformance with strategies around the low-carbon transition, a more inclusive economy, and the U.N. Sustainable Development Goals (SDGs). Already this year, US funds that employ environmental, social and governance, or ESG, analysis have attracted more than last year's record total of $21.4 billion.
>
> (Impact Alpha, 2020)

According to Wylie:

> While some business leaders argue shareholders should receive the lion's share of profits because they are the ones who bear the financial risks, the fallacy of this thinking has been laid bare during the pandemic, as companies asked the government and taxpayers to help them stay afloat. Corporations rely not only on shareholders, but also on stakeholders such as the country, consumers, and their own employees ... A stakeholder mindset is about more than just being socially responsible – it's also good for the bottom line. Stakeholder-minded businesses see reduced reputational risks and higher employee engagement, in addition to better investor evaluation and improved operating performance. Even consumers perceive products differently when businesses have a socially responsible reputation.
>
> (Wylie, 2020)

The built world's next learning mission is to grasp that there is no lasting socio-economic reform without changing existing power paradigms, and that there is no lasting power paradigm change without equality reforming structure. Pandemic winner and loser countries show that everything is downstream from culture. What is this new and better culture that is out there to be fulfilled and defined?

Culture change and demographics

Harvard Business School Professor, Rebecca Henderson, in her April 2019 newsletter declared:

> Unconstrained, capitalism is on the verge of destroying the planet and destabilizing society. The world is on fire. We're destabilizing the earth's climate, raising sea levels, and poisoning the ocean. Wealth is rushing to the top, while a toxic mix of rage and alienation is enabling a new generation of authoritarian populists to consolidate power. But the world could be different. We have the resources and the technology to build a just and sustainable world – and purpose driven businesses could be the catalyst that drives the global, systemic change we need to reimagine capitalism in a way that works for everyone.
>
> (Henderson, 2019)

In September of 2019, the US Business Roundtable discovered the downside of Milton Friedman's Shareholder Primacy and in February 2020, the World Economic Forum in Davos discovered Stakeholder Capitalism. These two 'reveals' implicate competitive values equations demanding better structures starting with more inclusive and expanded stakeholder culture where ownership is foundational.

We can unpack this process by recognising and organising the growing divide between US Worker Ownership & Employee Ownership communities – they used to be more or less the same but no more. The latter is now a dwindling subset of the former especially in the face of rising majority minority demographic transformation including gender, race, immigration status and origin, sexual preference, age, and generational identity composition. 'We whitewashed the middle class, and in the process, we legitimized a lie'. (Tankersley, quoted in Hohmann 2020).

America's rising, majority-minority working class seeking and deserving worker empowerment represents informal gig economy workers, formal free-lancers, 1099 contractors, temporary workers, organised labour, alternative labour, undocumented labour, commoditised labour including forced prison labour still sharecropping on privatised incarceration plantations, generational scholastic-graduating labour with nowhere to go, creatively destroyed, kicked-out and kicked-down labour, the unemployed, and under-employed. Ironically, these workers serve as the essential foot soldiers for the current crisis to flourish, it is how the 'Epicenter Pandemic Economy' (EPE) functions.

Moving on from today's labour snapshot where 'the white working class represents 44 percent of the electorate', (Teixeira, 2016) by 2040, in two decades, white Americans are projected to be less than 50% of the population. America's future majority minority workforce will be more race and gender diverse, older and with higher education levels starting with women. No single ethnic group is going to represent an absolute majority of the emerging US working class population.

Other direct and indirect 'cause and effect' working class change demographics to consider:

- According to latest census projections, in 2045 the US population is estimated to be 24.6% Hispanic, 13.1% black, 7.9% Asian, and 3.8% mixed race. (These figures will change after the highly conflicted 2020 census, already underway but now forced by a partisan US Supreme Court to cease its work counting undocumented immigrants – prematurely). The 65 and older working population will rise from 17% today to 22% in 2040, according to the US Census.
- Despite the current US administration's sadistic and criminal treatment of immigrants starting with accelerated family separation and putting brown babies in border cages (morally deserving of a domestic Nuremburg-like trial for crimes against humanity), America's increasingly gender and race diverse and older working class is on track to represent 65% of all who work.
- The immigrant share of the US population is approaching a record high but remains below that of many other countries and has been severely curtailed by the current Administration using the COVID-19 pandemic as cover for its cruelty and racist restriction policies against the wishes of the full spectrum US business community.
- The combining factors of low birth rates, workers who can't afford ever to retire, and now incoming immigration reduced to basically zero short-change the US economy with nationwide labour shortages that will become

critical as federal pandemic institutional leadership continues to fail citizens in advanced dire straits and all business sectors.

As a result, the US unauthorised immigrant population is at its lowest level in more than a decade. This sad statistic flies in the face of globally empowered competition from those countries who flattened their curves with greater success so that post pandemic demography becomes destiny. Barron's reports that 'Immigrants make up 14% of the USA population, but 28% of startup founders and 24% of patent holders. Without that entrepreneurial zeal, the United States would be much less innovative' (Gislason, 2019). Axios noted that 'immigrants and their kids founded 45 percent of US Fortune 500 companies' (Kight, 2019).

Flying in the face of these emerging demographics, white privilege among America's working classes is pervasive and lethal. 'A majority of Americans (56%) say that being black hurts a person's ability to get ahead a lot or a little, while 51% say being Hispanic is a disadvantage', according to a recent Pew Research Center survey. 'In contrast, about six-in-ten (59%) say being white *helps* a person's ability to get ahead in the US today' (Menasce Horowitz et al., 2019).

Why can't we practice, teach and advocate for a truly 'free' level playing field marketplace, one where so-called 'invisible hands' serve to eschew corporatist, rent-seeking corruption instead of the reverse? Why can't we support deepened and broadened self-reliance through individual worker ownership with equity, a voice, a vote and a 'Magna Carta' Labour collective bargaining agreement (CBA) to keep passive income powerbrokers, social media influencers, vulture investors and other would-be mandarins greed and dominance-checked?

Why can't America do better than yield to the forever pyramid, a top-down world formed by predatory-class economics practitioners where, to paraphrase Jean Jacques Rousseau's eighteenth century prophecy, humanity is born free yet everywhere finds itself in chains of imposed chaos, involuntary servitude, and deliberate politics of cruelty and abasement? Who determined society should categorise makers and takers as organically separate and keep them unequal when it so plainly takes an integrated, collaborating village to heal a pandemic? That how much we need each other is, in itself, a more mutually stimulating business ecosystem construct where inequalities are transformed into regenerative virtuous cycles, work is aspirational, and profits are more fairly shared. (Rousseau, 1998 [1762]).

The virus is proving that neither the pre-existing world of inherited comparative advantages and plantation privilege, nor its servile unequal markets for those whose labour is perennially commoditised can afford to be driven primarily by parochial self-interest. Narrowly defined economic perspectives charged with the care and feeding of rich people at the exclusion of everyone else has produced a neocolonialist straitjacket social order, a Joycean 'nightmare of history' from which the virus wakes us 'woke' unless it kills us first.

For the socially disenfranchised, economically abandoned and technologically 'creatively destroyed', aspirational and decent work is an oxymoron. Global, neoliberal-sanctioned labour arbitraging formulas and markets built on exterritorial, financialised commodity exchanges offshore, outsource and upend generationally sabotaged lives and communities for pennies on the labour dollar. 'Free' markets whitewash any philanthropic pretence to the contrary: in democracies these populations vote for Brexit and 'America First' because, to quote Kris Kristofferson (in a song most famously performed by Janis Joplin), 'freedom is just another word for nothing left to lose' ('Me and Bobby McGee', 1969).

Doing the opposite

Normally, much can be said for doing the opposite of what passes for annual Davos conventional wisdom. Increasingly, like the song Malvina Reynolds wrote for Pete Seeger, about green grass growing through dead cement (Pete Seeger, 'God Bless the Grass', 1966), the world belongs to a metaphorical Port Alegre of global citizenry rising up in their respective, unequal geographies, speaking truth to rancid and reactionary entrenched power, demonstrating against capitalistic 'droit de Seigneur' status quo, standing resolute for aspirational local economic democracy and sovereignty over their neighbourhoods, cities, countries and lives.

Davos 2020 offered paeans to stakeholder capitalism and continues publicly to pronounce on this theme by endorsing six 'Stakeholder Principles in the COVID Era'. These are: (1) workplace and employee safety, (2) shared business continuity through integrated and open supply chains and customer ecosystems, (3) fair prices and terms for essential supplies benefitting end consumers, (4) full support to governments and society, (5) long-term company viability and potential to create sustained value for shareholders, and (6) focus on long term sustainability goals including the Paris climate agreement and the United Nations Sustainable Development Agenda.

The American Sustainable Business Council (ASBC) in its recently released (2020), *Creating An Economic System That Works For All* report, with 1worker1vote as a content contributor, observes that:

> while capitalism remains a dynamic force, challenges such as income inequality, crumbling infrastructure, market consolidation, climate change, underinvestment, and the financialization of America's economy pose serious threats… Many across the country view our current capitalist system as rigged and not working for them… In recent history, management has focused on maximizing value for themselves and their shareholders. But a growing chorus of finance experts argues that this narrow focus has come at great cost to customers, employees, suppliers, and communities who have an even larger stake in the economy.
>
> If our economy is to work for *all* then business leaders have to implement ways to simultaneously address the priorities of *all* their stakeholders… The stated redirection in 'business purpose,' from a focus on

shareholders to stakeholders requires broad public policy changes as well as clear measurable goals, both of which are lacking in the Business Roundtable initiative. This critical transition will also require many changes in the culture, compensation, ownership, and the careful measurement of business performance as well as the passage of public policies that are based on serving the needs of all stakeholders. Such is our task and challenge.

(American Sustainable Business Council, 2020)

The ASBC report also notes that on 13 April 2020, the *New York Times* declared, in a piece titled 'Big Business Pledged Gentler Capitalism. It's Not Happening in a Pandemic', that 'CEOs who signed a celebrated Business Roundtable document, promising to elevate worker interests, are now resorting to furloughs' (Goodman, 2020). Axios reports:

The pool of American workers on the front lines of the coronavirus pandemic is getting a lot bigger... There are already around 55 million Americans working front-line jobs – defined as jobs that require exposure to a large number of people who could potentially carry the virus. Now add to that millions of teachers, retail sales reps, nail techs and other professionals who have returned or will return to work in the coming weeks as their workplaces reopen.

(Pandey, 2020)

In what I call the 'Streaming Stakeholder Economy', where digital platforms are co-operatively owned and shared, pull is more important than push and already benefits from a rising platform methodology. Environmental, Social, and Governance investing started in the 1960s as 'socially responsible investing' and has transitioned into three globally accepted and practiced metrics measuring the sustainability and societal impact of an investment in a company or business. Increasingly with the advent of social enterprises and social enterprise ecosystems, these criteria are used to measure and predict company financial performance across sectors. A further metric, the 2016 United Nations Sustainable Development Goals (SDGs), represent 17 goals with 169 targets that all 191 UN Member States have agreed to try to achieve by the year 2030 (UN, 2016).

Let's agree that how we face down the biomedical pandemic, co-operatively and collectively, will determine how society heals its cultural 'winners take all' capitalism fever. That the destiny of our remaining shared purpose lifetimes, within all of the ecosystems we impact directly and indirectly, mandates we reach for a more dynamic, inclusive, aspirational and multi-partisan, more united than divided, rising middle ground, middle earth, and expanding middle class. Where instead of more endless, toxic rounds boxing against ourselves, we no longer allow those who manipulate the siren songs and grievance heartstrings of false nostalgia culture to seize precious space in our collective minds and hearts through extractive eminent mental and physical domain.

Instead, let us commit to black belt, purpose-driven mastery in civic judo optimising stakeholder momentum organically from the bottom up to bring society more permanently forward. Rather than lifting our eyes and outlook to meet the artificial upper crusts of a socio-economic gravity circus imposed by others dedicated to holding us fixed and fixated in our commoditised places, unable to breathe freely, why don't we try something different, especially when it's profitable and works?

The past is prologue until it's not: the need for the union–co-op

Both the modern co-operative movement, which originated with the 1840s Rochdale principles in the UK, and the emergence of industrial unionisation to combat Industrial Age inequalities and inhumanity, developed in parallel. Today's union–co-op model draws its origin stories and evolving practices from the nineteenth century's Rochdale Pioneers, the Knights of Labor on three continents and four countries (UK, USA, Canada, and Australia), and from north-central Italy's ongoing Emilia-Romagna co-operatives, all founded within forty years of each other. This phenomenon is repeating two decades short of two-hundred years later.

In the twentieth and now twenty-first centuries, many (including this author) seeking proven, adapting and sustaining socioeconomic justice and workplace democracy find inspiration from seventy years of self-improving Mondragon industrial co-operative principles and experiences. The Mondragon Corporation is now Spain's tenth largest and fourth most important employment creator. Traversing three centuries, co-operatives and unions have evolved separately, and the development in Mondragón is an example of this, but today's extreme global solidarity deficit imperatives, nakedly exposed by the COVID-19 pandemic, compels a renewal and scaling-up of the union–co-op bond.

Starting in the 1970s, America has counterbalanced high per capita GDP with rising unequal income distribution. 'Winners-take-all' results and culture have produced stagnant wages, public sector operations outsourced to the lowest privatising bidder at precariat wage levels without benefits, declining mobility, multiple-track justice and healthcare depending on relative wealth and influence, increased economic class divisions and racial tensions at levels not experienced since the Great Depression. In today's America, globalised labour arbitraging commoditised and then cannibalised humanity, weakened unions and their ability to collectively bargain, and redlined majority minority neighbourhoods combined to gut America's 1964 Civil Rights and 1965 Voting Rights Acts, put lead into municipal water systems, cut off access to affordable healthcare in the middle of a pandemic, and ripped out the heart of existing societal compacts.

The 2008 Great Recession transferred trillions of accumulated rising middle-class wealth upwards to those designing and perfecting the Shareholder Primacy Economy's permanent, re-financialised trickle-down vicious cycles. Millions of working and middle-class homeowners from all ethnic backgrounds and geographies lost their lifetime nest egg equity and savings while not a single perpetrating banker or corrupt policymaker went to jail. Advertised 'change elections' betrayed their voter's once in power by doubling down on the financial status quo and allowed pseudo-populism to rear its ugly and destructive, bait and switch death-head.

The neoliberal global (and in the US domestically bipartisan) trade consensus shuttered over sixty-thousand American factories since 1992's NAFTA (North America Free Trade Act) signed by Mexico, Canada and the United States. Multiple deindustrialised generations later, the jury is no longer out for consultation and the verdict is epic.

Egregious shareholder exterritorial profits were prioritised over any basic moral and environmental principles associated with decent work conditions buttressing stakeholders. Already grotesquely socio-economically unfair, lethally polluting, and racially discriminatory towards industrial and service sector workers, America's leading business schools and their private sector acolytes celebrated stock option 'creative destruction' manna from 'free-market' heaven and then tilted every marketplace to be as 'unfree' and platform monopolised as possible. Any thoughts devoted to creative reconstruction for those so creatively destroyed are still missing in action.

Flattening labour curves – 'New Labor Organizing' defined

'New Labor Organizing' is a term defined and used by the 1worker1vote movement to describe additive changes in work culture including equity, agency, self-fulfilment, and community uplift through hybrid shared ownership models starting with a renewed union–co-op bond. Accelerated by a pandemic without mercy, a crossover electoral majority in the United States is demanding a new culture of honourable work. In a melting pot nation experiencing meltdown, hybrid labour organising opportunities abound. This process includes a democratic, co-operative and marketplace competitive approach to new work prospects, technologies, projects, missions and structures reflecting the values of self-reliance, boot-strapping entrepreneurialism, civic and workplace equity combined with wage solidarity, democratic inclusion, inter-co-operation, and social transformation.

Cooperatives that offer competitive marketplace examples of workplace democracy and represent significant scale are already uniting with Unions who bring solidarity culture and journeyman training including safety back to the American productivity table. Three examples include SEIU-UHW's 'AlliedUP' healthcare staffing firm, the International Association of Machinists Union's Lobster 207 and New England Loggers' Cooperative (https://vimeo.com/coopdevinst/troy-jackson), and Cooperative Homecare Associates (CHCA) represented by SEIU 1199.

As a more profitable and socially healing alternative, New Labor Organizing insists that first mover 'creative disruption' is paired with concurrent 'creative reconstruction' leaving no working-class community behind. New Labor Organizing rejects specious proclamations of a 'post-industrial' or 'post racist society' and instead recognises that only inclusive, comprehensive and organic restructuring from the bottom-up can be successful, involving all sector stakeholders such as corporations, unions, investors, government and advocacy influencers to rebuild America's new human talent ecosystems.

New Labor Organizing grasps that each new wave of dislocating technology, the latest being intrusive artificial intelligence (AI) applications, robotics, and surveillance platforms, coexists with a mandate to re-purpose and re-position human beings back into the centre, value-adding stage of each incoming socio-technological equation. New Labor Organizing offers a bottom-up, regenerative, democratic, 'fair share' (the worker ownership version of 'fair trade') wages, equity compensation and tax policies civic compact that seeds solidarity-infused, rising middle class-centric, local living economies. New Labor Organizing discards historically and consistently tried and failed wealth-centric strategies that trickle down and offers up a new Stakeholder Economy paradigm dedicated to 'bubble-up and gusher-up' (a 1worker1vote movement branded descriptor).

New Labor Organizing substitutes proven worker self-actuation models to reach higher and more durable remuneration standards and opportunities including equity shared with working class families and their communities. New Labor Organizing advocates for unalienable individual worker rights to compete with dominating corporate personhood rights starting with fair relative taxation rates with no exceptions for the wealthy and politically influential, participative workplace democracy and portable healthcare benefits to level and liberate the currently badly skewed, employer-employee-worker power paradigm playing field perpetuating an unnecessary and un-equalising top-down dependency.

New Labor Organizing repurposes collective bargaining agreements as enterprise 'magna cartas' benefitting management and workers based on transparent shared risks and shared rewards formulas, incentivising workplace democracy and 'one worker, one vote' equity participation. New Labor Organizing expands its outreach to include gig economy representation, crowd-sourced and crowd-funded technology platforms, and the enterprises they produce. In this brave new, 'pandemic as portal' world, monopolies are broken up in favour of both workers and consumers to pursue more socially resilient opportunities characterised by results and conclusions outlined in the World Happiness Report (https://worldhappiness.report/ed/2020/) and GINI index measuring place-based societal and structural inequalities.

Rob Witherell, innovative and resourceful organiser for the USW (United Steelworkers), who together with Chris Cooper, a Program Coordinator with the Ohio Employee Ownership Center (OEOC) at Kent State University, both 1worker1vote cofounders, co-authored the 1worker1vote movement's foundational union–co-op template in March 2012. Witherell envisions a new organising 'Union 3.0' concept. According to this, current Union models are no longer sufficient to organise many workers in today's economy. Membership under those models has been in decline for over 40 years, and there is an emerging labour movement outside of the current Union models with which Unions need to connect. The purpose of Union 3.0 is not to replace current models but to supplement them and to reconnect and grow the labour movement through job creation, business development, and worker ownership.

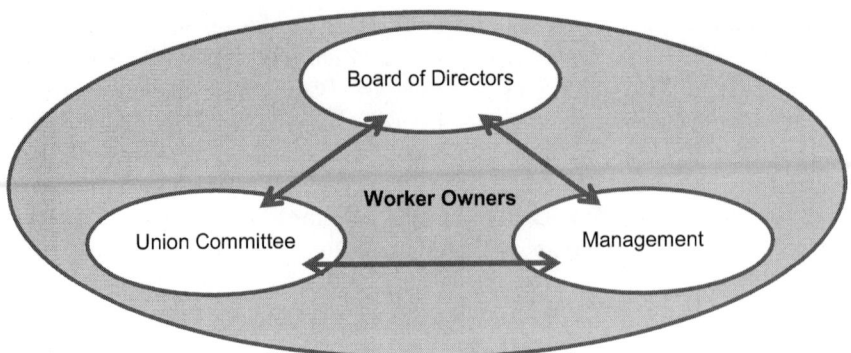

Figure 11.1 The USW-OEOC-1worker1vote Union-Coop Structure inspired by Mondragon's Social Committee

Source: Rob Witherell (http://1worker1vote.org/union-3-0-worker-ownership-and-the-future-of-the-labor-movement)

Equally relevant for beleaguered service and staffing sectors, Ra Criscitiello, SEIU-UHW's (Service Employee International's West Coast Nurses United Healthcare Workers Union) Deputy Director, Research Division and 1worker1vote advisory board member, is leading California's Cooperative Economy Act (CEA) legislative campaign (www.cooperativeeconomyact.org) to reimagine that state's gig economy contracting ecosystem. Previously cited in the ASBC *Creating an Economic System That Works For All* report (American Sustainable Business Council, 2020), which features the CEA as an innovative future of work paradigm for large scale adoption.

CEA pushes back on big business gig economy companies like UBER who decline to define drivers either as employees or even a core part of the business strategy, publicly admitting that doing so would decimate profit margins built on the back of arbitraging and commoditising human labour (Criscitiello, 2020) offering a new business model that provides for worker equity, workplace democracy, union representation, undergirded by a living family and community sustaining wage with competitive benefits.

Lisa Bolton, Vice President for Telecommunications and Technologies with the Communications Workers of America (CWA) and another visionary 1worker1vote advisory board member, led the Denver, Colorado metropolitan charge as President of CWA Local 7777 to create a union–co-op taxi movement with highly motivated immigrants East Africa. (Bolton, 2020).

To date, US Union Coops are purely private sector and represent business areas such as healthcare (includes homecare and nursing), food desert grocery stores, fishing, logging, energy efficiency, solar installations, child care, transportation, design printing, window manufacturing, agriculture, education, biking, software systems, marketing and communications, and soon medical cannabis. Scale exists and industry focus is broad and varied.

US Union Coops are located mostly along the Cincinnati-Dayton/Ohio corridor, in Western and Central Massachusetts, in Denver-Colorado, New York City, Madison-Wisconsin, Oakland/Berkeley/Los Angeles – California, in Olympia & Seattle – Washington, and the State of Maine but there are growth signs almost everywhere.

Participating, progressive Unions include the United Steelworkers, United Food & Commercial Workers, International Machinists, Service Employees International – SEIU, Transport Workers Union, United Electrical Radio & Machine Workers, Amalgamated Transit Union, United Farm Workers, and Communications Workers of America.

1worker1vote: the rising US union–co-op experience

QUESTION: What is a worker co-operative?

ANSWER: A worker co-operative is a for-profit business that produces goods and services and whose workers also own and democratically manage the business.

QUESTION: What is a Mondragon-inspired union co-operative?

ANSWER: A for-profit business, owned and directed by its workers; utilising the collective bargaining agreement process reflecting Mondragon's Social Committee approach; guided by the core principles of sustainability, solidarity, accountability, community as reflected in the ten Mondragon principles; paying close attention to seventy years of Mondragon co-operative ecosystem experiences and lessons learned.

The 1worker1vote movement, initially envisioned throughout the 2012–2014 timeframe, is a New York-registered 501c3 economic development non-profit catalyst formally launched in the Spring of 2015. 1worker1vote's legacy mission and practices spring from three founding sources:

- First, the October 2009 United Steelworkers and Mondragon International Collaboration Agreement intended as an antidote to the global socio-economic ravages of the 2008 Great Recession.
- Second, a thirty month nationwide incubation, reflection, feedback and consensus-building process resulting in the March 2012 public presentation of the union–co-op template by the United Steelworkers, the Ohio Center for Employee Ownership, and Mondragon International's North America delegate, co-presented by leaders of the US co-operative movement such as Dr Martin Lowery, EVP Emeritus of NRECA, in the atrium of the Steelworkers international headquarters in Pittsburgh, after two-and-one-half years of public reflection, feedback and consensus building.
- Third, collaboration MOUs signed with the leadership at that time of five Mondragon co-operatives in the spring of 2014 (Laboral Kutxa – Mondragon's co-operative bank, Mondragon University, Mondragon International, Saiolan –

Mondragon's co-operative incubator, and MIK – Mondragon's co-operative knowledge centre).

Given its dual Labor and Cooperative founding rationale and roots, 1worker1vote focuses on policies, practices, and projects to build shared purpose social enterprise ecosystems through hybrid shared ownership enterprise models starting with the union–co-op template. 1worker1vote helps to launch for-profit, hybrid model enterprise ecosystems and projects that are worker owned and managed. The focus is on developing economic self-reliance, inclusive entrepreneurship and civic equity culture in frontline communities across America by localising close to seventy years of Mondragón worker co-operative ecosystem principles and practices and then taking and localising those lessons learned 'across borders, markets and silos' (the 1worker1vote version of union co-ops beyond borders).

The 1worker1vote movement prioritises eliminating 'trickle-down' dependencies in all sectors (private, public, philanthropic) by replacing vertical relationships with 'flattened curve', horizontal ones (one worker/one vote equity, workplace democracy, agency, and solidarity) to design and inhabit aspirational and inclusive civic culture. Prized operational qualities include inclusivity, transparency, collaboration, professional excellence, follow-up and follow-through diligence.

1worker1vote believes and sets out to prove that ownership is the ineluctable human and democratic system condition. The transforming way forward for all of us rising from paycheck dependency to enterprise equity is to reflect on and then steward lessons learned from the Mondragón ecosystem where capital is labour's instrument, not its master.

Currently, 1worker1vote is governed by ten co-founders, ten members of our national advisory board and an executive director who is also a co-founder. 1worker1vote is a member of the American Sustainable Business Council (www.asbcouncil.org) and collaborates on hybrid shared ownership models policies with ASBC through a joint 'Ownership4All' campaign.

- As institutional co-founders, Coop Cincy (www.coopcincy.org) operates as the prototyping 'living lab' for the 1worker1vote movement and includes Coop Dayton (www.coopdayton.org).
- CUNY Law School's Community Economic Development Clinic (CEDC) in NYC leads 1worker1vote's intellectual property, legal and alliance structuring work. Recently, the CEDC founding executive director, Professor Carmen Huertas-Noble, a 1worker1vote co-founder, was inducted into the 2020 US Cooperative Hall of Fame, the highest honour accorded by this community and the first union–co-operator to achieve it.
- Other global partners include key thought and action leaders from Mondragon, the Institute for Innovation in Politics of Vienna, Austria, the Preston/UK Cooperative Development Network and UK Cooperative College, with our UK partners producing 'The Manifesto for Decent Work' (2020).

- Rebecca Henderson and Michael Norris of Harvard Business School have written a case study on '1worker1vote: Mondragon in the US' (Henderson and Norris, 2015).
- Boston's Tellus Institute 'Great Transition Initiative' GTI forum on CSR/corporate redesign: https://greattransition.org/gti-forum/corporations-in-the-crosshairs features 1worker1vote – http://1worker1vote.org/democratize-corporation/

Inspired directly as practitioners by seventy plus years of Mondragon co-operative ecosystem experiences, 1worker1vote began as a domestic (USA) and now emerging global non-profit catalyst for hybrid shared ownership models and their worker-stakeholder empowerment potential. As part of its 'truth to power' DNA, the 1worker1vote movement intentionally reaches across aisles that separate 'humanity@work' to 'reconcile opposites', partner and collaborate. The goal is to transcend and transform conventional thought borders and barriers, polarising and exclusive practice silos, and extractive status quo legacies with the basic ingredients to achieve broadened and deepened workplace liberation and fulfilment in marketplaces that are truly fair and free.

Conclusion

To summarise, let's legitimise and empower newly apparent 'humanity@work' truths and ecosystems.

Rising gender, race, immigration status and origin, sexual preference, age, and generational identity demographics are combining to form a new American workforce. This more diverse American workforce frame supersedes geographic labelling because its profile is practically ubiquitous throughout Blue/Democrat and Red/Republican States with a few exceptions. Embedded structural economic class inequalities within both rural and urban geographies made more visible during the pandemic starting with imperilled gig economy workers also combine to abuse America's newly diversified working class.

This diversity-reconfiguring workforce comes with new cultures and aspirations which have outpaced existing 'ownership models and formulas', reducing their relevance and requiring new hyphenated, hybrid ownership models (e.g. union–co-ops or Esoperatives) that deserve tax parity equal to more conventional tools such as democratic Employee Stock Ownership Plans (ESOPs). We should make the case that America's potential and current worker-owners and their hosting community stakeholders are best served through the freedom of choosing the ownership structure that's best for them. Free and open cultural as well as financial choices require tax parity among competing ownership structures that currently favour investors, boardrooms and passive-income, and usually ex-territorial shareholders with the goal of achieving a flat-level investor and financing playing field.

Those status quo resistors who argue for or against the conventional binary condition that society can either bring workers up to wealth or wealth down to workers, either through restructure or redistribution, either zero-sum or win-win, miss the reality of what's happening. America's new workplace and workforce reality revolves around a third dimension of local stakeholder choice, increased diversity, and zero-tolerance of 'plantation economics'. Using its power, a self-identifying indispensable workforce deserves and demands a better deal while carrying the rest of America on broad and vocal, collective shoulders.

Let's help others to build purpose driven businesses and ecosystems devoted to the common good by offering solutions supporting more transparent free markets, stronger and resilient free governments, and more inclusive, local stakeholder centric and equal democratic societies, concurrently and in tandem with leading by example.

To paraphrase one of many seminal conversations with Rebecca Henderson, let's be pebble rollers, hoping to start an avalanche.

Let's anoint a new Stakeholder Economy Bill of Rights sustained by better metrics and acknowledging that there is no workplace nor socioeconomic reform without changing existing power paradigms and there is no power paradigm change without broadened and deepened inclusive, hybrid-model shared ownership. The Stakeholder Economy starts with worker ownership as its enabling sociocultural technology app.

Aspirational, inclusive, and fulfilling, shared-purpose Stakeholder Ownership Culture will determine who and where is competitive, innovative, productive, societally equalising and fundamentally happy. Let's pursue, represent and organise this future. Other remedies, no matter how well intentioned or structured, function as band-aids treating reoccurring symptoms but do not cure or heal the originating viral diseases.

Hybridity is what America does best. Let's invent more useful hybrid, inclusive shared ownership models combining and integrating union–co-ops, Benefit

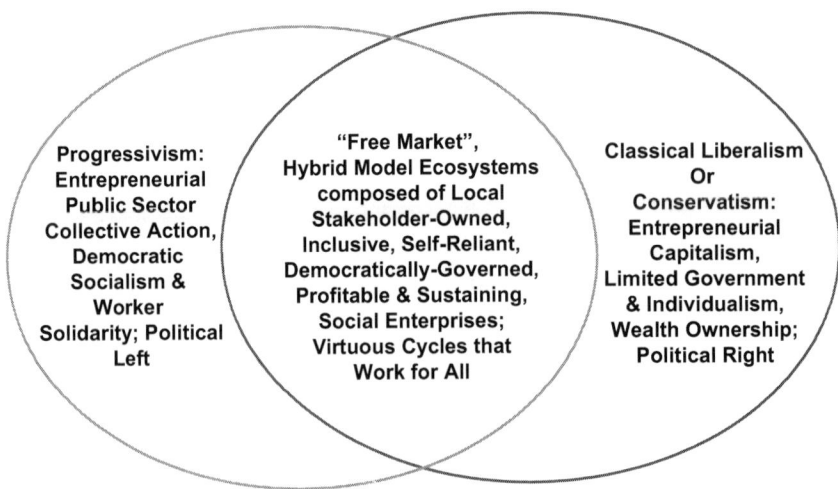

Figure 11.2 The Stakeholder Economy Dynamic Intersection
Source: Michael Peck, The Virtuous Cycle Collaboratory – tvc2

Corporations, Democratic-ESOPs, ESOPeratives, ESGs where the 'S' for Social measures Resiliency as the most important algorithm. Let's push the 17 UN Sustainable Development Goals (SDGs) to add worker ownership as goal number 18.

As examples, responding to 2020 COVID-plagued months, 1worker1vote is part of a team co-launching the People's Rising Sunshine Exchange (PRSE) – a shared services co-operative and digital platform for micro PPE purchases on behalf of frontline healthcare, homecare and emergency response workers – helping to save lives at risk for those saving others. 1worker1vote also helped to initiate and launch www.USPS.Coop to support US postal workers in frontline communities, America's largest and most diversified workforce.

1worker1vote's next upcoming joint global campaign is with the World Fair Trade Organization (WFTO – www.wfto.com – established in 1989, spanning 76 countries, WFTO is the global community and verifier of social enterprises that fully practice Fair Trade) so that more Fair Trade Enterprises (i.e. verified WFTO members) become increasingly connected with the global co-operative movement while more co-operatives become verified as Fair Trade Enterprises.

Together we will 'build back fairer' transparent markets and democratic workplace culture. Our goal in working together starts by joining forces at the grassroots enterprise level to grow and connect all interested global Fair Trade and co-operative (especially hybrid model shared ownership co-operatives) communities on an individual, regional and global outreach basis to explore, encourage and enable commercial B2B and policy opportunities by:

- flattening inequality curves through virtuous cycle fair trade and co-operative principles and practices;
- supporting Fair Trade enterprises and co-operatives throughout the COVID-19 process;
- building stakeholder capitalism foundations across borders, markets, and silos;
- expanding and converging our communities and strengthening our movements; and
- creating high-road, transformation-impacting change through shared structures, values, and purpose.

We are at the beginning of the beginning with enough mission pilgrimage for everyone's enduring and fulfilling lifetimes.

To echo the Indian novelist, Arundhati Roy, whose 'The pandemic is a portal' first appeared in the *Financial Times*:

> Historically, pandemics, biomedical and cultural, have forced humans to break with the past and imagine their world anew. This one is no different. It is a portal, a gateway between one world and the next. We can choose to walk through it, dragging the carcasses of our prejudice and hatred, our avarice, our data banks and dead ideas, our dead rivers and smoky skies

behind us. Or we can walk through lightly, with little luggage, ready to imagine another world. And ready to fight for it.

(Roy, 2020)

References

American Sustainable Business Council (2020), Creating an Economic System That Works For All, October. Retrieved from www.asbcouncil.org. Accessed 21 October 2020.

Bolton, L. (2020), Stories from the Organizing Front: Denver Colorado's Union Taxi and Green Taxi Union Coops. Retrieved from http://1worker1vote.org/stories-from-the-organizing-front-denver-colorados-union-taxi-green-taxi-union–co-ops/. Accessed 21 October 2020.

Criscitiello, R. (2020), Anchoring America's Solidarity Economy Helps to Heal Pandemic Inequality Challenges. Retrieved from http://1worker1vote.org/anchoring-americas-solidarity-economy-helps-to-heal-pandemic-inequality-challenges/. Accessed 21 October 2020.

Gislason, H. (2019), The Cost of Shutting Out Immigrants. Retrieved from www.barrons.com/articles/the-cost-of-shutting-out-immigrants-51546696800. Accessed 21 October 2020.

Goodman, P.S. (2020), Big Business Pledged Gentler Capitalism. It's Not Happening in a Pandemic. *New York Times*. Retrieved from www.nytimes.com/2020/04/13/business/business-roundtable-coronavirus.html. Accessed 21 October 2020.

Henderson, R.M. (2019), April 2019 Newsletter. Retrieved from www.hbs.edu/faculty/Pages/profile.aspx?facId=12345. Accessed 26 October 2020.

Henderson, R.M. and Norris, M. (2015), 1Worker1Vote: MONDRAGON in the US. Retrieved from https://store.hbr.org/product/1worker1vote-mondragon-in-the-us/315103?sku=315103-PDF-ENG. Accessed 5 November 2020.

Hohmann, J. (2020), Journalist Offers Mea Culpa, in New Book, for Undercovering Black Working Class. *The Washington Post*. Retrieved from www.washingtonpost.com/politics/2020/08/11/daily-202-journalist-offers-mea-culpa-new-book-undercovering-black-working-class/. Accessed 26 Octover 2020.

Horowitz, J.M., Brown, A. and Cox, K. (2019), Race in America 2019. Retrieved from www.pewsocialtrends.org/2019/04/09/race-in-america-2019/. Accessed 21 October 2020.

Impact Alpha (2020), Signals Ahead of the Curve. *Impact Alpha Newsletter*, October 14. Retrieved from https://impactalpha.com/get-impactalphas-newsletter-the-brief/. Accessed 26 October 2020.

Kight, S.W. (2019), Immigrants and Their Kids Founded 45% of US Fortune 500 Companies. Retrieved from www.axios.com/immigrants-founders-fortune-500-companies-7e883b5a-1b76-462c-83b5-be68e2e9cae4.html?utm_campaign=organic&utm_medium=socialshare&utm_source=email. Accessed 26 October 2020.

Manifesto for Decent Work (2020), A Manifesto for Decent Work. Retrieved from www.researchgate.net/publication/344388603_union–co-opsuk_A_Manifesto_for_Decent_Work_A_Manifesto_for_Decent_Work_Introduction_-A_Manifesto_for_union_co-ops. Accessed 21 October 2020.

Pandey, E. (2020), 1 Big Thing: The Second Wave of Essential Workers. *Axios*, 21 July. Retrieved from www.axios.com/newsletters/axios-atwork-ae127cd2-81dc-40df-958b-62a79620a980.html. Accessed 21 October 2020.

Rousseau, J.J. (1998 [1762]) *The Social Contract*. Wordsworth Editions, Ware.

Roy, A. (2020), The Pandemic is a Portal. *Financial Times*. Retrieved from www.ft.com/content/10d8f5e8-74eb-11ea-95fe-fcd274e920ca. Accessed 21 October 2020.

Teixeira, R. (2016), Demography Is Not Destiny. *Persuasion*. Retrieved from www.persuasion.community/p/demography-is-not-destiny?utm_medium=email&utm_campaign=cta. Accessed 21 October 2020.

UN (2016) Sustainable Development Goals Report 2016. Retrieved from www.un.org/development/desa/publications/sustainable-development-goals-report-2016.html. Accessed 1 October 2020.

Walsh, P. Peck, M.A. and Zugasti, I. (2018) Why the US Needs More Worker-Owned Companies. *Harvard Business Review*. Retrieved from https://hbr.org/2018/08/why-the-u-s-needs-more-worker-owned-companies. Accessed 1 October 2020.

Wylie, S. (2020), Why a Very Conservative Supreme Court Will Be Bad for Business. *Fortune*. Retrieved from https://fortune.com/2020/10/13/amy-coney-barrett-nomination-supreme-court-bad-for-business. Accessed 21 October 2020.

12 Basque industrial co-operative companies

A comparative analysis in terms of economic profitability and social welfare

Unai Elorza and Alaine Garmendia

Introduction

There are numerous co-operative business initiatives around the world. Among them is the Basque Country co-operative movement. It is considered an example of how economic co-operative initiatives can be undertaken as a means to favour the social development of the territory (Ormazabal, 2008). Unlike other regions of the world, where co-operatives tend to be agricultural or consumer-based, a number of industrial co-operative companies from different sectors consolidated in the Basque Country. They are industrial co-operatives that operate in international markets such as automotive, machine tooling, household appliances, among others. These industrial co-operatives are work organisations whose membership is restricted to those who work in them and that are owned and controlled by their workforce (Cornforth, 1992). They are managed on different management principles compared to the traditional companies. For example, each worker is a co-owner (member) who has one vote in the company's highest decision-making body, regardless of the capital he or she holds in the company. Any co-owner worker can be elected by the rest of his or her colleagues to form part of the co-operative company's day-to-day governing bodies for a limited time (Azurmendi, 1984). In the Basque Country, there is a high concentration of industrial co-operative initiatives of these characteristics in a limited geographical area.

All the industrial co-operative initiatives that have developed in the Basque Country have sought to maximise their social impact. To this end, they have actively sought to grow and develop new employment and make those new employees members (co-owners) of the company. Growth has been a desired goal for two reasons. One, to be more competitive in the market. Growth helps to maximise economic profitability, thus contributing to the survival of the company in the future. Two, to develop as much employment as possible around them, since the co-operative understands that work is a means for the development of people and society. The better the results, the more sustainable the co-operative, the greater the growth that leads to more employment, the higher the number of members, the greater the distribution of results among members and above all, the more social transformation and/or educational projects in the region can be financed.

Therefore, to grow is something inherent to Basque co-operatives because their ultimate purpose is to develop the society in which they are located. The enterprise and the capital it generates, is a means of transforming society. Examples of this transformation are the development (not only professional) of the people who are part of the co-operative and/or the educational development of the region. Therefore, the co-operative is a business project that seeks the well-being and development of the people and the society in which it is located. Economic profitability is a means to make the business project sustainable and to favour the development of people/society (Azurmendi, 1984).

The study of industrial co-operatives in the Basque Country may be an opportunity to understand to what extent industrial co-operatives are successful business cases (in economic terms) and to what extent they are cases where people's well-being is maximised (in terms of satisfaction and proactivity). One of the requirements for any company to be sustainable is a good economic performance. However, in the case of co-operatives they should also offer good social welfare. This is because the enterprise is but a means through which to develop people and by extension society. Are industrial co-operatives successful from an economic point of view? Are they also an example from a social point of view? Currently, there is little empirical evidence on the reality of industrial co-operatives in general. The aim of this research is to explore this reality empirically and to understand to what extent industrial co-operatives deliver good economic profitability and beneficial social welfare.

Hypothesis development

Previous research shows that large companies in general (as opposed to small ones) have better economic profitability (e.g. Halil and Hasan, 2012; Ilaboya and Ohiokha, 2016; Papadogonas, 2007; Pervan and Višić, 2012). The underlying logic is that the larger the organisation becomes, the better it takes advantage of economies of scale. In other words, a higher volume of activity helps to maximise the economic performance (Porter, 1985). In turn, greater economic profitability allows companies greater capacity for investment and growth, thus increasing the possibilities of being competitive in the medium term (through investment, new technology, and so on (Becker-Blease et al., 2010)). Research shows evidence that relates the size of the organisation with economic profitability (Ilaboya and Ohiokha, 2016). However, these studies are mainly from English-speaking regions and/or studies that do not incorporate the reality of co-operatives. There is a lack of evidence from samples that include industrial co-operative companies and from other geographical areas. Therefore, the following hypothesis is proposed:

Hypothesis 1: In the Basque Country, larger industrial companies have a better economic profitability (measured in terms of EBIT) than smaller industrial companies.

The industrial co-operatives of the Basque Country have sought to grow for various reasons. On the one hand, they have been partly motivated by the need to be competitive in an increasingly globalised market, which requires a greater international presence; on the other hand, also partly motivated by the desire to develop local employment and by the desire to contribute to the development of the society in which they are located. Basque Country co-operatives often implement unusual flexibility mechanisms when facing market difficulties. They adopt measures to reduce wages in order to deal with crises, thus avoiding loss of knowledge that is key to competing in the market (Arando et al., 2010, 2011). They also have mechanisms for inter-co-operation or mutual aid between different co-operatives. This mutual aid takes the form of an exchange of workers between different co-operatives that might have different market realities or even mutual economic aid. The combination of these flexibility mechanisms allows co-operatives to face difficult situations and at the same time to remain in relatively good condition by the time the market recovers. When this happens, the co-operative is usually in a favourable position to grow organically because it has not been decapitalised (in terms of knowledge). If successful, this deliberate mechanism of survival and growth should be visible through a larger size of co-operative companies compared to other non-co-operative companies. Therefore, it would seem likely that industrial co-operatives in the Basque Country should be, in general, larger than non-co-operative companies. There is no previous research analysing this characteristic of industrial co-operatives, so the following hypothesis is proposed:

Hypothesis 2: Industrial co-operatives are larger than non-co-operative industrial companies in the Basque Country.

If hypothesis 1 is confirmed (that large companies show better economic profitability) and if hypothesis 2 is confirmed (that industrial co-operatives are larger compared to those non-co-operative companies), it is logical to assume that industrial co-operatives will have better economic profitability compared to the non-co-operative companies. So far, there are no studies analysing this proposal among industrial co-operatives in the Basque Country. The following third hypothesis is therefore proposed:

Hypothesis 3: Industrial co-operatives in the Basque Country have a better economic profitability (measured in terms of EBIT) than the non-co-operative industrial companies.

Traditional management literature usually focuses on the well-being of people as a means of obtaining better organisational performance (Guest et al., 2012; Peccei and Van De Voorde, 2019). That is, people are a means of achieving better economic profitability. However, for the industrial co-operatives of the Basque Country, the development and well-being of people is an end in itself (Azurmendi, 1984). This logic of developing the well-being of people is rooted in the co-operative principles. For the co-operative, economic profitability is essential to make the business sustainable over time, but it is still a means to a greater end: the development of people and society. Given that the development of people is a purpose of the co-operative, it is to be supposed that in the co-operatives there will be better levels of well-being compared to other non-co-operative companies. Moreover, in the case of the industrial co-operatives of the Basque Country workers are co-owners or members of the company. This is why, many of the people management policies proposed by the Strategic Human Resource Management (SHRM) literature as desirable to foster people motivation and well-being (Kaarsemaker and Poutsma, 2006; Kruse and Blasi, 1995; Poutsma et al., 2017) are implemented in these industrial co-operatives. People management policies such as transparency/information, participation in strategic decisions, profit sharing, participation in decision-making bodies, and more, are policies that are formally established and practised in the co-operative.

There is a lot of empirical evidence that shows a significant and positive relationship between participation policies, information and profit sharing, with people satisfaction (e.g. Boxall and Macky, 2014; Wood and De Menezes, 2011; Zatzick and Iverson, 2011). Given that a co-operative seeks the development of people (as an end in itself), and implements people management policies that foster workers' well-being (because the workers are co-owner-members) it is probable that they will present better well-being levels than non-co-operative companies. One way to measure people's well-being is through their level of satisfaction. The more satisfied people are, the lower their levels of absenteeism are (Hausknecht et al., 2008). Therefore, people satisfaction can be a measure of their well-being.

On the other hand, previous research has shown that greater individual satisfaction is related to greater proactivity (Strauss et al., 2015). The theory of social exchange proposes that when people perceive favourable treatment from the organisation (for example, in terms of policies of transparency, participation, and profit sharing) they tend to generate proactive behaviour in favour of the organisation (Gouldner, 1960). That is, when people feel satisfied with the organisation (because of the way they are treated, because of their working conditions, and the implemented policies) they tend to generate proactive behaviour favourable to the interests of the company (Elorza et al., 2016). This proactivity will also be partly fostered by the fact that the people in the co-operative are co-owners of the organisation. The feeling of responsibility they accept because they feel they are also the owners of the business also favours greater proactivity. Therefore, either because people are more satisfied or because people feel they own the organisation (or both), it seems likely that in co-operatives, people will show more proactive behaviour than in non-co-operative companies. To date there are few previous studies that analyse the level of satisfaction and proactivity of people in industrial co-operatives (Arando et al., 2011). Therefore, because of the above, this research proposes the following fourth hypothesis:

Hypothesis 4: People from industrial co-operatives are more satisfied and proactive than people from non-co-operative industrial companies in the Basque Country.

Method

Sample

The data sample consists of 23,435 surveys from 199 industrial organisations. These are data collected in the period 2017–2019. The companies belong to different industrial sectors. The most important are: machine tooling, automotive components and home appliance components. Table 12.1 shows the summary of the characteristics of the sample. The first column refers to the data collected from the co-operative companies. The second column refers to the data collected from non-co-operative companies. Finally, the third column shows the total of the sample (including both co-operative and non-co-operative companies).

More or less one-third (34 %) of the organisations in the sample are co-operatives while the rest of the organisations are mainly public limited companies. Specifically, 12,949 surveys belong to 132 non-co-operative companies; while 10,486 surveys belong to 67 co-operative industrial companies (see Table 12.1). The percentage of people who completed the survey in the case of co-operatives was 77% while in the case of non-co-operatives it was 86%. The average size of co-operative companies is larger than that of non-co-operative companies. In the case of co-operatives, it is 198 persons per company, while in the case of non-co-operatives it is 141. It should be noted that there are two non-co-operative companies with a much larger size than the rest of the sample (with 4,178 persons in one case and 2,456 in the other). Both cases (of non-co-operatives) are an exception and increase the average size of non-co-operative companies to 141.

Table 12.1 Characteristics of the sample

	Co-operatives	Non-co-operative	Total sample
No. of companies	67	132	199
% of co-operative companies	100%	0%	34%
Average size (min; average; maximum)	5; 198; 828	5; 141; 4.178	5; 163; 4.178
No. of surveys collected	10.486	12.949	23.435
% participants (min; average; maximum)	27%; 77%; 100%	10%; 86%; 100%	10%; 83%; 100%
Co-operative members	77 %	0 %	35%
Male gender	82 %	74%	78%
Tenure (less than 5 years)	13 %	21 %	17 %
Tenure (between 5 and 10 years)	24 %	18 %	21 %
Tenure (between 10 and 20 years)	42 %	37 %	39 %
Tenure (more than 20 years)	21 %	25 %	23 %

It should also be noted that 77% of the surveys collected in the sample of co-operative companies are co-owners (or co-operative members). Because the sample is composed of industrial companies, the percentage of male surveys is high (82% in the case of co-operatives and 74% in the case of non-co-operatives). Finally, and with regard to tenure of the people participating in the sample, it should be noted that the most frequent period of tenure of the workers is between 11 and 20 years (both in co-operatives and in non-co-operatives). In summary, the characteristics of the data sample of co-operative and non-co-operative companies are similar both in terms of demographics and as a percentage of participation. This provides confidence that comparisons of means will be made between survey groups with similar characteristics.

Data collection procedure

The data collection procedure began with the dissemination and pitch to companies about the benefit of surveying people in order to understand the level of well-being of the people working in the company. The dissemination process was carried out by university researchers. The companies targeted were both co-operative and non-co-operative. Companies were motivated to participate by being offered the possibility of finding out the level of satisfaction and proactivity of the people with regard to their sector. This comparison with respect to the sector offers the company a useful information to become aware of the level of satisfaction and proactivity of people with respect to other companies in the same sector. It helps to raise awareness of the situation and to define action plans for improvement in the company. Once the companies agreed to carry out the survey, the greatest possible participation was sought. 100% of the people in the organisation were invited to participate in a survey that was psychometrically validated in previous research (Elorza et al., 2016; Rafferty and Griffin, 2006). The company informed people about the objective of the survey and organised them in groups, summoning them at specific times to a meeting room (each group at a time). The researchers attended the groups in the room and briefly presented the survey to the people, clarified doubts and collected the surveys. The researchers then processed the surveys with the aim of developing a report for the company. At the same time, the researchers accumulated the data collected in order to be able to perform this research.

Measures

Economic profitability. This was measured through EBIT archive data. The average EBIT of the previous four years was used in order to obtain a more stable indicator far from the economic fluctuations of a given moment.

Organisational size. This was measured through the number of people. As in the previous case, the average of the last four years was used.

In order to normalise both measures (size and EBIT) the original data were transformed to their logarithm. Given that in the case of EBIT there may be negative indicators, before calculating their logarithm, an index was added (to all measures) so that the highest negative value was transformed into zero. In this way, negative cases were not lost when using the logarithm in the transformation process. Once the logarithmic transformations were carried out, both measures met the normality criteria. This transformed version of the measures was used in subsequent analyses.

Satisfaction. The three original items of the scale proposed by Rafferty and Griffin (2006) were used to measure satisfaction. A sample item is: 'Overall, I am satisfied with the kind of work I do'. Response options ranged from 1 ('strongly disagree') to 6 ('strongly agree').

Proactivity. Measured through three items of the individual task proactivity scale developed by Griffin et al. (2007). A simple item is: 'I initiated better ways of doing my core tasks'. Response options ranged from 1 ('strongly disagree') to 6 ('strongly agree').

A confirmatory factor analysis was performed (with AMOS v.7) to test a two-factor structure. Six items loading on two factors: three items for satisfaction and three items for proactivity. No cross loadings were allowed, neither item errors were correlated between each other. The fit indices of the model yielded acceptable results: $\chi^2(194) = 305.8$, $p < 0.001$; TLI = 0.98; CFI = 0.99; RMSEA = 0.04. No refinement of the items was necessary. The $\chi2$ statistic is significant since it is very sensitive to large sample sizes (as is the case here) and tends to reject models that should not in fact be rejected. The rest of the fit indices yielded good results, so overall the model was acceptable. Table 12.2 shows details of item loadings and factors reliabilities. All factor loadings are higher than 0.70. Therefore, results provide support for convergent and divergent validity of the constructs. The internal consistency (composite reliability) of satisfaction was 0.87 and proactivity 0.88. Both exceeded the commonly accepted cut-off values of 0.70. Therefore, data

Table 12.2 Standardised item loadings (standard errors) and factor reliabilities

Items	Satisfaction	Proactivity
Overall, I am satisfied with the kind of work I do	0.88 (–)	
Overall, I am satisfied with the organisation in which I work	0.70 (.008)	
Overall, I am satisfied with my job	0.90 (.007)	
I Initiated better ways of doing my core tasks		0.82 (–)
I came up with ideas to improve the way in which my core tasks are done		0.88 (0.007)
I made changes to the way my core tasks are done		0.83 (0.008)
Extracted variance (cut-off value of 0.50)	0.69	0.70
Composite Reliability (cut-off value of 0.70)	0.87	0.88

Note: all factor loadings were statistical significant at $p < 0.01$.

also provided support for the internal consistency of the constructs. In sum, the measures are good enough to test the Hypotheses.

Results

Table 12.3 shows the basic statistics of the variables involved in this study. It is worth noting that the correlations of satisfaction and proactivity with size are statistically significant and negative. EBIT and size have a positive and significant correlation. The same occurs with satisfaction and proactivity. Finally, no correlation is observed between satisfaction, proactivity and EBIT.

To test the hypotheses, Student's *t*-test was used. In the case of Hypothesis 1, the EBIT measure was dichotomised using the K-means clustering technique. So, companies were classified into two groups: (i) a group of 84 companies with an average size (log) of 2.36 and (ii) a group of 115 companies with an average size (log) of 1.15. To perform the test of Hypothesis 2, the classification of co-operative (n=67) and non-co-operative ($n = 132$) companies in the sample was used.

Table 12.4 shows the results of the mean comparisons. Hypothesis 1 proposed that larger firms have better economic profitability (assessed by the EBIT). The average EBIT (log) of the larger companies is significantly higher than the average of the smaller companies (Student's $t = 4.5$). Therefore, Hypothesis 1 is confirmed. Hypothesis 2 proposed that co-operative companies are larger than the non-co-operative ones. The average size of the co-operative companies is 2.0 while the average size of the non-co-operative companies is 1.6. These are statistically significant differences according to Student's *t*-test ($= 4.5$). Therefore, Hypothesis 2 is confirmed. Hypothesis 3 proposed that co-operatives have better economic profitability indicators (EBIT) than non-co-operatives. The table shows that the average EBIT in co-operative companies is significantly higher than in non-co-operatives ones (Student's $t = 4.5$). Therefore, Hypothesis 3 is confirmed. Finally, Hypothesis 4 proposed that co-operative companies have better measures of satisfaction and proactivity. Table 12:4 shows that the average satisfaction level is lower in co-operatives companies (4.3) than in non-co-operatives companies (4.5). The difference is

Table 12.3 Descriptive statistics and correlations

Variables	M	SD	1	2	3	4
1. Size (log)	1.8	0.56	1			
2. EBIT (log)	3.0	0.41	0.59**	1		
Satisfaction	4.5	0.43	−0.32**	−0.01	1	
4. Proactivity	4.2	0.38	−0.30**	0.00	0.65**	1

*: statistically significant at $p < 0.05$; **: statistically significant at $p < 0.01$

Table 12.4 EBIT, satisfaction, proactivity and size comparisons for bigger vs. smaller and co-operative vs. non-co-operative companies

Hyp.	Groups	Variable	N	Mean	SD	Student's t	p-value
Hyp. 1	Bigger companies	EBIT (log)	34	3.2	0.49	4.5	0.000
	Smaller companies		31	2.8	0.12		
Hyp. 2	Co-operative comp.	Size (log)	67	2.0	0.53	4.5	0.000
	Non-co-operative		132	1.6	0.53		
Hyp. 3	Co-operative comp.	EBIT (log)	36	3.2	0.37	4.5	0.000
	Non-co-operative		29	2.8	0.35		
Hyp. 4	Co-operative comp.	Satisfaction	67	4.3	0.39	−2.3	0.019
	Non-co-operative		132	4.5	0.43		
	Co-operative comp.	Proactivity	65	4.1	0.30	−4.1	0.000
	Non-co-operative		114	4.3	0.40		

statistically significant (Student's $t = -2.3$). Similarly, the average level of proactivity in co-operative companies is lower (4.1) than the average level of non-co-operatives companies (4.3). The differences are also statistically significant (Student's $t = -4.1$). Therefore, the evidence does not confirm Hypothesis 4; rather it contradicts it.

Discussion

This research had the aim of understanding whether co-operatives (compared to non-co-operative companies) have better economic profitability and better social indicators (assessed in terms of satisfaction and proactivity of people). The evidence collected in the data sample suggests that the size of the organisations is a major determinant of the response. Evidence has shown that the larger the company, the better is the economic profitability. Therefore, Hypothesis 1 is confirmed. Economies of scale might partially explain this phenomenon. The larger the firm, the greater the economies of scale it achieves and as a consequence the greater its economic profitability. Evidence also shows that co-operatives are generally larger than non-co-operative companies in the Basque Country. Thus, Hypothesis 2 is also confirmed. This may make sense because co-operatives have always sought to maximise their impact on society. They have pursued the development of as much employment as possible. Work is seen as a way to foster the personal growth of people. Therefore, the more employment is created the higher the development of the society in which co-operative is located. To sum up, growth is an inherent part of being a co-operative.

On the other hand, evidence also shows that co-operative companies present better economic profitability (EBIT). Collected evidence confirmed Hypothesis 3. This hypothesis is confirmed, partly because co-operatives are larger and economies of scale offer an advantage over smaller companies. Therefore, in view of the data, developing co-operative businesses is something desirable for any region as co-operatives seeks to grow, generate employment and its growth helps to obtain economic returns which, in turn, will help its future growth.

However, the evidence in this study has shown that co-operatives do not present better indicators of satisfaction and proactivity compared to non-co-operative companies. Thus, Hypothesis 4 is not confirmed. The collected sample data contradicted the proposals made from theory. The co-operatives in the Basque Country seek to generate employment. People that enter to work in co-operatives are invited to become members of the company. That is why most of the workers in an industrial co-operative in the Basque Country are members. The members of the co-operative have all the information about the company, they have mechanisms for participation in strategic decision-making, they participate in the annual assembly, they benefit from profit sharing, they can be elected to represent the governing board of the co-operative for a period of time, etc. In theory, people in the co-operative (compared to others in non-co-operative companies) should feel more informed, trained, engaged in participation and responsible. Evidence from the SHRM field shows that a greater perception of information, participation, responsibility, profit sharing, etc. is related to greater satisfaction and proactivity of people (Peccei and Van De Voorde, 2019). However, the data collected in this research does not present evidence in that direction. Despite the fact that the people in co-operatives (in theory) have more information, more training, more participation, etc., the workforce responses present worse levels of satisfaction and proactivity than those in non-co-operative companies.

This result can be explained by the size of the company. A mean comparison between large and small companies shows statistically significant differences for satisfaction and proactivity (Student's $t = -3.1$ for satisfaction and -3.0 for proactivity). That is, the data confirm that the smaller the organisation, the better the satisfaction and proactivity of people. Co-operatives are large companies, and this could explain why satisfaction and proactivity are lower. This evidence suggests that people's satisfaction and proactivity may be more influenced by issues of size, rather than just by being (or not being) a co-operative. It is possible that people day-to-day may be different in a large company versus a small company. Why should satisfaction and proactivity in a large company be lower than in a small company? One possible explanation may be the way growth has been organised. That is, the structuring of the organisation as the company has grown, discussed below.

According to Mintzberg (1979), large companies have more complex organisational structures than small companies, making it difficult to align the attitudes and behaviours of workers with the objectives of the organisation. In a large company, departmentalisation and specialisation is greater, which favours a loss of general vision of the business by people. At the same time, a large company has a more complex structure, which means greater hierarchy systems and responsibility levels that distribute and supervise the execution of tasks to people on the shop floor. The bigger the structure, the more likely it is that people will feel a loss of: (i) autonomy and responsibility, (ii) information/transparency, and (iii) informal communication, among others. It is important to emphasise that we are talking about 'feeling', 'experience' or 'perception' of people, because it is logical to assume that in large companies there are more formal systems implemented compared to small companies, that is to say, formal systems to share information, make people participate, to provide feedback, and so on. However, these formal systems do not necessarily guarantee a higher perception of information or a higher perception of participation by people. In a small company, despite not having formally implemented systems, the perception of information, communication, participation in the day-to-day business is probably more intense (despite being more informal) than in a large company. This feeling (or experience) of less perception of transparency and less participation may be amplified with a more departmentalised (or local) vision of the company and a lesser sense of autonomy (because there is a greater structure of supervisors). All this may be conditioning the feeling of satisfaction and proactivity of people. This may also be applicable to co-operative companies, as they have followed the same principles of structuring and organising growth as the non-co-operative companies.

In the case of co-operatives, it is likely that this phenomenon of organisation/structuring of growth will be compounded by the fact that there is a greater risk of producing disillusionment in people. Disappointment may result from unfulfilled expectations about what it means to work in a co-operative company and/or to be a co-owner. As the co-operative grows, it takes on new members. These members are likely to come with higher expectations in terms of conditions, rights, and voice within the company (compared to other traditional companies). However, after a while, disillusionment might be generated by a lack of fulfilment of expectations. This lack of fulfilment might be motivated by an insufficient sense of information and participation (despite the formal systems that are implemented in co-operative companies).

All of the above might be arguments that explain why people have less satisfaction and proactivity in large co-operative companies (compared to smaller ones). However, it also suggests interesting future research questions for co-operatives: Is the growth strategy suitable for a co-operative? Growth leads to gains in economies of scale that help to improve economic profitability and this growth also helps to generate co-operative employment. These are benefits of growth, but it can also have a negative side: it can present some social shortcomings represented, for example, by the lower satisfaction and proactivity levels highlighted by this study. Assuming that the ultimate purpose of the co-operative is to develop the people and society in which it is located, it is probably not an option to stop growing as much as possible. This suggests a second question: if it is not feasible to stop growing, could growth be organised differently? Would it be possible to grow in order to maximise its impact on society and gain economies of scale in economic terms, but at the same time maintain people's social satisfaction and motivation? Co-operatives have organised growth in the same way as other non-co-operative companies: through specialisation, departmentalisation and the establishment of a structure of authority that usually takes the responsibility to overcome the challenges of the company. However, this research suggests that a growing co-operative should look at other ways of organising growth. This is something that has not happened in the industrial co-operatives of the Basque Country, and given the growth they have had, this is a key issue for their sustainability in the future.

The present investigation should be treated as preliminary, as it has major limitations. Four major limitations can be highlighted. First, the research is focused in a very limited geographical area so it might not be appropriate to generalise its conclusions to all industrial co-operatives in other geographical areas. Second, the research is focused on industrial co-operatives and therefore its conclusions may not be useful for other co-operatives such as agricultural or consumer co-operatives. Third, statistical analyses are mean comparisons and correlations. Therefore, this is a descriptive research that cannot pretend to provide clear guidelines for the practice within the company. Fourth, the data sample may not be entirely representative of the industrial companies of the Basque Country, as the participating companies (co-operatives and non-co-operatives) are companies that have agreed to carry out a diagnosis of their social situation. The research team has met with many companies (especially non-co-operatives) that did not want to carry out such a social diagnosis. Therefore, it is possible that the study is biased in the sample with evidence of companies that have shown social sensitivity and without evidence of companies that do not have such social sensitivity.

Despite the limitations, the study suggests important implications for the practice of industrial co-operative companies. Not growing may not be an option, for two reasons. First, because the increasingly globalised market requires it and there is a risk of disappearing if there is no growth. Second, they will seek to grow because co-operatives seek to generate employment and the development of the society in which they are located. Therefore, growth in co-operative employment is an objective that co-operatives should not exclude from their agenda. However, co-operatives must be aware of the importance of organising their growth; that a different organisation of growth is a vital element that will significantly influence the feeling of well-being. A classic way of organising growth (similar to any other non-co-operative organisation) that tends to departmentalise and establish hierarchical levels of responsibility and supervision will likely have a social cost in terms of satisfaction and proactivity. This will probably be a higher cost in co-operatives than in non-co-operative companies, because of the risk of unfulfilling the expectations of members. This is because in co-operatives newly integrated members might develop some expectations that are disappointed through the practice of everyday management (based on similar management principles as in non-co-operative companies). This disappointment could generate the loss of satisfaction and proactivity. This latter effect of disillusionment may not occur so much among non-co-operative companies because such initial expectations are not generated. Managers of growing co-operatives should be cautious and aware that they cannot organise growth as traditional companies usually do.

Conclusions

This study presents evidence that industrial co-operative companies in the Basque Country are usually large companies (in terms of number of jobs) in their region. These companies perform economically better than small companies, probably due to economies of scale. This finding is an empirical evidence of the growth strategy that has always accompanied co-operative companies. These companies have sought to grow in order to generate co-operative employment and to foster the development of the society in which they are located. In this way, the industrial co-operatives of the Basque Country are an example of business success and growth.

However, this entrepreneurial success seems to have a social cost as well, as these large co-operative companies also show worse social indicators (in terms of satisfaction and proactivity) compared to the non-co-operative companies. It seems that growth, or rather the way growth is organised, leads to a social cost. Generally speaking, people feel satisfied and are proactive in autonomous working environments, where they feel responsible, with information, and participation in decision-making. Data collected in this research is showing that people working in large co-operatives do not seem to perceive such working environments. This is probably partially explained by the way in which growth has been organised: usually through departmentalisation, specialisation and through a hierarchy of managers and a larger intermediate structure. It is possible that this structure takes responsibility for the running of the organisation and generates (over time) a vacuum of responsibility in the people working on the shop floor. This could lead to a situation where shop-floor workers might feel like a 'resource' at the service of the structure/ supervisors, without any real possibility of taking responsibility, deciding and being proactive.

Therefore, the evidence suggests that it is necessary to reflect on how the growth of co-operative companies is being organised. It also raises the question of whether there could be other ways of organising this growth, so that people do not feel the loss of autonomy, responsibility, information and, as a consequence, a loss of satisfaction and proactivity.

Acknowledgement

We acknowledge the Gipuzkoa Provincial Council for the Bateratzen initiative.

References

Arando, S., Gago, M., and Derek, C.J. (2011), Efficiency in Employee-Owned Enterprises: An Econometric Case Study of Mondragon, *International Labor Relations Review*, 68 (2): 1–28.

Arando, S., Gago, M., Takao, K., Derek, C.J., and Freudlich, F. (2010), Assessing Mondragon: Stability and Managed Change in the Face of Globalization. Retrieved from www.iza.org/publications/dp/5711/efficiency-in-employee-owned-enterprises-an-econometric-case-study-of-mondragon. Accessed 5 November 2020.

Azurmendi, J. (1984), El hombre cooperativo: Pensamiento de Arizmendiarrieta. Retrieved from www.euskomedia.org/PDFAnlt/mono/arizmendiarrieta/elhombre.pdf. Accessed 5 November 2020.

Becker-Blease, J.R., Kaen, F.R., Etebari, A., and Baumann, H. (2010), Employees, Firm Size and Profitability in U.S. Manufacturing Industries, *Investment Management and Financial Innovations. Business Perspectives*, 7 (2): 7–23.

Boxall, P. and Macky, K. (2014),' High-Involvement Work Processes, Work Intensification and Employee Well-Being, *Work, Employment and Society*, 28 (6): 963–984.

Cornforth, C. (1992), Co-operatives, In Széll, G. (ed.), *Concise Encyclopaedia of Participation and Co-Management*, Walter De Gruyter, New York, 186–192.

Elorza, U., Harris, C., Aritzeta, A., and Balluerka, N. (2016), The Effect of Management and Employee Perspectives of High-Performance Work Systems on Employees' Discretionary Behaviour, *Personnel Review*, 45(1): 121–141.

Gouldner, A.W. (1960), The Norm of Reciprocity: A Preliminary Statement, *American Sociological Review*, 25(2): 161.

Griffin, M.A., Neal, A., and Parker, S.K. (2007), A New Model of Work Role Performance: Positive Behavior in Uncertain and Interdependent Contexts, *The Academy of Management Journal*, 50(2): 327–347.

Guest, D.E., Paauwe, J., and Wright, P.M. (eds) (2012), *HRM and Performance: Achievements and Challenges*, John Wiley and Sons, Chichester.

Halil, E.A. and Hasan, A.K. (2012), The Effect of Firm Size on Profitability: An Empirical Icelandic Firms, *Bifröst Journal of Social Science*, 1: 33–42.

Hausknecht, J.P., Hiller, N.J., and Vance, R.J. (2008), Work-Unit Absenteeism: Effects of Satisfaction, Commitment, Labor Market Conditions, and Time, *Academy of Management Journal*, 51(6): 1223–1245.

Ilaboya, O.J. and Ohiokha, I.F. (2016), Firm Age, Size and Profitability Dynamics: A Test of Learning by Doing and Structural Inertia hypotheses, *Business and Management Research*, 5(1): 29–39.

Kaarsemaker, E.C.A., and Poutsma, E. (2006), The Fit of Employee Ownership with Other Human Resource Management Practices: Theoretical and Empirical Suggestions Regarding the Existence of an Ownership High-Performance Work System, *Economic and Industrial Democracy*, 27(4): 669–685.

Kruse, D. and Blasi, J. (1995), Employee Ownership, Employee Attitudes and Firm Performance. National Bureau of Economic Research Working Papers 5277. Retrieved from www.nber.org/papers/w5277. Accessed 5 November 2020.

Mintzberg, H. (1979), *The Structuring of Organizations: A Synthesis of the Research*, Prentice-Hall, Englewood Cliffs, NJ.

Ormazabal, P. (ed.) (2008), *Cooperativismo en el País Vasco*, S. Minerva Ediciones, Madrid.

Papadogonas, T.A. (2007), The Financial Performance of Large and Small Firms: Evidence from Greece, *International Journal of Financial Services Management*, 2(1–2):14–20.

Peccei, R. and Van De Voorde, K. (2019), Human Resource Management–Well-Being–Performance Research Revisited: Past, Present, and Future, *Human Resource Management Journal*, 29(4): 539–563.

Pervan, M. and Višić, J. (2012), Influence of Firm Size on its Business Success, *Hrvatsko Društvo Za Operacijska Istraživanja*, 3(1): 213–223.

Porter, M.E. (1985), *Competitive Advantage: Creating and Sustaining Superior Performance*, Free Press, New York.

Poutsma, E., Ligthart, P.E.M., and Kaarsemaker, E.C.A. (2017), Employee Ownership and High-Performance Work Systems in Context, *Advances in the Economic Analysis of Participatory and Labor-Managed Firms*, 17, 5–22.

Rafferty, A.E. and Griffin, M.A. (2006), Refining Individualized Consideration: Distinguishing Developmental Leadership and Supportive Leadership, *Journal of Occupational and Organizational Psychology,* 79(1):37–61.

Strauss, K., Griffin, M., Parker, S.K., and Mason, C.M. (2015), Building and Sustaining Proactive Behaviors: The Role of Adaptivity and Job Satisfaction, *Journal of Business and Psychology*, 30(1): 63–72.

Wood, S. and De Menezes, L.M. (2011), High Involvement Management, High-Performance Work Systems and Well-Being, *The International Journal of Human Resource Management*, 22(7): 1586–1610.

Zatzick, C.D. and Iverson, R.D. (2011), Putting Employee Involvement in Context: A Cross-Level Model Examining Job Satisfaction and Absenteeism in High-Involvement Work Systems, *The International Journal of Human Resource Management*, 22(7): 3462–3476.

13 Adult education, economic democracy, and local economic development

Jonathan Michie

Introduction

This chapter argues that successful local economic development requires a vibrant educational system in that locality. It also argues that economic democracy can be conducive to sustainable economic development, and that economic democracy too depends on adult education. Thus, what I would term 'adult education and lifelong learning' is central to both economic democracy and successful local economic development. This term subsumes community education, continual professional development (CPD), and part-time study at university and elsewhere.

What is required, in short, is the full range of post-18- and post-23-year-old educational provision, being available to citizens at the different stages of life when it might prove helpful, whether in relation to life events or work requirements. Such educational provision needs to be available in all communities, and at work. It should be provided through universities that collaborate actively with other local organisations, contributing to individual welfare, local communities and regional economies. And it needs to be part of national strategies to promote educational opportunities at all stages of life.

The chapter is arranged as follows. The following section considers the factors that foster successful corporate performance, and thereby the successful economic development of those areas in which those firms are based or operate; and conversely, what factors foster successful economic development, and how these factors operate by encouraging the founding of companies and their successive growth and development.

The subsequent section analyses in particular the role played in these processes by economic democracy and education. After that, the Report of the Centenary Commission on Adult Education is considered, before a final concluding discussion.

Organisational performance and economic development

Productive collaboration within firms – and between them – plays a crucially important role in corporate success and economic development. Yet this is often overlooked within mainstream economic theory, for which the firm is all too often a 'black box', and in which firms should be competing not collaborating. But not all processes need involve competition.[1]

There are two aspects to the importance of collaboration – firstly, within the firm, and secondly collaboration by a firm with other firms and organisations (such as universities).

Collaboration within the firm

Adam Smith's *Wealth of Nations* stressed the importance of collaboration within the firm. This enabled a division of labour which increases efficiency, reducing costs, which enables lower prices that drive increased sales that in turn create both the incentive and opportunity for a still greater division of labour as employment and productive collaboration expands within and across the firm (Smith, 1904 [1776]).

A key point that needs to be appreciated is that the output from production processes – in terms of quantity and/or quality – cannot, or rather should not be 'read off' from the inputs according to a 'production function'. That 'production function' approach of mainstream economics is at best simplistic and at worst misleading. The actual outputs will in practice depend on how effectively – and productively – the workforce collaborates, and what use they make of their capital equipment, which again cannot be 'read off' in a production function approach. How productive capital equipment will prove to be will depend on what the employees make of it. Often they will find innovative and productive uses that the inventor or designed had never contemplated.

This is analysed in the high-commitment work systems literature, which researches the policies and practices that firms pursue in order to get the best from their workforce. A key finding is that to maximise their productivity requires three things.

Firstly, employees need the *capabilities* to be productive. This requires education and training.

Secondly, they need to be *motivated* to put those capabilities to good effect. A range of 'Human Resource' policies and practices can be utilised to enhance employee motivation and commitment, including policies of involvement and participation. This is one area in which corporate ownership and governance structures play a part. To motivate employees to 'go the extra mile', corporate leaders will invariably declare that 'our employees are our greatest assets'. In cases where the employees have ownership and governance rights in the company, that commitment has some force. Where the company is owned by external shareholders, whose financial interests the management is seeking to maximise, then the declaration may have less of an impact on employee motivation. On education and training, while the provision of this by companies for their employees will have the first point of capabilities in mind, receiving such support from their company may also have a positive motivational effect for employees.

Thirdly, it is not enough for employees to have the capabilities and motivation unless they also have the *opportunity* to contribute additional effort or innovation, and hence appropriate work organisation is necessary. This includes the use of suggestion schemes through to the use of work teams. But again, corporate ownership and governance may prove relevant in this regard, and having employee education and training may well contribute positively towards such opportunities. If the employees are the owners, with a concomitant governance voice, they can create the opportunities.

Michie and Sheehan (2003) report that these sort of high-commitment work systems are found to be positively correlated with corporate performance, whereas the 'hire and fire' type of 'flexibility' is not:

> [T]he links between what is often broadly referred to as labour 'flexibility' on the one hand, and corporate innovation and performance on the other, depended crucially on the *nature* of this flexibility. Specifically, the sort of 'hire-and-fire' flexibility that firms might be tempted to resort to given a deregulated labour market – particularly if put under short term pressure (by, e.g. an uncompetitive exchange rate) – was found to be negatively correlated with innovative activity.
>
> [O]ur results suggest that policies aimed at increasing labour market 'flexibility' (proxied by contract type and part-time employment), while in some cases having a positive effect on short-term financial performance, invariably have a *negative* effect on labour productivity, product quality and innovation.
>
> (Michie and Sheehan, 2003, p. 188)

These high-commitment work systems often include explicit employment guarantees – in stark contrast to the 'gig economy' style of flexibility. But perhaps ironically, they may result in the employees then behaving in more flexible and innovative ways than they otherwise might have. Firstly, there may be a motivational effect, with employees seeing they are being invested in, and treated with respect, and this engendering a degree of employee commitment and motivation. And also, faced with an idea that might boost productivity by doing away with the need for their own job, would an employee pass the idea on to management? In the absence of an employment guarantee, probably not.

Collaboration between a firm and other firms or organisations

Firms that innovate tend also to collaborate. In the case of collaborating with universities or other research institutes this may seem obvious. But innovative firms tend to also collaborate with other companies. The fact is that most innovations are not going to be invented by your staff in your firm – they are going to occur in other firms. Hence the benefits of collaborating with other companies. But the ability to benefit from such collaboration will depend on the firm's own absorptive capacity – i.e., their ability to learn from innovations

introduced in other companies. Such absorptive capacity will be positively correlated with the degree of education and training amongst the workforce.

Using data from the ESRC Centre for Business Research, Kitson and Michie
(2000) found that 'fast growth' firms (measured in terms of employment) were
almost twice as likely to have collaborated compared to firms with negative or
no growth. They conclude that:

> The fostering of collaborative structures may be an important element in
> creating a competitive and successful economy – an economy capable of
> closing the output gap with its major competitors. This opens up a very
> different policy agenda than that which was pursued in the UK during the
> Thatcher and Major Governments of the 1980s and 1990s. Instead of the
> 'freeing up' of labour and product markets through policies of deregulation
> and casualisation we need new industrial innovation, and macroeconomic
> policies which will: develop new forms of corporate finance and create
> effective mechanisms of corporate governance; provide a modern produc-
> tive infrastructure which private firms can utilise, in many cases in a
> cooperative fashion; ensure a macroeconomic regime conducive to the
> creation of new industrial capacity, including low interest rates and a
> competitive exchange rate; ensure the expansion of employment opportu-
> nities so that investment in education and training will translate into the
> increased output levels which in the long run will repay such investments;
> and promote productive cooperation and industrial innovation.
>
> (Kitson and Michie, 2000, p. 156)

So, for successful corporate performance, a degree of competition is usually
important. But the *nature* of that competition is also important – encouraging
firms to compete over the long term on the basis of innovation and enhanced
quality of output, rather than a race to the bottom in cost-cutting. And alongside that sort of competitive environment, *collaboration* is also an important
part of a successful economic ecosystem. And underpinning these processes lies
the work organisation within those companies, and the provision of education
and training.

Economic democracy and education

As indicated above, economic democracy – entailing consultation and participation – and employee education and training are key factors in corporate
success and economic resilience. This raises the question of how to create that
economic democracy, and how to promote that employee education and
training?

One way is to tackle the fundamentals, of corporate ownership and control.
When companies are owned by external shareholders, and the fiduciary duty of
company directors is to maximise the financial returns for those external
shareholders, then the danger arises of the interests of shareholders and their

financial returns taking precedence over the interests of the employees, their engagement with the organisation, and their interests.

This is one reason why companies with employee ownership may deliver better for the organisation's long-term success, because what is in the interests of employees – involvement and engagement, participation and consultation, and education and training will thereby be prioritised.

So, companies with employee ownership may prove more successful for those reasons. Companies with customer ownership may prove successful because of their focus on the key issue of what the customer wants. Companies with local ownership may prove successful for local economic development, for the obvious reason that they will have an interest – in every sense – to promote the interests of the locality.

Thus, having a variety of corporate forms is to be welcomed, as it is likely to deliver the range of economic (and social) benefits indicated in the preceding paragraph. In addition to that, there is a further reason why having a variety of corporate forms should be encouraged, which is to provide resilience to the economy. Companies with different ownership structures – for example being owned by the firm's employees, or customers, rather than shareholders – tend to have different governance structures, corporate purpose and culture, and policies and practices. This means that when the system gets hit by some shock, such as an international financial crisis, these different types of firms react and behave in different ways. This reduces the risk of a domino effect, with companies all reacting in the same way, potentially into a downward spiral.

The Ownership Commission

The UK's Ownership Commission was established in 2010 to review the state of ownership in the UK, to examine the extent to which it supports or inhibits successful, long-term value creation by business in all its ownership guises. This was based on the recognition that given the scale of Britain's economic challenges, it was time to reassess whether the balance of ownership obligations and rights had been struck correctly. The Commission noted that in Britain one ownership type, the shareholder-owned public limited company (PLC) dominates all others, to a degree not seen in other countries, nor seen in Britain prior to the privatisations and demutualisations from the 1980s. The Commission concluded that there are three broad preconditions for good ownership. Firstly, a healthy economy needs diverse ways through which ownership can express itself and be applied to various business models. The consequent diversity will give the system more resilience and more opportunity to experiment with ownership forms. Secondly, an ownership culture is needed which enables and encourages decisions to be taken on the basis of long-term results and outcomes, and takes its responsibility for good stewardship seriously. And thirdly, owners need to participate and engage in the strategies and behaviours of the firms they own. As *The Economist* put it: 'Just as an ecosystem benefits from diversity, so the world is better off with a multitude of corporate forms' (Economist, 2010, p. 58).

I would argue that a major contribution to ensuring the necessary systemic stability is to create a more diverse financial services sector, otherwise, the big shareholder-owned banks will inevitably tend to support only those sorts of structures in the rest of the economy. We need financial institutions that understand and appreciate the range of alternative corporate forms available, each with its own strengths and weaknesses, and each perhaps more appropriate for any given circumstance, depending on what the purpose and nature of the company is.

Corporate diversity in the financial services sector

The chief economist at the Bank of England argues that one of the factors behind the 2007–8 international financial crisis was that individual financial institutions had been diversifying – for example moving into more speculative operational areas – and that while this might be thought to reduce risk, it does not do so if all are diversifying in the same way, so instead the system as a whole becomes less diverse (Haldane, 2009, pp. 18–19.)

The Centre for European Policy Studies (CEPS) produced two comprehensive studies of diversity in European banking (Ayadi et al., 2009, 2010). Both reports emphasise the advantages of having diversity in banking structures and models, and illustrate this with case studies of several countries. Thus:

> The most important conclusion is that the current crisis has made it even more evident than before how valuable it is to promote a pluralistic market concept in Europe and, to this end, to protect and support all types of ownership structures.
>
> (Ayadi et al., 2009, p. 3)

The importance of place, and local knowledge, plays an important part in creating the necessary supportive ecosystem, from the financial services sector to the rest of the economy, together with knowledge of the relevant industrial sector. I once heard this illustrated by the example of what would happen if one went to a bank with an idea on how to create a new variety of tulip. In the Netherlands one would be taken to talk with the person who dealt with the tulip sector. In the UK, they would call security.

The Centenary Commission on Adult Education

The question of how the economy – and society – could recover and rebuild after the devastation and destruction of the First World War was posed by Britain's prime minister, Lloyd George, establishing the Ministry of Reconstruction. Arguably the most impactful outcome from the Ministry was the 1919 Report published by the Ministry's Adult Education Committee. This argued for a major and sustained national investment into what today would be variously referred to as adult and community education, professional development, and lifelong learning. The need then remains relevant today – perhaps increasingly so.

Firstly, they argued, the great issues of the day needed all citizens to be able to participate in discussion and debate, and this in turn required 'a degree of education for all. They no doubt had in mind the great questions of war and peace. Today we also need to talk about the climate crisis, and the need for resilience in face of future pandemics.

Secondly, they warned in 1919 that new industries were on the horizon, which would involve new technologies, making it inadequate at best to be 'training' employees for today's skills, when what was needed was the capabilities and capacity to respond imaginatively to new technologies and process innovations as these arose. Today is no different, with developments in machine learning, artificial intelligence, robotics, and the whole range of emerging and as yet unknown innovations and technologies.

Thirdly, with the extension of the franchise, the new electors needed education not just on the issues to be decided, but also to ensure the ability to think critically, weigh evidence, and differentiate between on the one hand genuine political arguments, from on the other hand demagoguery. Again, the need is as great today.

The 1919 Report called on all universities to establish departments for continuing education, to deliver adult education and lifelong learning in collaboration with other providers. Although the government of the day failed to do much to implement the Report's recommendations, all universities did sooner or later respond positively to this call, and over the following decades there was widespread adult education and lifelong learning provided by universities, local authorities, the Workers Educational Association (WEA) and others, with much public funding and support from government.

What became a national consensus around the benefits – economic, social and individual – of such educational provision, led in the 1970s to the establishment of the Open University, which became seen to be a world leader in flexible and distance learning for adults – firstly through lectures provided on BBC TV, and now of course, using online methods.

The importance of adult education and lifelong learning has not been questioned or challenged. None of the political parties in the UK have campaigned to save money by cutting its funding. Yet a series of unfortunate actions over the past 20 or 30 years have eroded many of the gains made over the previous 70 or so years. Thus, while all political leaders in the UK, and many corporate and other leaders, will stress the importance of adult education and lifelong learning, they have failed to deliver. Quite the contrary, in fact.

Underlying much of the damage has been the managerial fad of 'deliverables' and 'metrics', which translated into accreditation and funding changes. The Gordon Brown government introduced the 'Equivalent and Lower Qualifications' (ELQ) policy, which meant that funding would no longer be provided if the student already had a qualification at that level. In other words, funding would only be provided for a course which was at a higher level than the student had ever received previously. This made a nonsense of Gordon Brown's speeches and policy measures to promote 'flexibility' in the economy. Funding would be provided if you kept doing higher qualifications in the subject you started out on initially – philosophy, classics, or whatever. But if you wished to switch to electrical engineering or machine learning, which would require studying initially for a qualification at a lower level, funding would be denied. This did huge damage to the Open University and university departments for continuing education, many of which closed as a result.

The subsequent 2010 Coalition government then tripled student fees for degree programmes, including for part-time students. This was disastrous for adult learners. It led to a huge fall in part-time study. And the Open University and departments for continuing education suffered still further. For a school student wondering whether to go to university, the funding mechanism is not necessarily the major issue. Whether it was to be paid for through a student loan which would be recouped through taxation, and written off if not paid off after a certain number of years, is not in most cases the key factor. It is rather more of a life choice.

But for adult students, the idea of taking a student loan to pay for a course feels far more like having to take a loan to replace the family car, or to be able to have a family holiday that year. Faced with those choices, many abandoned the idea of studying. The government minister responsible subsequently admitted that raising fees for part-time students in this way had been his biggest mistake in office, not to understand this basic dynamic, and hence the huge damage he was inflicting on individuals, society, and the economy.

The Coalition government's policies of austerity were continued by the subsequent Conservative government, and these austerity policies did still further damage to adult education and lifelong learning, starving the providers of funding – universities, local authorities, and others – and weakening the demand from companies and individuals on whom the austerity policies also impacted.

This was the backdrop to the decision to establish a commission to publish a follow up to the 1919 Report, published a century later almost to the day, in November 2019, by the Centenary Commission on Adult Education, entitled *A Permanent National Necessity… Adult Education and Lifelong Learning for 21st Century Britain.* [2]

The Centenary Commission's Report makes 18 recommendations, which I will not list here, but which range from the need for Government to frame and deliver a national ambition, through to requiring 'any organisation that wishes to describe itself as a University to provide adult education and lifelong learning, of types appropriate to their role in the local community, compensating for past disadvantages, and utilising radical and engaged forms of education'. On the world of work, the Commission called for the 'Apprenticeship Levy' to be made more flexible; for employers to provide paid time off for learning; for learning representatives in all workplaces; for employers to report on their spending on employee education and training; and for 'contract compliance' to be used to ensure contractors meet the same high standards where these are in place in the contracting company.[3]

In a preface to the report, the Bank of England's chief economist argued that:

> People born today can be expected to live 90 or 100-year lives and to spend the larger part of it – maybe 60 years – in work. This means it is now an arithmetic fact of (longer) life that lifelong learning – for long a convenient slogan – needs to become a practical reality.
>
> At the same time, the world of work is being up-ended by a new technological revolution, with widespread automation and artificial intelligence. This will see many, perhaps most, jobs disrupted and a large number destroyed. This too will make a necessity of reskilling those displaced and disrupted on a systematic and comprehensive basis.
>
> For three centuries, the UK's education system has had a singular – and very successful – focus: developing cognitive skills in the young. That model is not fit for tomorrow's purpose. The education system of tomorrow needs to span the generational spectrum – young to old – and the skill spectrum – cognitive to vocational to interpersonal.
>
> (Haldane, 2009)

All workplaces and organisations can benefit from increased educational provision. This can be focussed on particular skills, but there are also benefits to be had from educational provision in general, regardless of subject area, in helping people to think in new ways and from different angles. Further, if employers provide this as an employee benefit, it is likely to be repaid in the form of employee commitment and motivation, which may feed through to improved corporate performance, which in turn may contribute positively to the local economy.

Conclusion

An article about the documentary being produced on the book *Capital in the 21st Century* reports that Piketty 'blames the stagnation in educational spending (as a proportion of national income) for the slowdown in growth in developed countries' (Mance, 2020). Certainly, the relatively high levels of educational spending from 1945 onwards formed an important part of the Welfare State, contributing in a variety of ways to economic growth, as well as social cohesion and individual wellbeing. And as indicated above, in the UK – as in many other countries – such educational provision included adult and community education, professional development and lifelong learning, targeted at individual wellbeing as well as community cohesion and upskilling for the world of work.

The leading expert on organisational theory and behaviour, Professor John Child, has stressed the importance of promoting organisational participation for 'building back better' following the global COVID-19 crisis (Child, forthcoming). He sets out not only the benefits to be had from such an approach, but also the mechanisms by which to deliver it and reap the full potential benefits.

Michie (2019) argues that alternative corporate forms – such as employee benefits – can contribute in exactly the way that Child (forthcoming) elaborates, and identifies the obstacles to progress in this direction. Compelling examples are given by the range of contributors to the collection compiled by Michie et al. (2017). There is thus no shortage of evidence as to the need for a change of course, and in what direction to travel. But as always, there are powerful forces who wish to defend the status quo, who wish to 'build back' to how it was before, which was so profitable for them, in every sense. Because while one of the problems that has been created since the breakdown of the 'Bretton Woods' era of 'the Golden Age of Capitalism', from the 1980s onwards has been the growth of inequality in income, wealth and power, such inequality creates winners as well as losers, and those winners are in a powerful position within each country and globally.

So, developing an alternative path that is more sustainable socially, economically, and above all environmentally will not be straightforward, but is both necessary and urgent. As argued above, part of the approach must be to recognise the importance of place, and of creating resilient communities and local economies. A second key ingredient is education, available to adults at the various times when it may prove to be important, and provided in communities as well as at work. We need adult education and lifelong learning to support democracy at work and local economic development and resilience. These goals and policies are entirely synergistic, and need to be pursued together if we are to take full advantage of the opportunities that new technologies and extended life expectancies are offering.

Notes

1 A stand-up comedian once asked, 'Why is there only one Competition Commission?'.
2 Full disclosure: I was the Joint Secretary to the Centenary Commission.
3 The report is available free of charge from www.centenarycommission.org

References

Ayadi, R., Arbak, E., Valverde, S., Carbo, F., Rodriguez, F., and Schmidt, R.H. (2009), *Investigating Diversity in the Banking Sector in Europe: The Performance and Role of Savings Banks*, Centre for European Policy Studies, Brussels.
Ayadi, R., Llewellyn, D.T., Schmidt, R.H., Arbak, E., and De Groen, W.P. (2010), *Investigating Diversity in the Banking Sector in Europe: Key Developments, Performance and Role of Co-operative Banks*, Centre for European Policy Studies, Brussels.
Centenary Commission on Adult Education (2019), '*A Permanent National Necessity…*' *Adult Education and Lifelong Learning for 21st Century Britain*. Retrieved from www.CentenaryCommission.org. Accessed 5 November 2020.
Child, J. (forthcoming), Organizational Participation in Post-Covid Society – Its Contributions and Enabling Conditions, *International Review of Applied Economics*.

Economist (2010), The Eclipse of the Public Company, *The Economist*, 19 August (online). Retrieved from www.economist.com/business/2010/08/19/the-eclipse-of-the-public-company. Accessed 5 November 2020.

Haldane, A. (2009), Rethinking the Financial Network, speech to Financial Student Association in Amsterdam, April. Retrieved from www.bis.org/review/r090505e.pdf. Accessed 5 November 2020.

Kitson, M. and Michie, J. (2000), Markets, Competition and Innovation, in Kitson, M. and Michie, J. (eds), *The Political Economy of Competitiveness*, Routledge, London.

Mance, H. (2020), 'Thomas Piketty on going from data-crunching to documentary', *Financial Times*, 14 September. Retrieved from www.ft.com/content/4969eb37-7d36-4d63-959f-4ea5548c4ad8. Accessed 5 November 2020.

Michie, J. (2017), The Importance of Ownership, in Michie, J., Blasi, J. and Borzaga, C. (eds), *The Oxford Handbook of Mutual, Co-operative, and Co-owned Business*, Oxford University Press, Oxford.

Michie, J. (2019), Employee-Owned Companies Perform Better, but are Resisted by Banks, Lawyers and Governments. Retrieved from https://theconversation.com/employee-owned-companies-perform-better-but-are-resisted-by-banks-lawyers-and-governments-117154. Accessed 5 November 2020.

Michie, J. and Sheehan, M. (2003), Labour 'Flexibility' – Securing Management's Right to Manage Badly? In Burchell, B., Deakin, S., Michie, J. and Rubery, J. (eds), *Systems of Production: Markets, organisations and performance*, Routledge, London.

Smith, A. (1904 [1776]), *An Inquiry into the Nature and Causes of The Wealth of Nations*, 5th edition, compiled by Cannan, E., Methuen and Co., London.

Conclusion

The future past

Philip B. Whyman and Julian Manley

This book has sought to examine, from a range of different perspectives, a fascinating example of policy innovation, designed and implemented locally by citizens, businesses, political representatives and communities in a small city in the northwest of England seeking to respond to the challenges created by the aftermath of the 2008 global financial crisis and the austerity policy implemented by the national UK government. At a time when the external environment had become particularly challenging, and reliance upon external agencies to facilitate social and economic development within the local economy had become more problematic, the Preston Model looked inward, to focus upon those assets and policy levers that were within its control. Rather than feeling powerless amidst forces of globalisation or national policy priorities, it allowed local people to take back a greater vestige of control over their lives and livelihoods. The Preston Model, therefore, represented both a practical accommodation to the realities prevailing at the time, but also reflected a desire to better utilise the talents and innovation within the existing population. Necessity, in this case, truly was the mother of invention.

This is not to suggest, however, that the development of the Preston Model was purely reactive. In a real sense, it reflected a desire for the area to 'take back control' – to determine its own priorities and realise these goals. Part of this impetus was to strengthen the local economy, and thereby create more sustainable, high skilled and high waged jobs for local people. In addition, an essential feature was the encouragement of greater participation from the local community, whether through involvement in designing the programme of interventions or through greater involvement at work. The combination of economic improvement and citizen participation was also intended to generate renewed pride in the area and in what local people had achieved. The implications for other areas, particularly those 'left behind' areas within the UK and beyond, are potentially profound. Certainly, the approach has proved of interest to local authority districts such as Newham, Oldham and Sandwell, who are ranked among the most deprived areas of England,[1] yet, as Brookes et al. point out, the Preston Model can additionally prove to be an inspiration to relatively affluent areas who are equally as frustrated with orthodox approaches to economic regeneration and wish to explore more innovative approaches to deliver co-operative, participatory, empowerment and equality goals. Hence, the policy experiment, taking place in a part of the UK that policymakers too often ignore, has received a considerable amount of attention.

In essence, the Preston Model represents an interesting combination of a fairly simple concept – one local community taking back control – yet seeking to do so through a multidimensional and complex set of initiatives. As a result, contributors have sought to examine the Preston Model from a number of different perspectives – philosophical, social, educational, its impact on the local community and governance more generally, interaction with trade unions, the impact upon the local community, together with the potential for efficiency gains.

The aspect where most attention (whether supportive or critical) has been focused, is the economic impact that the Preston Model may arguably be able to deliver (Whyman). The economic interventions have sought to better utilise existing resources by reducing leakages from the local circular flow of income to achieve end goals such as raising GNI and hence living standards, together with a procurement strategy aimed at enhancing local supply chains and supplemented by attempts to steer local capital to regenerate key elements of the local economy. The economic literature additionally suggests that there is the *potential* for democratic organisations to improve efficiency (micro) while reducing economic instability (macro), and therein creating better job opportunities and reducing deprivation. Critics, however, claim that this approach is protectionist and hence is likely to be inefficient or self-defeating, if all areas of the country adopted similar inward-focused approaches. These criticisms tend to be based upon neo-liberal economic assumptions or prejudices, a point subtly made by Farrelly in his study of the language used in media discussion of the Preston Model, which are themselves not altogether realistic, and ignore weaknesses with the current UK economic model, such as the need for rebalancing of activity to facilitate smoother and higher growth rates. Nevertheless, this critique needs to be tested against a robust set of data which is not yet available. Hence, while there are suggestions that the economic impact delivered by the Preston Model is positive for the local economy, more work needs to be done to reach a definitive judgement on the relative merits of the approach if wider adoption is to be considered.

Reducing the Preston Model to a set of economic imperatives, however, as some of its critics tend to do, is to diminish the approach. It is a far more interesting and richer phenomenon. The significance of the Preston Model for local governance and the potential for enhancing citizen participation, whether through formal channels or informal fora, were highlighted in the chapters authored by Aiken, Farrelly, Prinos, and Ridley. The ability for the Preston Model to strengthen civic society and voluntary organisations, such as citizen forums and trade unions, were indicated by Peck, Aiken, and Bird et al. In particular, the latter argues that, by displacing neoliberalism, the Preston Model has the potential to enhance democratic participation and thereby increase trust and legitimacy in local decision-making. As Manley points out, democratic participation emerges from a sense of a genuine flattening of structures, rhizomatic as opposed to hierarchical, and democracy is expressed through such affective commitments to agency in participation among citizens, both in community and in the workspace, leading to enhanced feelings of wellbeing, motivation, determination, resilience, hope and pride. Indeed, the very fact that Preston – a proud city, but one which may seem peripheral when viewed from the standpoint of London – gave its name to this initiative, is itself a source of pride for many Prestonians.

A central feature of the Preston Model, relates to its encouragement of co-operatives and other forms of municipal and social enterprise. Co-operation, here is to be understood as a way of working and living a life as well as the creation of co-operative businesses. As Ridley demonstrates, there is a case for saying that a healthy community is also a co-operative community. Motivations vary, but may include a desire to enhance employee participation in the workplace (Michie, Whyman), promoting wellbeing and personal fulfilment for working people (Manley, Peck), reducing inequality (Bird et al., Peck, Whyman), enhancing resilience and reducing economic instability (Manley, Whyman), promoting social solidarity (Ridley), promoting plurality of ownership through stakeholder capitalism (Peck, Whyman).

The evidence pertaining to worker co-operatives delivering on all of these objectives is mixed, but there is a fairly consistent data trail indicating the potential for enhanced labour productivity leading to greater efficiency, combined with reduced rates of workplace conflict, which equates with high performance workplace literature. Interestingly, the analysis of industrial co-operatives in the Basque region, outlined by Elorza and Garmendia in their chapter, support this conclusion regarding co-operative efficiency. Yet, their work additionally suggests that, once co-operatives grow above a certain size, their potential for creating worker satisfaction may decline. Bearing in mind that Elorza and Garmendia are writing from the perspective of arguably the most successful and durable co-operative groups in the world – in Mondragón and the Basque Country – this speaks to the shifting nature of such workplace and social organisations and how success is riddled with questions and failures along the way. Similarly, it becomes clear from the contributions to this book that the Preston Model is not 'done and dusted' but rather in a state of constant development, with possibly no definitive end. Perhaps the nature of a complex, democratic organisation of work and life is to be such: always on the move. The idea, therefore, of the Preston *Model* is perhaps in itself unhelpful, suggesting, as it may, that it represents some concrete template or fixed model to be reached, where in fact there is only a lively sense of creative thinking at work.

A second key feature of the material presented in this book, pertains to the importance of adult (citizen and worker) education providing the knowledge, skills, and confidence, for members of the local community to participate in multiple aspects of the Preston Model, whether in the workplace, political debate, policy development or engaging with resulting economic opportunities.

The significance of education to underpin economic democracy initiatives and in the sustainable creation of co-operative businesses can be viewed in relation to the Mondragón co-operative network (Wright and Manley). In noting the need for culture change and in tracing the development of this change in Mondragón through 13 years of education before the first co-operative was born, Wright and Manley suggest that there is a longer-term balance to developments in Preston, as opposed to the shorter term gains of the procurement policy with anchor institutions. The Preston Model can be seen, therefore, as a long term social and economic transformation of work, life and place which can only be made sustainable and resilient through education. Michie notes that education facilitates local economic development through strengthening economic resilience and creating the combination of trust and functional flexibility which are identified in the high-performance business literature as important contributors to innovation and productivity. Indeed, key founders of the economics discipline, such as John Stuart Mill and Alfred Marshall, both anticipated that education would promote self-fulfilment and facilitate self-governance, while the resulting democratisation of the workplace would enable latent productive energies to be released and thereby increase productivity (Whyman). In the case of the resonances between Mondragón and Preston, the writings of Arizmendiarrieta postulate co-operativism as being indistinguishably both an economic and an educational movement (Wright and Manley).

While individual elements can be assessed separately, Farrelly, Manley and Whyman have all argued that the Preston Model should best be considered as an inter-connected set of elements which, when combined, do indeed make a sum greater than its constituent parts. Indeed, the case for retaining the complexity of the Preston Model forms a central feature of the Introduction to this book, and a recurring theme throughout many of the chapters. The encouragement of co-operative enterprise reinforces the boost to the economy generated by procurement policy, as democratic firms are by their nature more rooted in the area from whence they sprang, while procurement provides additional opportunities for these same co-operatives, in addition to other SMEs, to expand and thereby strengthen indigenous supply chain networks. Anchor institutions have sought to amplify their individual impacts through coordination of procurement activity, while local educational institutions and political representatives from Preston City Council have sought to both facilitate the development of a Preston Co-operative Development Network which simultaneously provides the education and skills training to underpin successful business development. This degree of inter-connectivity, producing mutually-reinforcing impacts, would appear to replicate the type of 'Mondragón ecosystem' that Ridley identifies as playing a critical role in the growth and long-term viability of the Basque co-operative network.

Not all of this has worked as planned, of course, and Prinos notes the perceptions, even among active participants, that the Preston Model contains contradictions and that its outcomes, to date, have proved to be 'a rather mixed bag'. Not all sections of the community have benefitted from the approach and many members of the community regard it as more of a 'leadership' project, rather than being a truly grassroots movement. Perhaps this is inevitable, given that the Preston Model breaks with orthodox models of development, and hence it does rely upon the vision of key individuals to construct an alternative approach. Thus, while it has not yet developed into a true social movement, the potential exists for this to occur. Moreover, it is important to remember that, when evaluating the strengths and weaknesses of the Preston Model, *the phenomenon is only seven years old*. Consequently, while evidence is emerging to hint at the areas where impact does appear to be occurring, in other important aspects, it is simply too soon to draw definitive judgements. Perhaps this book should be viewed as delivering an interim appraisal of the Preston Model, with definitive judgements awaiting further work, examining developments over a longer time period. Or, perhaps that is the natural conclusion to be reached by academic researchers, for whom additional evidence is always welcome to strengthen the robustness of conclusions.

Another way of evaluating the strengths and weaknesses of the Preston Model is to attempt to trace its influence or potential outside Preston, in the UK and internationally. Certainly, the Preston Model has attracted a lot of attention outside the northwest of England (Appendix). A fuller analysis of the Preston Model as an element of a global trend lies outside the scope of this book, albeit that some of this work is scheduled to be presented in forthcoming research (e.g. Davies 2021). However, the contributions to Part II of the present edition suggest that perhaps this is indeed the case and that the Preston Model, distinct as it is in its details, is nevertheless part of a panorama of change that is emerging in many different guises – such as community wealth building, the commons, the green economy, the Doughnut Model, and others – and indicates a social and economic transformation that appears to be emerging from a tired and depleted neoliberal system. This sense of urgent change is acutely expressed by Peck.

Perhaps the final point, to be acknowledged in the book, is to highlight the fact that the Preston Model is simultaneously unique and yet stands firmly on the shoulders of giants; a future based on a past. Its inspiration may be traced back to insights provided by a long history of economic democracy theory and debate, combined with practical examples provided by the Mondragón co-operative network and the community wealth building initiatives introduced in Cleveland and elsewhere. Yet, it is quite distinctive, whether in terms of the absence of the degree of top-down control that has applied in other international examples of CWB, as noted by both Manley and Whyman, or because, however imperfect, it does embody the 'made by people in Preston for people in Preston' concept outlined by Prinos. It has received a lot of attention because it challenges received (orthodox) wisdom, that local communities are relatively powerless in the face of global forces, and because it emerged at a time when fiscal austerity was squeezing the life out of many communities. The emergence of the Preston Model demonstrated that there was another way to regenerate local economies, which appeared to be more consistent with egalitarian and democratic objectives, and provided hope to many communities across the country. What is more, it appears to work. Granted, such conclusions are provisional, pending the further development of the initiative creating the data required to produce more robust and definitive conclusions.

The Preston Model, therefore, raises as many questions as it has, thus far at least, been able to answer. Yet, in demonstrating the potential for a different pathway to social and economic development, it creates a space within which policy makers, businesses, workers and others within the local community, can investigate the plausibility of alternatives to orthodoxy, and in so doing, stimulate new thinking about issues pertaining to democracy, participation, development and deprivation. It is both brave and new. Challenging and inspiring. That is why the Preston Model is important.

Note

1 See www.gov.uk/government/statistics/english-indices-of-deprivation-2019

References

Davies, J.S. (2021) *Between Realism and Revolt: Governing Cities in the Crisis of Neoliberal Globalism.* Bristol: Bristol University Press.

Abbreviations

1W1V	1Worker1Vote
ACEVO	Association of Chief Executives of Voluntary Organisations
ACF	Adventure Capital Fund
APSE	Association for Public Service Excellence
BBF	Bilbao Innovation Factory
CCIN	Cooperative Councils Innovation Network
CCT	compulsory competitive tendering
CEPS	Centre for European Policy Studies
CIC	community interest company
CLES	Centre for Local Economic Strategies
CLG	company limited by guarantee
COVID-19	coronavirus disease 2019, caused by severe acute respiratory syndrome coronavirus 2 (SARS-CoV-2); global spread became a pandemic in 2020
CPD	continual professional development
CSBA	Community Savings Bank Association
CWB	community wealth building
EBIT	earnings before interest and taxes
EIMD	English Index of Multiple Deprivation
ELQ	equivalent and lower qualifications
EPE	Epicenter Pandemic Economy
EPP	polytechnic school – became the Faculty of Engineering for MU
ESFA	Education and Skills Funding Agency
ESG	environment, social, governance
ESOPs	Employee Share Ownership Plan
EU	European Union
GINI index	Gini index or Gini coefficient – a measure of the distribution of income across a population
GVA	gross value added – the regional equivalent to gross domestic product (GDP)
ICA	International Co-operative Alliance
IMD	Index of Multiple Deprivation
IPS	Industrial and Provident Society

LCC	Lancashire County Council
LGP	Lancashire Government Pension Fund
LM	Labour-managed firms
LM3	three stage (Keynesian) multiplier approach; utilised to identify the boost to the local economy resulting from an initial injection multiplied by the effect of money circulating within the local economy
LSE	London School of Economics
LSOA	lower-layer super output areas
MCC	Mondragón Co-operative Corporation
MU	Mondragón Unibertsitatea
NAO	National Audit Office
NCVO	National Council of Voluntary Organisations
NUTS-3	Nomenclature of Territorial Units for Statistics – EU categorisation of regions. For the UK, NUTS-1 equates to the four primary regions (i.e. North West England), NUTS-2 the sub-regions (i.e. Lancashire) and NUTS-3 upper tier local authority areas (i.e. Blackburn with Darwen, Blackpool, Chorley and West Lancashire, East Lancashire, Mid Lancashire [including Preston], Lancaster and Wyre)
ONS	Office for National Statistics
OSF	Open Society Foundations
PCC	Preston City Council
PCDN	Preston Cooperative Development Network
PCEC	Preston Cooperative Education Centre
PHE	Public Health England
PLC	public limited company (private sector company with limited liability)
PM	Preston Model
PwC	PriceWaterhouse Coopers
RIBA	Royal Institute of British Architects 2019 National Award
SBC	Stevenage Borough Council
SDG	UN Sustainable Development Goals
SHRM	strategic human resource management
SIB	Social Investment Business Ltd
SMEs	small and medium-sized enterprises
TSO	third sector organisation
UCLan	University of Central Lancashire
VSCEs	Volunteer, Social, Community Enterprises
WCC	Wales Co-operative Centre
WEA	Workers Educational Association
WFTO	World Fair Trade Organization (not to be confused with World Trade Organization (WTO))

Appendix

A selection of media resources tracking the impact of the Preston Model since 2013

1Worker1Vote (2018). The Mondragón Experience to the Preston Model. Available: http://1worker1vote.org/mondragon-experience-preston-model-stir (Accessed: 20.03.2019).

1Worker1Vote (2018). An Emerging US/UK Union Co-ops Consensus. Available: http://1worker1vote.org/emerging-us-uk-union-co-ops-consensus (Accessed: 20.03.2019).

Albrecht, E. (2019). Kehrtwende in Preston Englische Stadt hat genug vom Kapitalismus. Available: www.deutschlandfunkkultur.de/kehrtwende-in-preston-englische-stadt-hat-genug-vom.979.de.html?dram:article_id=437405 (Accessed: 20.03.2019).

Bauwens, M., Onzia, Y. (2017). The Commons Transition Plan for the City of Ghent. Available: https://stad.gent/sites/default/files/article/documents/Commons%20Transitie%20Plan%20Gent.pdf (Accessed: 20.03.2019).

Beckett, A. (2019). The New Left Economics: How a Network of Thinkers is Transforming Capitalism. *The Guardian*. Available: www.theguardian.com/news/2019/jun/25/the-new-left-economics-how-a-network-of-thinkers-is-transforming-capitalism (Accessed: 25.06.2019).

Bermuda Economic Development Corporation (2018). An Evening with Dr Julian. Available: https://bedc.bm/economic-cooperative-development-unit/an-evening-with-dr-julian-manley-nov-20–2018 (Accessed: 20.03.19).

Bernews (2018). Presentation on Community Wealth Building. Available: http://bernews.com/2018/11/presentation-on-community-wealth-building (Accessed: 20.03.2019).

Brown, M. (2016). The Road to Socialism is the A59: The Preston Model. Available: www.renewal.org.uk/articles/the-road-to-socialism-is-the-a59-the-preston-model (Accessed: 20.03.2019).

Brown, M. (2018). Our Towns and Cities Operate in a Straight- jacket, but Community Wealth Building Offers Hope. Available: https://party.coop/2018/06/07/our-towns-and-cities-operate-in-a-straight-jacket-but-community-wealth-building-offers-hope (Accessed: 20.03.2019).

Chakrabortty, A. (2018). In 2011 Preston Hit Rock Bottom. Then it Took Back Control. *The Guardian*. Available: www.theguardian.com/commentisfree/2018/jan/31/preston-hit-rock-bottom-took-back-control (Accessed: 20.03.2019).

Chakrabortty, A. (2019). In an Era of Brutal Cuts, One Ordinary Place Has the Imagination to Fight Back. *The Guardian*. Available: www.theguardian.com/commentisfree/2019/mar/06/brutal-cuts-fight-back-preston-dragons-den (Accessed: 20.03.2019).

Community Wealth Building Unit (n.d). Co-operatives. Available: www.communitywealthbuilding.org.uk/resources/co-operatives (Accessed: 29.05.2020).

GoToStage (2020). Co-operation and the Preston Model: Beyond "Urban Regeneration" with Julian Manley. Video added by International Centre for Co-operative Management (ICCM). Available: www.gotostage.com/channel/6ec860805f9e42c3868151624fea6b14/recording/524f2dce541541358475bbfaced93552/watch?source=CHANNEL&utm_source=May+E-Newsletter&utm_campaign=Prospects+2020+Co-operative+Management+Education+%28March%29&utm_medium=email (Accessed: 16.11.2020).

Co-operative Councils' Innovation Network (n.d). Case Studies. Available: www.councils.coop/case-studies (Accessed: 20.03.2019).

Co-operative Party (2017). John McDonnell Pledges Funding for a New Generation of "Co-operatively Owned" Ubers and AirBnBs. Available: https://party.coop/2017/02/17/john-mcdonnell-pledges-to-fund-a-new-generation-of-co-operatively-owned-ubers-and-airbnbs/?fbclid=IwAR1ILfY8TPbRMd8RWbEidp9IYEiFORS6tx9DaosrgmvvlHu1Hd1-fWwcTuI (Accessed:17.11.2020).

Eaton, G. (2018). Corbynism 2.0: The Radical Ideas Shaping Labour's Future. *New Statesman*. Available: www.newstatesman.com/politics/uk/2018/09/corbynism-20-radical-ideas-shaping-labour-s-future (Accessed: 20.03.2019).

Eaton, G. (2018). How Preston – the UK's "Most Improved City" – Became a Success Story for Corbynomics. *New Statesman*. Available: www.newstatesman.com/politics/uk/2018/11/how-preston-uk-s-most-improved-city-became-success-story-corbynomics (Accessed: 20.03.2019).

The Economist (2017). Preston, Jeremy Corbyn's Model Town. Available: www.economist.com/britain/2017/10/19/preston-jeremy-corbyns-model-town (Accessed: 20.03.2019).

Everything Co-op (2019). Michael Peck, Pat Conaty & Dr. Julian Manley,Discuss Co-op Development in the UK on Everything Co-op. Podcast. Available: https://soundcloud.com/user-913981455/michael-peck-pat-conaty-dr-julian-manley-discuss- co-op-development-in-the-uk-on-everything-co-op (Accessed 20.03.2019).

Fernandez, M. (2019). The British Left Look at the Mondragon Experience. Available: www.naiz.eus/eu/hemeroteca/gara/editions/2019-05-26/hemeroteca_articles/la-izquierda-britanica-mira-a-la-experiencia-mondragon (Accessed: 17.11.2020).

Harris, J. (2018). Politicians May Finally Be Catching on: Towns Now Hold the Key to Britain's Future. *The Guardian*. Available: www.theguardian.com/cities/commentisfree/2018/oct/18/politicians-may-finally-be-catching-on-towns-now-hold-the-key-to-britains-future (Accessed: 20.03.2019).

Hopkins, R. (2018). A Report from #CTRLshift2018. Available: www.robhopkins.net/2018/03/31/a-report-from-ctrlshift2018 (Accessed: 20.03.2019).

Howard, T. (2018). Addressing the Systemic Challenge at the Heart of Escalating Inequality and Environmental Destruction, The Next System Project. Available: https://thenextsystem.org/learn/stories/addressing-systemic-challenge-heart-escalating-inequality-and-environmental (Accessed: 20.03.2019).

Keegan, S. (2019). The Preston Model Becomes International Trailblazer. Available: www.insidermedia.com/publications/north-west-business-insider/north-west-business-insider-november-2019/the-preston-model-becomes-international-trailblazer (Accessed:17.11.2020).

Kent, J. (2018). Free Event to Feature Preston Economic Model. *The Royal Gazette.* Available: www.royalgazette.com/economy/article/20181115/free-event-to-feature-preston-economic-model (Accessed: 20.03.2019).

Lancashire Evening Post (2016). Could Spanish Town Help Solve Our Identity Crisis? Available: (Accessed: 20.03.2019).

Lancashire Evening Post (2017). Jeremy Corbyn praises Preston. Available: www.lep.co.uk/news/jeremy-corbyn-praises-preston-674782 (Accessed: 20.03.2019).

Lancashire Evening Post (2018). Why Boris Johnson was wrong to sneer at Preston. Available: (Accessed: 20.03.2019).

The Laura Flanders Show (2019) Special Report: Building the Democratic Economy, from Preston to Cleveland, Youtube video added by. Available: www.youtube.com/watch?v=qnXsteyfiUg#action=share (Accessed: 20.03.2019).

Lusuardi, A. (2018). Preston – The Model for Cooperative Future. Available: www.principle5.coop/wp-content/uploads/2018/09/Sheffield-Co-operator-September-2018.pdf (Accessed: 20.03.2019).

Manley, J. (2017). Local Democracy with Attitude: The Preston Model and How it Can Reduce Inequality. Available: https://blogs.lse.ac.uk/politicsandpolicy/local-democracy-with-attitude-the-preston-model (Accessed: 20.03.2019).

Manley, J. (2018). Preston Changed its Fortunes with "Corbynomics" – Now Other Cities Are Doing the Same. Available at: https://theconversation.com/preston-changed-its-fortunes-with-corbynomics-now-other-cities-are-doing-the-same-106293 (Accessed: 15.07.2020).

Manley, J. (2019). New Model Economy Benefits Business and the Community. Available: www.uclan.ac.uk/business_at_uclan/new-model-economy.php (Accessed: 17.11.2020).

Morgan, J. (2018). Towns and Universities: UK Labour's New Civic Thinking. *Times Higher Education.* Available: www.timeshighereducation.com/news/towns-and-universities-uk-labours-new-civic-thinking (Accessed: 20.03.2019).

Morgan, J. (2019). Is Cooperation the Antidote to Higher Education's Competitive Anxiety? *Times Higher Education.* Available: www.timeshighereducation.com/features/cooperation-antidote-higher-educations-competitive-anxiety (Accessed: 06.03.19).

Mudie, K. (2017). How One City is Beating Tory Austerity with "Radicalism on a Shoestring". *The Mirror.* Available: www.mirror.co.uk/news/politics/how-one-city-beating-tory-11468663 (Accessed: 20.03.2019).

New Prosperity Devon (2020). Community Wealth Building in Practice: Sharing Experience in Devon. Available: www.youtube.com/watch?v=cf2YsVlqrsA (Accessed: 4.11.2020).

Preston City Council (n.d.). The Preston Co-operative Initiative. Available: www.preston.gov.uk/article/1577/The-Preston-co-operative-initiative (Accessed: 20.03.2019).

Preston City Council (n.d.). What is Community Wealth Building? Available: www.preston.gov.uk/article/1335/What-is-Community-Wealth-Building- (Accessed: 20.03.19).

Preston City Council (n.d.). What is Preston Model? Available: www.preston.gov.uk/article/1339/What-is-Preston-Model- (Accessed: 20.03.2019).

Raikes, N. (2019). Preston Model: Bringing Democracy to Local Economy. Available: www.bbc.co.uk/news/av/uk-politics-48559059 (Accessed: 07.06.2019).

Richardson, I. (2018). Preston Meets Mondragón: Worker Ownership and Democratic Businesses for Preston. Available: www.thersa.org/fellowship/fellowship-news/fellowship-news/preston-meets-mondragon-worker-ownership-and-democratic-businesses-for-preston (Accessed: 20.03.2019).

Schaefer, L. (2018). The Preston Model of Community Wealth Building in the UK. Available: www.centreforpublicimpact.org/case-study/the-preston-model-of-community-wealth-building-in-the-uk (Accessed: 16.11.2020).

Scotland's Rural College (2017). Mondragón Cooperatives: Links with Culture, Land and History. Available: https://vimeo.com/241045579 (Accessed: 20.03.2019).

Scottish Communities Action Network (2020) Dr Julian Manley: The Preston Model: Going Local – SCCAN Tuesdays4Climate. Available: www.youtube.com/watch?v=20nRLl0-qBw&feature=youtu.be (Accessed: 16.11.2020)

Sheffield, H. (2017). The Preston Model: UK Takes Lessons in Recovery from Rust-Belt Cleveland. Available: www.theguardian.com/cities/2017/apr/11/preston-cleveland-model-lessons-recovery-rust-belt (Accessed: 20.03.2019).

Sheffield, H. (2019). The Original Solution of a British City for Austerity. Available: https://tvxs.gr/news/egrapsan-eipan/i-prototypi-lysi-mias-bretanikis-polis-gia-ti-litotita (Accessed: 16.11.2020).

Singer, C. (2016). The Preston Model. Available: https://thenextsystem.org/the-preston-model (Accessed: 20.03.2019).

Smith, J. (2019). If Labour Wants to Beat a Big-Spending Boris, it Must Be Far More than just an Anti-austerity Party. *The Independent*. Available: www.independent.co.uk/voices/boris-johnson-labour-public-spending-anti-austerity-preston-model-economic-democracy-a8996721.html?amp&__twitter_impression=true&fbclid=IwAR2suYWc7vCCBYO19wSz2Y7wFA1ZtU1X105vzk2CU9FQWJkZk0Rw9Hy9AqY (Accessed: 11.07.2019).

Stäuber, P. (2019). Applied "Corbynomics". *Die Wochenzeitung*. Available: www.woz.ch/-9cdd (Accessed: 16.11.2019).

Stubbington, T. (2017). Buy Local, Hire Local: Preston Blossoms on Corbynomics. *The Times*. Available: www.thetimes.co.uk/article/buy-local-hire-local-preston-blossoms-on-corbynomics-xkbtq0t90 (Accessed: 20.03.2019).

Té Con Gotas (2019). Modelo Preston: un éxito desde o local e o cooperativismo. Podcast. Available: www.ivoox.com/11-modelo-preston-exito-desde-
o-local-audios- mp3_rf_36964748_1.html?fbclid=IwAR13gz3chs1QVw-kDIN3
MXHhDJt0D4b6nMKBxxNO5bUloS8JQunUl77EMtc (Accessed:17.11.2020).

Titley, M. (2019). Funding for Network of Co-operative Start-ups in Preston to be
Finalised. *Lancashire Evening Post.* Available: www.lep.co.uk/your-lancashire/p
reston/funding-for-network-of-co-operative-start-ups-in-preston-to-be-finalised-
1-9633042 (Accessed: 20.03.2019).

University of Central Lancashire (2019). Ambitions Are High for the Next
Phase of the Preston Model. Available: www.uclan.ac.uk/news/ambitions-
high-for-preston-model.php (Accessed: 06.03.2019).

Walker, E. (2018). New Preston Council Leader Decided by Labour Group. Available: www.blogpreston.co.uk/2018/05/new-preston-council-leader-decided-by-
labour-group (Accessed: 20.03.2019).

Walker, E. (2019). What Next for the Preston Model? Investing in Worker Owned
Co-operatives in the City. Available: www.blogpreston.co.uk/2019/03/what-
next-for-the-preston-model-investing-in-worker-owned-co-operatives-in-the-city
(Accessed: 20.03.2019).

Watkins, S. (2018). How the Left-Behind Took Back Control in Preston.
Available: https://moneyweek.com/487565/how-the-left-behind-took-back-
control-in-preston (Accessed: 20.03.2019).

Zeldin-O'Neill, S. (2018). The Preston Model – Event Review: "Cities Are
Looking to Us for Hope". *The Guardian.* Available: www.theguardian.com/
uk-news/2018/mar/17/the-preston-model-event-review-cities-hope-localism
(Accessed: 20.03.2019).

Index